U. S. POLICY TOWARDS INDIA
A Post Cold War Study

U.S. Policy Towards India
A Post Cold War Study

Amulya K. Tripathy
Rabi Narayan Tripathy

Reference Press
4831/24, Ansari Road, Darya Ganj,
New Delhi-110002
Tel. : 23260807, 41563444
Fax : 011-41563334
E-mail: info@essessreference.com
url:http://www.essessreference.com

REFERENCE PRESS
4831/24, Ansari Road,
Darya Ganj,
New Delhi-110 002.

Tel.: 23260807, 41563444
Fax: 41563334
E-mail: info@essessreference.com
www.essessreference.com

Rs.725/-

First Published - 2008

ISBN: 81-8405-041-0 (10 Digit)
978-81-8405-041-7 (13 Digit)

Published By Reference Press and printed at Salasar Imaging Systems

PRINTED IN INDIA

Dedicated
To

Mr. Arun Kinkar Tripathy, I.P.S. (Retd)
Smt. Haripriya Tripathy
(Parents of Dr. Rabi Narayan Tripathy)

Preface

An effort has been made in the present study to analyse the American policy towards India in the Post-Cold War period and particularly during the Presidency of Bill Clinton. It was during the Cold War period relationship between the two democracies the US and India was strained. The relationship was strained due to the conflicting perspective in the Cold War. The main focus of US foreign policy was containment of Communism. India being a leading non-aligned country was opposed to the Cold War. India became particularly concerned after Pakistan entered into military alliance with the US.

But things changed dramatically after the Cold War. The end of Cold War provided new opportunities for improving relations between the US and India. Indian adherence to democratic path, secularism, free market economy and above all the vast consumer market attracted the Americans. India also relinquished its non-aligned policy as there were no more two super powers. Pakistan has been sidetracked and the US is now India's largest trading partner. The study presents the relationship between India and America in the Post-Cold War period and seeks to analyze the relation between the two countries during the Presidentship of Bill Clinton.

The present study consists of nine chapters. While chapter one provides an introduction which is the objective of the study, chapter two provides the setting of the problem. Chapter three to six comprise its substantive portion. Chapter seven to nine describe the summary of the study as well as concluding observations.

For purposes of the present study we have consulted materials related to United States policy towards India both from primary as well as secondary sources. Primary source materials such as the Department of State Bulletin, the Congressional Record, the Congressional Hearings, Foreign Policy Statements, Memoirs of Public Officials, US documents as well as secondary source materials from books, periodicals and selected articles from learned journals have been consulted. Several news papers belonging to the United States and India as well as Press clippings from newspapers namely New York Times, The Washington Post, Asian Age (Kolkata), The Hindu (Madras), Statesman (New Delhi), Times of India (New Delhi), Telegraph (Kolkata), Indian Express (New Delhi), Hindustan Times (New Delhi), Economic Times (New Delhi), Financial Express (Mumbai), Financial Times (London), Amrit Bazar Patrika (Bangladesh), International Herald Tribune (Paris), National Herald (New Delhi), Patriot (New Delhi), , Tribune (Chandigarh), Dawn (Karachi) have been consulted.

The present researchers had no opportunity of undertaking a field trip to United States for collection of materials pertaining to the study and hence the research report is based entirely on materials available from public libraries in India. In this connection we have made a number of visits to the following libraries in India: Indo-American Centre for International Studies, Hyderabad (formerly ASRC); Osmania University, Hyderabad; Indian Council of Social Science Research,

Hyderabad; National Library, Kolkata; American Centre, New Delhi; Indian Council of World Affairs, New Delhi; Institute for Defence Studies and Analysis, New Delhi; Jawaharlal Nehru University, New Delhi; Teen Murti Bhawan Library, New Delhi; Parliament Library, New Delhi; Delhi University Library, New Delhi; American Centre, Bombay; Bombay University, Bombay and Indian Council of Social Science Research, Bombay.

Amulya K. Tripathy
Rabi Narayan Tripathy

Acknowledgements

In Course of our research work we had the benefit of inspiration from eminent scholars like Prof. L.N. Mishra (Presently, Vice-Chancellor , Utkal University, Orissa), Prof. Chintamani Mahapatra , Centre for American Studies, S.I.S. , J.N.U. , New Delhi, Prof. R.G. Pradhan, Sambalpur University, Orissa , Prof. J.K. Mahapatra, Berhampur University, Orissa, Prof. Santishree Pandit, University of Poona, Prof. Digambar Mishra, Miles College, Birmingham, U.S.A. and Prof. Beverly Hawk, University of Alabama, U.S.A. . We wish to thank Them.

We are to express our gratitude to Sri Arun Kinkar Tripathy, I.P.S.(Retd) and Smt. Hari Priya Tripathy (Parents of Rabi Narayan Tripathy) for their inspiration and encouragement. We wish to thank Sri Sachindra Kumar Mishra, Smt. Susama Mahapatra and Prof. Kalidas Mishra for their inspirations.

We wish to thank to Sri Krushna Chandra Sahu and Smt. Meera Mahapatra(in-laws of Amulya K. Tripathy) for their regular encouragement.

Finally, we are to thank to our respective family members Dr.Nandini Sahu, Associate Prof. in English, IGNOU, Delhi and Parthasarathi (wife and son of Amulya K. Tripathy), and Smt. Sanjukta Dash, Lect. in History, S.Rampur College, Orissa and Debasis (wife and son of Rabi Narayan Tripathy for their timely help and encouragement.

Amulya K. Tripathy

Rabi Narayan Tripathy

Contents

1
Introduction

Objective of the Study

During the Cold War years there were ups and downs in the relations between US and India. But in fact, there were more downs than ups. The strain in their relation was primarily due to their conflicting perspectives, divergent approach towards various issues during the Cold War. During the Cold Wars, there were two super powers, the USA and the USSR and both were applying different strategies to woo different countries to their sides. The US was the architect of the policy of containment against the Soviet Union. In order to contain and roll back communism, the US built several multilateral and bilateral defence alliances. India being a leading non-aligned country was opposed to the Cold War. India's apprehension was that alliances and counter alliances would breed war rather than peace. India became particularly worried when Pakistan entered into military alliance with the US. India feared that the presence of Cold War in the sub-continent would endanger her security and thereby would be forced to divert its scarce resources from development to military preparedness.

My thesis seeks to analyze the under currents in American attitude and policies towards India during the Post-Cold War period in general and Clinton's Presidency in particular. It is noteworthy to mention here that the Clinton phase represents a 'Refreshing change' in American perspective towards India, which is a marked contrast to the earlier phase, namely, the period of Cold War. To begin with the period of the Cold War had witnessed such ugly features and phenomena in their bilateral relationship like 'estrangement', 'antagonism', 'failure', 'confrontation', 'interventionism' and 'enmity'. Scholarly works embracing the Cold War period have further characterized the US-India relations as one of 'Amissed partnership', 'the unfriendly friends', 'the dialogue of the deaf', 'the old peace', and 'the politics of encounter'. The Post-Cold War phase, however, represents positive steps towards one of accommodation amidst discard in their bilateral relations. Actually things changed dramatically in the Post-Cold War period. The mistrust was modified into mutual trust. It was a remarkable change which no body had expected.

The key of American perspective vis-à-vis India during the Cold War had been the strategic importance of its military ally namely, Pakistan, to whom it had funneled some $650 million under Military Assistance Programme (MAP) alone between 1950 to 1980. In fact, Pakistan had become the second largest recipient of MAP aid (after Iran) and that this assistance had been provided as part of a general "Northern Tier" strategy to limit Soviet expansion into the middle East, South Asia and the Indian ocean. Following the fall of the Shah of Iran in January 1979 and the Soviet invasion of Afghanistan in December 1979 as well as the Iran-Iraq war of 1980, the American policy makers had decided to reinforce their military assistance to Pakistan in reaction to these adverse and threatening situation in South and South West Asia. In return, Pakistan acted as the "Front-Line State" a conduit for US weapons sent to Afghan guerillas. In the process Pakistan became important in US eyes and played an international role quite disproportionate to its actual size and capabilities. This was the Cold War situation when Pakistan got primary importance because of its strategic location. As we know nothing is permanent in international politics. The situation however underwent drastic transformation because of the bold experiments launched by the USSR President Michael Gorbachev which paved the way for the disintegration of the Soviet Union and thereby end of the Cold War. The withdrawal of Russian troops took place from Afghanistan and Russia was degraded to a second rank power. In the process, Pakistan forfeited its status and role as a front line state as mentioned earlier. After the collapse of the Soviet Union, the US remained as the only super power in the world and Pakistan also lost its importance in the US scenario.

So a drastic change occurred in US attitude towards India after the end of Cold War. India also relinquished its non-aligned policy as there were no more two super powers. The end of the Cold War provided new opportunities for improving relations between the US and India, incidentally the two largest democracies in the world. Indian adherence to democratic path, secularism, free market economy and above all the vast consumer market attracted the Americans. USA is a country which stands for democracy every where in the world. India from its independence has not deviated from democratic principles. This is probably another reason for the closeness of US and India. The upsurge of Islamic fundamentalism and its alleged links with Islamic terrorism had contributed to the downgrading of Pakistan's status in the eyes of American policy makers. On the contrary, the American policy-makers discovered the profound importance of India in the Post-

Cold War period, whose alignment with the Soviet Union had been a thing of the past after the expiry of the twenty years Indo-Soviet treaty of friendship.

In fact the Indian armed forces which had relied heavily on soviet military supplies had lost access to weapons on concessional terms after the expiry of the treaty in 1991. Further, not only did Russia demand market price, but also continuity of supply was no longer assured. So India had no other way but to look towards US for help to fulfill its demand on weapons. Significantly enough the Russian need for American assistance had very soon prompted the Soviet Union to renege in July 1998 on its agreement with India for transferring cryogenic rocket technology as had been pledged earlier. Moreover, the vast potential of India market for American goods and the prospect of huge collaboration between the two countries in the field of joint venture and technology transfer became great attraction for the US. India's open door policy, liberalization of its economy attracted the Americans. Again, Americans needed the Indian Navy to help and keep the Indian Ocean sea-lanes open. In the Post-Cold War period, the US emerged as the largest foreign investor in India. Bilateral trade between India and the US have gained momentum from the year 1991. The Clinton Administration has identified India as one of 10 emerging markets for US exports along with China, Indonesia, South Korea and several other countries. Now the US of America has emerged as the largest investing country in India having committed over an investment amounted to US $ 2 billion in the last three years (1991-1994) and it is hoped that the same remains at the top of the heap in the future too[1]. The US is now the single largest investor in India accounting for almost billion $4 out of a total of about $12 billion worth of foreign investments cleared by the Government of India since 1991[2]. Besides this, the ambit of US-India military relations had received a further impetus when the navy of the respective countries held joint military exercises for the first time in 1992.

The end of the Cold War also witnessed marked improvement in Sino-Indian relationship. In fact a joint working group has been established to determine as how to ensure peace and security along the Sino-Indian border. As the JWG continued its deliberations, Sino-Indian trade has increased by more than seven folds from 1989-1990 to 1992-93. This has been supplemented by the exchange of visits of the Indian and Chinese Prime Minister to respective countries in 1988, 1991 and 1993. But if we take the regional considerations from security perspective, the remote threat to India is from the People's Republic of China. Of course both the countries have moved a long way from the confrontationist stand of the 1970s to the closer bilateral relations in the 1990s. First security concern is that China is a nuclear power. Secondly there is an unresolved border dispute between India and China. My thesis will examine US-China relation vis-à-vis US-India relation and how China is going to be increasingly a major factor in Indo-American relations.

Against this background the study of US-India relations gains importance. It will find out whether the end of Cold War will lead to close friendship between US and India and how it will affect the US-Pakistan relations on the one side and Indo-Pak relations on the other.

In recent years non-proliferation and human rights have been the two cardinal principles of American foreign policy irrespective of the party which wins the presidential elections. The American Government pursues these two objectives with vigour and determination. These two issues have been the bone of contention between US and India and in the coming years they may continue to affect the relations between the tow countries. Of course Bill Clinton pursued a pragmatic foreign policy. According to him the things in which both the countries disagree should be sidetracked and things should progress in positive dimensions. Regarding human rights violation by the Indian security forces the US is now convinced that it was a false propaganda by the Pakistan Government. Rather the US has cautioned Pakistan to stop cross boarder terrorism in Kashmir.

President Clinton's policy towards India has been marked as more downwards than previous democrat Presidents. US-India relation touched to new heights during the Clinton era. US-India economic relation, strategic relation made new landmarks during his period. Besides these ups some downs were also witnessed during his time in the case of cryogenic engine and the other was the Pokhran II explosion when sanctions were imposed by US on India and Pakistan. Of course sanctions were later on lifted to facilitate US-India economic relation.

References

1. Iqbal B.A. and Khan A.O., T.N.Cs: India in the World Perspective: India Quarterly, Vol.1, No.3, July-September 1994, pp.95-102.
2. India-US Relations in a Changing World: M.J. Vinod, Strategic Analysis, Vol.XX, No.3, July 1997, pp.441-442.

2

The Setting of the Problem : The US Policy Towards India Under Bill Clinton's Presidency

In a real sense, India and the USA are two influential and important countries. While the USA is three times the area of India, the population of India is two and a half times that of the USA. The one is a highly developed country and the other is at the takeoff point. As these countries constitute two different market economies, they are not competitive but are largely complementary.

These two countries have many things in common: (i) both India and the USA are secular democracies, (ii) both are wedded to the rule of law, freedom of the Press and individual liberty, (iii) both cultures represent a synthesis of various cultures, races and religions of the world, (iv) both have guided the destinies of the modern world through the forum of the United Nations and outside it and have contributed to preserve peace and freedom.

Jawaharlal Nehru, India's first Prime Minister said, "Between the US and India, there had existed friendly relations even before India gained her independence. No Indian can forget that in the days of our struggle for freedom we received from your country a full measure of sympathy and support. Our two republics share a common faith in democratic institutions and the democratic way of life and are dedicated to the cause of peace and freedom".

The US was the sanctuary of several freedom fighters of India. Among them were eminent scholars, journalists, scientists and thinkers like Tarak Nath Das, Har Dayal, G.B. Lal, S.N. Ghosh, M.N. Roy, Dhengopal Mukherjee to name a few.

Ghadr Party originated in California and the trial of the leaders of this party made a sense of feelings on the Americans that that party was no less patriotic than those of George Washington[1].

After independence, India was forced to develop friend2ly relations with the US. The Indian leaders acknowledged with gratitude the positive role played by the American President in exerting pressure on the British Government to expedite the grant of independence of India. The democratic ideals of America facilitated the Indian leaders, specially Nehru and they tried to develop intimate relations with the USA. But relations between the two could not develop in friendly lines. The main factor which hampered the development of intimate and mature relations between the two countries was difference in their foreign policy perception. India decided to keep out of the prevailing Cold War and refused to join either of the two power blocks because it would have restricted her freedom of action. India decided to pursue policy of non-alignment based on the principle of seeking friendly relations with all and judging each issue on its merits. This was not liked by the US, which considered this as an unfriendly act towards her. The US Secretary of State, John Foster Dulles declared, "Those who are not with us are against us"[2]. The refusal of India to join the military alliances sponsored by the USA was quite annoying to the American leaders.

During the Cold War years the policy of containment of Communist Soviet Union and People's Republic of China through military alliances initiated by the US in mid fifties also did not find approval with India. India felt that the forging of military alliances in which Pakistan was a member, would endanger her security through supply of huge quantities of modern arms to Pakistan. Though US administration assured India that the arms supplied to Pakistan were meant for use against communist countries, India apprehended that these would be used by Pakistan against India. In the face of all these developments, India drew closer to the Soviet Union which caused further bitterness in the US-India relations.

In 1956 Jawaharlal Nehru, India's first Prime Minister undertook a visit to USA with a view to improving relations with her. This visit failed to produce the desired results except that India was able to secure some food aid from the US. Some improvement in their relations took place as a result of their common stand on Suez crisis. But the reluctance of India to criticise Soviet intervention in Hungary and opposition to the American involvement in Lebanon further led to cooling of relations between the two. Again relations improved when the US President Eisenhower visited India in 1959. Again the relations improved under Kennedy when he became the US President. He demonstrated his friendship for India in the wake of Chinese invasion by shipping small arms and assuring air support for the defence of Indian skies. India felt obliged for this timely help. But difference persisted between the US and India because India refused to give up the policy of non-alignment.

During the tenure of Lal Bahadur Shastri as Prime Minister of India, the US-India relations continued to make steady progress because President Johnson of the US continued the liberal policy of Kennedy. In 1963 the two countries signed an agreement for the supply of enrichment of uranium fuel for Tarapore Atomic Power Station in India. He also continued to extend food aid to India. But suddenly in 1965 the relation of the US-India suffered a set back because of Indian criticism of the US bombing of North Vietnamese positions. The relation became worse during the Indo-Pak war in 1965 when Pakistan attacked India with the help of American Patton tanks which the US had provided to Pakistan for the containment of communism. The dominant role played by the Soviet Union to stop the war by arranging a meeting of both India and Pakistan at Tashkent also contributed for straining of relations between United and India.

After this incident slowly and steadily India and Soviet Union became closer to each other and the US-India relation could achieve limited success. The US-India relation became worse when President Nixon assumed power in America. He followed an international policy to check the expanding role of the Soviet Union. The US-India relation reached an all time low in 1971 when India signed a treaty of peace, friendship and co-operation with the Soviet Union. Again during the Indo-Pak war of 1971, US took a pro-Pakistan stand and charged India of interfering in the internal affairs of Pakistan. The US administration even used Gun Boat Diplomacy to pressurize India and dispatched the US 7th fleet to the Bay of Bengal.

In 1960 India had entered into PL480 agreement with US under which the later agreed to supply food grains to India against rupee payment. Some improvement in the relations between India and the USA took place in 1973 when the USA decided to write off nearly 2/3rd of the accumulated PL480 funds. But soon differences over Vietnam, Diego Garcia, and resumption of the US military supplies to Pakistan gave a set back in relations between the two countries. During the Prime Ministership of Mrs. Indira Gandhi India exploded the nuclear device in 1974. The USA bitterly criticized India's peaceful nuclear explosion which was not liked by India. In October 1974, the US Secretary of State Henry Kissinger paid a visit to India with a view to improving relations. On 28th October 1974, the US and India signed an agreement for the establishment of joint Indo-US Commission on economic, commercial, scientific, technological, educational and cultural cooperation. The prospects of improvement of relations between India and the US further improved due to the end of the Vietnam War, emerging détente between the USA and the Soviet Union and resumption of the US economic aid to India. Again in 1975 emergency was imposed in India by Prime Minister Mrs. Indira Gandhi. The USA has always stood for democracy, democratic ideals, democratic ethos. I can say it is the breeding ground of democracy next to the UK. The USA bitterly criticized India's imposition of democracy. This criticism was but natural because a country which has made democracy as the high ideal, high moral will never like the act of crushing of democratic values. So due to this coldness came in the US-India relation and India became closer to the Soviet Union.

My point is that India starting from independence had always banked upon Soviet Union for her security. All the defence supplies were made by the Soviet Union. Since independence, India has got an enemy Pakistan.

India got another enemy China in 1962 when China attacked India. Nehru was very much shocked by the act of China. When the then Foreign Minister of China Chou-en-Lai was questioned about the Chinese aggression on India, his reply was "all is fair in love and war". So India had two enemies close to her borders. The Soviet Union was the nearest friend. A Cold War was going on between the US and the Soviet Union. Even though India pursued a policy of non-alignment it was pro-Soviet in its attitude. The main task of the US at this time was containment of communism. So the USA got an ally Pakistan from the very beginning for her own interest. The USA always wanted to crush communism, to check the spread of communism. The geo-strategic position of Pakistan helped the USA to further her own interest. As we all know that national interest is the prime factor for the pursuance of any country's foreign policy, the USA got a very good platform Pakistan in that scenario and India's relation with the US was sometimes up and sometimes down. One can say, it was issue-based relation. So during the Cold War years the US-India relation was not up to the mark, sometimes good and sometimes bad. The saddest part of the thing is that even though both were democratic countries, they could not come closer for all times to come and for this the international situations were to be blamed not the USA or India.

Let us now examine the US-India relation from 1977 to 1979 when the Janata party came to power in India after 30 years of the Congress rule. The most important event during this period was the visit of the US President Jimmy Carter to India in January 1978. This gave a new warmth to the US-India relation. This visit did not bring any good result as differences arose between the US and India on the issue of Non-Proliferation Treaty (NPT). India refused to sign this treaty on the ground of being discriminatory and harmful for the national interests of India. Then in June 1978 Indian Prime Minister Morarji Desai paid a visit to America to promote greater cooperation between the two countries. The main motive of Morarji Desai to undertake the US visit was to promote greater cooperation between the two countries and to secure some agreement regarding supply of enriched uranium for use in the Tarapore plant which America had been delaying. During this visit President Carter assured Prime Minister Morarji Desai that America would try to honour her commitment. Thus the visit helped in removing some prevailing misunderstanding between the two countries even though the two could not reach any agreement on the issue of NPT. Thus, during the Janata Government, despite best efforts by the Indian Government, India's relations with the USA could make only limited progress.

In 1980 leadership change occurred both in India and the USA. While in India Mrs. Indira Gandhi became the Prime Minister, in the USA Ronald Reagan assumed office. Both the leaders tried to have cooperative and friendly relations between the two countries but relations between the two countries could not improve to a considerable level due to several factors. Let us examine the factors which hampered the US-India relations in the 80's. The first factor was the presence of Soviet troops in Afghanistan. The USA advocated the withdrawal of Soviet troops from Afghanistan. India being a friendly country of the USSR did not side with the US in this issue. To counter the spread of communism, the US sold sophisticated weapons to Pakistan. India protested against the sale of sophisticated weapons to Pakistan, as it would contribute tension between the two countries divided on the basis of religion. There were also other factors which fuelled the US-India tension. Another factor was the Tarapore Atomic Power Plant. The USA did not like to supply nuclear fuel to the plant on the plea that India had not signed the Non-Proliferation Treaty (NPT). But the USA did not insist on similar conditions in case of China. Other factor was the growing presence of the US in the Indian Ocean, i.e. in Diego Garcia. India's main contention was that the US should not try to make her presence felt in the Indian Ocean and the ocean should be demilitarized. In this case the USA's direct enemy was the Soviet Union, not at all India. I can say India was trapped by the US-USSR conflict. Pakistan got tremendous help from the US, in the Cold War scenario by taking advantage of the situation.

In 1984, Mrs. Indira Gandhi, the most popular courageous Prime Minister was assassinated and her son Rajiv Gandhi became the youngest Prime Minister of India. President Reagan was in power in the US. The most important contribution of Rajiv Gandhi in the US-India relation was the procurement of super computers from the US. He had undertaken a visit to the US in 1985 to repair the badly strained relations. US agreed for the transfer of high technology including the sell of high-speed computers and also offered advanced military technology. On 5th September 1987 both Prime Minister Rajiv Gandhi and President Reagan signed an agreement on cooperation in high technology. But again the relation between the two countries became strained because of supply of sophisticated weapons to Pakistan. India also disfavoured the growing presence of the US in the Indian Ocean. On Afghanistan issue both the US and India were like two diversified beings. India fully supported the Najibullah Government in Afghanistan and even established diplomatic contacts with that Government. The USA was fully against the Najibullah Government and was willing to replace it by a friendly Government in Afghanistan. India did not approve the aid provided by the US to the Mujahideens and regarded it as an interference in the internal affairs of Afghanistan.

Another factor for the cooling of relations between the US and India was the imposition of Super 301 law on India branding it as an unfair trade partner.

Rajiv Gandhi's party lost the election in 1989 and the National Front Government with the leadership of Viswanath Pratap Singh came to power to India. In the USA also change of leadership took place. George W. Bush became American President. Both the new Governments tried to improve relations. The US government at this time suspended action against India under Super 301. Not only this, for the first time the US warned Pakistan for extending support to terrorists and militants operating in Kashmir. The US stressed that this violates the UN charter. The US attitude on Kashmir changed significantly. Previously the US was urging for a plebiscite on Kashmir under the UN supervision. But at this moment the US came out from her previous statement and stressed that India and Pakisthan should resolve their dispute bilaterally according to the Shimla Accord. It was definitely a good sign for India. Both the countries came closer. The Indian appreciation in the US stand was marvelous. The Gulf war started in 1990-91 because of Iraq's occupation of Kuwait. The Indian Government, at this time provided refuelling facilities of American fighter planes. India cooperated with the US by providing this facility in spite of national and international criticism. So from George Bush period the US and India came closer and closer. The law of political gravitation constantly attracted India and the US to one another because of their physical size, large population, democratic way of life and the role they play in world affairs. Gone were the days of the US policy of isolation. Now the US being the strongest power of the world could not remain indifferent to world events and got directly involved in whatever happened in any part of the world. In case of India, the US could not remain as a silent spectator. A sea change occurred in the US-India relations.

The Cold War going on between the US and the Soviet Union came to an end with the collapse of the Soviet Union in 1989. As the Cold War came to an end, the Soviet troops withdrew from Afghanistan, the Soviet control over East European countries faded, the Soviet Union underwent a period of internal political pandemonium. Actually a series of international events took place at this time. The Berlin wall fell and the German unification took place. The Vietnamese troops withdrew from Cambodia. All these international events marked the end of the Cold War. Bipolarity ended and unipolarity stood up. America became the unchallenged super power in the world. Let us now examine how America and India became closer in the turn of these events. The Gulf war took place to liberate Kuwait from Iraqi military occupation. India in a significant departure from past policy, allowed American military transport planes to refuel at Bombay's Sahara Airport on their way to the Gulf. Although this permission was later withdrawn due to domestic political pressures, this gesture marked the inauguration of a much closer level of defence and security understanding between the US and India in subsequent years, compared to earlier years. There was appreciation in the US policy-making circles of India's cooperative action and attitude during the Gulf war. Lee Hamilton, Chairman of the House Foreign Affairs Committee said in April 1994: "... India in recent years has proved to be a reliable American partner. Military to military exchanges are routine. Indian forces have patrolled alongside the US and the UN peacekeepers in Somalia and have given their lives. During the Gulf war three years ago, the Indian Government, at considerable political risk, permitted the US air plains to refuel in India on their way to the Gulf"[3]. So the Gulf war was an aberration from the general trend of détente and cooperation in the world after the Soviet withdrawal from Afghanistan. India had high stakes in the Gulf region, where 1.5 million Indian nationals were stationed and 172,000 in Kuwait. India used to get about 40 percent of its oil imports which originate in Iraq and Kuwait. India issued a statement reiterating its firm position against the use of force in relations between states and called upon Iraq to withdraw its troops from Kuwait. The Ministry of External Affairs issued a statement that the "Government of India is opposed to use of force in any form in relation between states and that it sincerely hopes that Iraq would soon withdraw its troops from Kuwait"[4]. In addition, India took a series of initiatives designed to seek a non-military solution to the Gulf crisis, including the two meetings of the non-aligned countries on this subject held in Belgrade in September 1990 and January 1991. Not only this but also India adhered to all the 12 mandatory UN Security Council Resolutions on sanctions against Iraq and took effective steps to implement them. In this manner by opposing Iraq, India became closer to the US. The US-India ties became stronger and stronger.

Let us now briefly analyse what went wrong with Pakistan, the US former ally at this moment. Two months after the outbreak of the Gulf crisis, the Bush administration distanced itself from Pakistan by expressing its inability to certify that country's nuclear virginity which led to imposition of the Pressler Amendment and cut-off of all American assistance to Islamabad. In December 1990, a sizeable American defence delegation, led by Assistant Secretary of Defence for International Security Affairs Henry Rowen, came to India, giving rise to concerns in Islamabad about an American tilt towards India.

Defence is a subject which no country in the world overlooks. Every country in the world gives utmost importance to its defence. Now we shall examine how and why the US and India defence cooperation progressed. During the Cold War period it was the Soviet Union which was fulfilling India's defence requirements. The Mig-21 aircrafts, T-72 tanks were all purchased by India from the Soviet Union. After the disintegration of the Soviet Union, Russia could not remain in a position to fulfill India's defence requirements. So after the Cold War, in the 1990s, New Delhi and Washington were coming closer and closer. A few months after the Gulf war, a former Commander of the US army in the Pacific, Claude Kickleighter, brought forth a proposal to augment the level of Indo-US defence cooperation in April 1991. The Kickleighter proposal envisaged enhanced level of military to military cooperation through joint seminars, training and establishment of steering committees. Such cooperation was fundamentally different from the kind of defence ties India had with the former Soviet Union. The prospect of military cooperation received a further boost with the visit of the Commander in Chief of the US Pacific Command in October 1991 and the visit of the Commanding General of the US Army in the Pacific and Chief of Naval Operations in January 1992. As a result, joint steering committees of Army, Navy and Air force were set up. Not only this, exchange of visits of military officers to each other's military facilities and installations also increased. The most concrete and visible defence cooperation between India and the US was reflected in the joint naval exercises by the two Navies in the waters of the Indian Ocean in May 1992 and September 1994. Of course India had made such exercises with a host of other countries. But this naval exercises between the US and India shows confidence building measures between the two countries. It is definitely a step forward for military to military cooperation between the two countries. It may be appropriate here to quote what acting Secretary of State Lawrence Eagleburger told Indian Foreign Secretary J.N.

Dixit in March 1992. He said, "putting aside nuances and semantics about issues on which India and the USA disagree, it is time now to adopt a practical approach. Our joint effort (USA's and India's) should be to adopt a problem solving orientation in policies towards each other. Scoring points and old attitudes of irrelevant confrontation should be abandoned. Both sides predicate developing bilateral relations on positive lines while clearly acknowledging that there are some on which there are fundamental differences which will remain constant between the US and India". To which Dixit's reply was, "... as far as US did not over interpret or misinterpret India's differences opinion with that country (USA) on basic issues such as nuclear non-proliferation, transfer of technology and intellectual property right and as far as the US policies did not negatively affect India's national security in all its dimension, India would be willing to adopt the practical approach". From this we came to know that a new relationship developed between the US and India after the Cold War. Both the countries were willing to come forward to have good, progressive and practical relations leaving aside the subject in which both disagree. When the USSR no more existed, the Indian leadership wanted to have positive relations with new power centres of the world, out of which the US was the most important one. India's attitude was not to compromise with the fundamental interest of India and to develop economic, technological and defence relations with the US. There was convergence of the US-India attitude in many areas. For example the US and India had similar concerns for the growing international terrorism, the spreading of AIDS, religious extremism, illegal drug trafficking, support for human rights, regional stability, unrestricted navigation on the Indian Ocean and the adjoining Persian Gulf region.

The Commander-in-Chief of the US Pacific

Command, Robert Mackey in his trip to India in 1995 gave clear hints that India and the US were at that moment considering the possibility of more military exercises between the defence forces of the two countries. The idea was to gradually enhance the level of such exercises and other types of military contacts between the military establishment of the US and India. At this moment both the leadership of the two countries were trying to chalk out positive dimensions in their relations to one another leaving aside the dimensions of divergence. Robert Macckey made it clear that this US-India defence cooperation was not intended to harm any third party either Pakistan or China. So Pakistan or China need not interpret the US-India security understanding targeted against either of them.

This military to military contacts between the US and India continued during the Clinton administration in the spirit of Kickleighter proposal and the US-India naval exercises in the Indian Ocean were more than just symbolic of the changing nature of Indo-American security cooperation. The Indian Ministry of External Affairs and the US State Department kept up a series of dialogues to remove misperceptions and to improve mutual understanding on other international political and security issues, particularly the problems related to nuclear and missile proliferation. Washington also made use of this bilateral dialogue to pressurize India to soften its opposition to the NPT extension and to concede certain concessions on some strategic policies, particularly on its missile development programme. All these things, the joint naval exercises, military to military cooperation is perceived as one of the confidence building measures to remove decade-long misunderstanding.

One of the notable outcomes of Indo-American strategic understanding is the signing of an "Agreed Minutes on Defence Relations between the US and India" [illegible] the visit of the US Defence Secretary William Perry to India in 1995. Perry remarked at New Delhi, "The ending of the Cold War [illegible] the US-India security relations. Old barriers to our cooperation have been replaced by new opportunities. We in the US are excited by these opportunities and want to increase the security links between our two democratic nations. Doing so will allow us to better pursue our common security interests and provide a base of understanding for working out differences".

The agreement that is signed pointed out, "The Governments of the US of America and India recognize the importance of enhancing our defence cooperation as an important part of our overall bilateral relationship". The growth of bilateral defence relations in new areas will be evolutionary and related to convergence on global and regional issues. The enhanced defence cooperation between our two countries is designed to make a positive contribution to the security and stability of Asia. These measures will also promote the maintenance of international peace and security in the Post-Cold War world.

So this broad formulation of the US-India strategic cooperation to ensure peace and stability in Asia is an acknowledgement of the growing role of India in international affairs and in the maintenance of international peace and security. Both the US and India have important economic and security stakes in the Asia-Pacific region and it would be in the interest of both countries to cooperate in maintaining peace and stability in the region. India's status as a full dialogue partner of ASEAN and India's entry into the ASEAN Regional Forum (ARF) are significant developments of the Post-Cold War era. From the US point of view, despite the closure of its military bases in the Philippine Islands, it continues to maintain a substantial military pressure in the region and its economic interaction with the Asia-

Pacific countries is ever increasing. [illegible] was the worsening of the US-Pakistan security ties because of the imposition of the Pressler Amendment in 1990. Beijing was also at the moment carefully monitoring the US-India defence cooperation. Here it was made clear that the US-India cooperation was not targeted against any third party, including Pakistan and China. This military to military relation did not cover any arms transfer or joint development technologies.

There is little doubt that notable improvement in the US-India security ties and understanding has occurred after the end of the Cold War in comparison to earlier years. The positive trends in the security understanding between India and the US are off and on overshadowed by the divergent views between the two on proliferation issues. At the same time, the strategic community in both countries appears to have developed an understanding over the need for cooperation for maintenance of international peace and security and to deal with some of the trans-national security challenges of the Post-Cold War era, such as international terrorism, drugs trafficking and international organized crime.

Let us now examine the economic perspective on the US-India relations after the Cold War. Before analysing the Post-Cold War perspective it will be wise to hint on the background, from Cold War to Post-Cold War. India and the US have been engaged on economic interactions from the last two centuries. During the British rule in India it was between colonial India and the US as an independent country. But after independence it was between a poor country like India and economically the most powerful country the USA. So at this moment the US-India economic relation was like donor-recipient syndrome. This donor-recipient tie was not a happy experience. Sometimes the food aid given to India was guided by American arrogance. In the post-world war second period, India faced a serious famine. At this time the United Nations Relief and Rehabilitation Administration (UNRRA) had been set up. When India approached the UNRRA, it was argued that the famine in India was outside the purview of the UNRRA as it was argued that the UNRRA was only meant for population of areas liberated form enemies. Since India was neither invaded nor occupied by any enemy, the famine-stricken people of India did not qualify for emergency food aid.

Many more instances can be given. India faced famine once again in 1946. On March 1, 1946, Herbert Hoover was appointed as the Head of the Emergency Famine Committee by President Harry S. Truman, to undertake a detailed study of famine situations in various parts of the world. But India did not figure on Hoover's list. Truman felt that the Indian famine situation was exaggerated[5].

At that time India was pursuing the democratic socialist pattern of economic development where as the USA was the votary of free market economy. So the two divergent economies could not become convergent so to say. During the Cold War years India was always depending on the US assistance with a begging bowl. The USA was sometimes giving food aid but sometimes was reluctant. Various factors were responsible at that time for the reluctance of the US. For example, India's recognition of People's Republic of China and her support in favour of the PRC's membership in the UN. This discouraged American legislation from supporting a substantial economic assistance programme for India. Next was the pursuance of India's non-aligned policy.

India was a backward country having backward infrastructure facilities, low agricultural productivity and massive poverty. So during this time the Indian economy failed to attract the US businessman and investors and the nature of economic interactions between the two countries was largely like donor-recipient one. Then the political differences between the two countries had tremendous influence over the economic ties.

But things changed tremendously after the Cold War when disintegration of the Soviet Union took place in 1991. A remarkable thing happened in Indian economy when India adopted the economic liberalization programme and pursued the free market economy. For the first time India adopted the open door policy in 1991. Even before Bill Clinton entered the Oval Office as the first Post-Cold War the US President in January 1993, a report on India and America after the Cold War, co-authored by Selig Harrison and Geoffrey Kemp and signed by 34 members of the study group was released, urging the US Government to give increased priority to India as the world's largest democracy and to treat India as a potential partner in efforts to resolve the global disputes[6]. A study by the Asia Society Study Mission, South Asia and the US after the Cold War, subsequently recommended to the US Government that economic relation should be the focal point of the US engagement in South Asia because successful economic reform and deregulation in South Asia will offer extensive commercial opportunities for the US, especially India.

In 1991 the Congress party under the leadership of P.V. Narasimha Rao formed the Government at the centre in India. The famous economist, today's Prime Minister was at that time the Finance Minister. So Man Mohan Singh started the policy of economic reforms to make the Indian economy part of international economic activities. He started the process of making the Indian economy global. This caught the imagination of the American commerce, Treasury and Energy departments as well as American corporations and business houses.

Of course neither the Carnegie Report nor the Asia

Society Report had any positive impact on the State Department Official's thinking, at least during the first year of the Clinton administration. The threat to impose sanctions under Super and Special 301 clauses of the US Trade Act against India, unpalatable remarks and undue delay in sending an Ambassador to New Delhi created bad blood between India and the US.

But by early 1994, the State Department's judgment on prospects for enhanced level of economic interaction between the two countries was considerably optimistic. Assistant Secretary of State for South Asian Affairs Robin Raphel stated on February 5, 1994: "The US economic relationship with India expanded rapidly in 1993. There was more investment by American companies in India last year than in all the years since independence. Major US corporations recently launched an India Interest Group. This group includes AT&T, Coca Cola, Enron, Ford, General Electric, IBM, International Equity Partners, Morgan Stanley, Raytheon and Unisys. I am certain trade and investment will grow at an increasing pace. This is fueled by continuing Indian economic reforms and increased willingness by US business to pursue commercial opportunities there. Twenty per cent of all Indian exports come to the US, and the US is the largest source of foreign investment and commercial technology for India. The Commerce Department has designated India as one of the ten big emerging markets in the world to receive special attention as we formulate our worldwide export strategey"[7].

Robin Raphel and her boss, Deputy Secretary of State Strobe Talbott had visited India in 1994 to remove misunderstandings and to augment political relations between the two countries to facilitate further trade and investment relations. Robin Raphel asserted in New Delhi that the US supports a strong, stable and prosperous India and emphasized the growing commercial and business ties and the long-standing agreements on scientific and technological collaboration between the two countries. In a prepared speech at the American Centre in New Delhi, she further commented: "India is becoming an increasingly important trade partner. We expect the partnership to grow even more in the coming years. Prime Minister Rao and his economic team deserve great credit for launching India into the front ranks of the world's emerging markets. The new opportunities for cooperation and rapidly expanding economic relationship that I have outlined will shape our relationship in the decades ahead"[8].

The US House of Foreign Affairs Committee Chairman, Lee Hamilton, stressed the need for better ties with India in a speech to the Asia Society on April 29, 1994. Hamilton said: "For decades South Asia has been a forgotten stepchild of American foreign policy. Yet the US should care about India. Why? First, India is simply too important to ignore. One quarter of the world's population lives in South Asia – most of them in India. Early in the next century, India will overtake China as the world's most populous country. It is the world's largest democracy and the second largest English speaking country. It has the fifth largest economy, the fourth largest army, the largest scientific and technical community and the second largest number of software professionals. Fortunately there are forces drawing our two nations together. After four decades of socialism, India began in 1991 a far-reaching programme of economic reform and deregulation. The Government lowered trade barriers, eliminated government monopolies, slashed taxes, encouraged foreign investment, opened the banking sector and capital markets and made its currency convertible. The results have been dramatic. GDP is up, while inflation has fallen. Foreign investment is pouring into the country and foreign currency reserves are ballooning. New factories are churning out an ever-expanding supply of goods. India's middle class already rivals the total population of the US and is growing. The sheer size of this pool of potential customers starved for consumer goods is a powerful magnet for US business. ... US business has seized this opportunity ... the Commerce Department recently named India one of the world's big emerging markets. ... US companies with business interests are also active. They recently formed the India Interest Group, an informal network aimed at improving bilateral commercial ties"[9]. He also stressed that the Indian economic revolution must be pushed forward. Indian industries must fire the surplus workers. The money losing companies should be privatized etc.

Prime Minister P.V. Narasmiha Rao had undertaken a visit to the US in May 1994. He conveyed there the desire of India to enhance Indo-US economic cooperation. Prime Minister Rao stressed that the US and India share common interest in addressing global environmental crises, combating international terrorism and stemming the tide of international narcotics trafficking. He pointed out that in these areas both US and India have worked together. But in one thing where both have not worked well together are trade, investment and transfer of technology. India has opened its economy. The transition of a closed economy to an open, export oriented economy has taken place. As India has a vast domestic market, huge educated, skilled and semi skilled work force, sound financial institutions and time tested democratic system, the US companies have tremendous opportunities to invest in India. Prime Minister Rao had also spoken in the US that the US had become the largest trading partner and the largest foreign investor in India.

So the US has a totally new outlook about India after the Cold War. India's economic reform programme attracted the American and the Indian market got a special status in the US scenario. A totally new perception about India took place on the part of the US. Both the US and India pursued the market economy and so both economy became convergent. They became unified.

In his speech at the United Nations on September 29, 1994, Secretary of State Warren Christopher said, among other things that "India's economic reform plan has cleared the way for unprecedented trade and investment between our two countries, a matter that's certainly been noted by more and more of our business community. Our investment in India has increased more in the last year than in the preceding four decades of Indian independence"[10].

The US investment in India kept on rising in the Post-Cold War environment. The US also remained as the single largest investor in India in terms of direct foreign investment.

The long standing economic presence of the US in the region and its heightened activity in the wake of recent reforms have given it a comparative advantage vis-à-vis Europe and Japan. Enhanced economic ties will help moderate the US-South Asian political discord and will create a deeper private and public engagement between the US and the region. The most important the US interest in South Asia is continued economic reform leading to faster and well-distributed growth. The economic relation is therefore be the focal point of the US engagement with South Asia particularly India.

The committee on foreign affairs and its sub-committee on Asia and the Pacific in its 103 Congress session opined that:

Table 1: India's Major Trade Partners (Top Five Buyers) (April 1994 – March 1995).

Rank	*Countries*	*India's exports in $ million*
1.	USA	5,526.0
2.	Japan	2,220.0
3.	UK	2,011.0
4.	Germany	1,986.0
5.	Hong Kong	1,821.0

Table 2: Top Five Sellers (March 1994 – April 1995).

Rank	*Countries*	*India's exports in $ million*
1.	USA	3,384.0
2.	Germany	3,142.0
3.	Japan	2,414.0
4.	Saudi Arabia	2,020.0
5.	Kuwait	1,972.0

Table 3: Indo-US Trade (in $ million).

Sl. No.	*US-India Trade*	*1993/94 (Est.)*	*1994/95 (Est.)*	*1995/96 (Est.)*
1.	Exports to India	2,761	2,296	3,000
2.	Imports from India	4,551	5,302	3,362
3.	US share of India's imports (%)	11.84	8.93	9.80
4.	US share of India's exports (%)	20.00	19.20	23.20

To support and benefit from South Asia's economic reforms the US should:

1. Open the US markets further to South Asian exports.
2. Avoid linking human rights issues to trade or attaching environmental and labour conditions to

Table 4: Foreign investment in India (in $ million).

Sl. No.	*Country*	*1992*	*1993*	*1994*	*1995*
1.	Total approvals	1,577.1	2,835.0	4,577.0	776.9
2.	USA	499.6	1,107.8	1,125.2	276.6
3.	Germany	20.7	56.3	183.7	49.6
4.	UK	47.7	119.3	419.1	35.0
5.	Singapore	28.2	24.1	85.6	18.7
6.	Hong Kong	26.7	31.8	53.2	14.4
7.	Australia	36.4	10.7	125.2	14.1
8.	South Korea	18.5	10.6	34.5	7.6
9.	Japan	—	247.6	82.4	129.3
10.	Italy	41.9	42.4	126.1	3.2
11.	Netherlands	39.3	102.9	66.8	3.1

Sources of the Tables: (1) Secretariat for Industrial Approvals, Ministry of Industry, February 1995 and (2) Indian Investment Centre, March 1995.

bilateral and multilateral trade agreements.

3. Make South Asia a major focus of the US Government's trade and investment promotion activities
4. Review and revise Cold War era export controls to ensure that sales of the US technology and know-how to South Asian countries are not necessarily restricted.
5. Actively promote assistance to South Asian economies through international financial institutions.
6. Expand scientific and technical cooperation with South Asia.
7. Assist South Asian Governments in developing the technologies and strategies necessary to feed their rapidly growing populations[11].

So a change of the US attitude towards South Asia, particularly India took place after the Cold War. It was American State Department which formulated a totally new approach towards South Asia, particularly India. For this the golden prize should be given to the economic reforms programme pursued by India after the Cold War.

Before the Cold War, South Asia was viewed by the American policy makers, opinion leaders and citizens as fraught with problems like poverty, overpopulation, ethnic and religious conflict and natural disasters. It was seen as static, closed and backward. But after the Cold War South Asia had become a opportunity for the US in both short-term and long-term. American business could benefit from the region's economic opening and growth. The US Government could expand cooperation with South Asian countries on many issues with relatively little additional effort and resources. American non-governmental organizations, Universities and think tanks could broaden their agendas and impact through more extensive links with South Asian counterparts particular India.

Many tariffs have been lowered and import restrictions and licensing requirements had been either relaxed or removed. In India the peak tariff had been dropped from 400 per cent in 1990 to 65 per cent in mid 1994 and the average tariff had been dropped from 87 per cent in 1990 to 33 per cent in mid 1994. India has also reduced the number of items that require an import license. In India economic reforms had taken place to attract foreign investment. Privatization of Government owned enterprises running in losses had been pursued cautiously and selectively. In 1991 the actual foreign direct investment jumped from $128 million to $544 million in 1993. And in this foreign direct investment America remains at the top.

One of the most hopeful and exciting aspects of future US relations with India is the increased opportunity for private sector collaboration. Given the recent progress towards more open markets and democracy, American businesses, non-governmental organizations, media, Universities have a wider scope for cooperation. India expresses a strong interest in business, cultural, professional and educational ties with the US.

One of the areas for the US-India disagreement is the Nuclear Non-proliferation treaty. This has remained as the bone of contention in the Cold War years as well as the Post-Cold War period. This non-proliferation treaty came into existence in 1970. It obligated its signatories not to manufacture or otherwise acquire nuclear weapons or other explosive devices. This treaty signed by the USA, the USSR and England was designed to prevent non-nuclear countries from developing nuclear weapons capacity. At present 39 nations have not signed and 13 signatories have not ratified the treaty. Two categories of countries have agreed to accept and ratified the provisions of the treaty. (1) those not capable of manufacturing nuclear armaments and (2) those that are dependent upon nuclear powers for their national security. But a country like India which is capable of developing nuclear weapons has not accepted the treaty. India and other non-signatories have clear and convincing reasons for not accepting the NPT. In India's view the treaty seeks to disarm the unarmed allowing the armed to keep arming. The NPT would cage the puppy of horizontal proliferation while leaving the tiger of vertical proliferation free to maraud the world[12]. Really it seems illogical when the USA and other nuclear power states can manufacture and keep nuclear weapons, others cannot keep or manufacture. India's stand is that the NPT is discriminatory. Every country including the USA should eliminate the nuclear weapons and then only India will sign this NPT.

India detonated nuclear device in Rajasthan desert on 18th May 1974. When there was outcry in the western media, India made her stand clear by proclaiming that it was a peaceful device. India's refusal to sign the NPT evoked the US to stop supply of nuclear fuel to feed Tarapur reactor under Nuclear Non-proliferation Act 1978 (NNPA). A section of the Act prohibits export of the US nuclear goods and services to any non-weapon country which does not allow its nuclear facilities under International Atomic Energy safeguards. Actually the development of agreement with the US for Tarapur power station started in 1963 and it came into force on 25th October 1963. The tenure of the agreement was thirty years. Under Articles 11, the US Atomic Energy Commission agreed to supply all the enriched uranium fuel requirement for this plant during the term of the agreement[13].

Again India exploded nuclear bombs in may 1998. The result was the US economic sanctions. At this time Pakistan also exploded atom bomb. Looking at it the US termed India-Pakistan zone as the dangerous zone in the world. Till today India has not signed the NPT. The most interesting thing is that India could become able to explore the nuclear bomb by the US technology. Pakistan could become able to manufacture the bomb by the help of Chinese. India and Pakistan are competitive in manufacturing the bomb. Of course India has proclaimed no first use of nuclear weapon against Pakistan. But it could not satisfied the Americans. So the US imposed sanctions against both India and Pakistan.

Relations between India and the US have improved considerably since the end of the Cold War. But they are still punctuated by controversies over nuclear non-proliferation. To a significant extent, these conflicts seem to be the result of persisting American beliefs that India is obstinate about Nuclear Non-Proliferation Treaty.

In India's view, the NPT curbs the spread of nuclear weapons to non-nuclear states without providing adequate security guarantees. Furthermore, it fails to reduce or eliminate stockpiles of the weapon states and thus legitimates them. India regards vertical and horizontal proliferation of nuclear weapons as equal threats to peace, and contends that elimination efforts ought to proceed in tandem. It also believes the US unfairly singles it out from Pakistan and Israel, two other non-signatory states. Although undeclared, Israel is surmised to have a sizable nuclear arsenal[14].

No doubt the US wants non-proliferation of nuclear weapons. But India had no option out but to go nuclear. Neighbouring China has steadily advanced the size and sophistication of its nuclear weapons programme. Pakistan became a nuclear weapon state by the help of China. So India became nuclear because of her security despite US stress on NPT.

In the Post-Cold War period, there are signs that the US is stepping up efforts to limit the transfer of dual-use technologies to developing countries. Technology denial is considered a workable form of containing proliferation. Of course this assumption seems misplaced, especially in the case of India which already has a mature technological base[15].

Actually the foreign policy of a nation changes when the world scenario changes. After the fall of the Berlin wall, the disintegration of the Soviet Union, the world scenario changed completely. Before the Cold War the equation was (India and the USSR) and (the USA and Pakistan). But now the new equation became the USA and India. Both the vibrant democracies came closer to have fruitful relations. Of course many many years before also both the countries imbibed from each other. India incorporated the Bill of rights in her constitution. The spirit of America's declaration of independence so moved Indian spiritual leader Swami Vivekananda that on July 4th, 1898, he wrote a poem titled, "To the fourth of July". Move on, O Lord, in the resistless path!

Till the high noon overspreads the world.

Till every land reflects thy light

Till men and women with uplifted head behold their shackles broken, and know in springtime joy, their life renewed[16].

Again Martin Luther king was also inspired by Mahatma Gandhi, who learned from Gandhi that "non-violent resistance paralysed and confused the power structure against which it was directed".

Hundreds of American Missionaries spread into the remotest tribal areas of India, learned their complicated languages and numberless dialects and served the people there with unparallel devotion.

My point of stating of all these things is that US-India relation does not start only after the Cold War. It is age old. Of course the relationship at government-to-government level became more stronger, became more reliable after the Cold War.

Out Prime Minister P.V. Narashima Rao had addressed to a joint meeting of the US Congress on 18th may, 1994. He said, "India has undertaken the first step to shape the history for the next generation. After decades of centralized economic policies, India recently embarked on a reform programme designed to modernize our economic potential. We welcomed private investment and competition and encouraged free market growth. As a result India is becoming globally competitive and the standard of living of our citizens is gradually on the rise. The momentum of these reforms will carry India into the next century as the single largest free market in the world.

Perhaps the most impressive aspect of India's ambitious economic reform programme is the smoothness with which the transition from a closed, protected economy to an open, export oriented economy has occurred. Far reaching changes have been undertaken, in a short span of three years, at the same time devising prompt and effective steps to obviate several social consequences which could have threatened future reforms. With these steps, coupled with popular support and a broad consensus across India's diverse political spectrum the reform process has acquired a momentum of its own.

The impact of the changes in India has had a profound effect on Indo-US economic relations and has benefited both countries. American firms have been in the forefront of forging a new economic relationship. India's vast domestic market, huge educated, skilled and semi-skilled work force, sound financial institutions and time tested democratic system offer tremendous investment opportunities for forward-thinking companies.

In shaping our history for the next century, we must look ahead to greater trade between nations. An unfortunate by-product of the past half-century was the introduction of weapons of mass destruction around the world. The difficult and complex question of nuclear weapons proliferation can be effectively addressed only when we consider their global reach, requiring similar global solutions.

Every nation large or small, rich or poor is sovereign and possesses an inherent right and responsibility to its people to ensure their security. I firmly believe that the way to ridding the world of weapons of mass destruction lies in creating a world order based on the universal principles of equality and no-discrimination as means of enhancing security The answer that we as nations choose will shape the destiny of the world in the coming century.

And so much more remains to be done. A nuclear 'no first use' agreement to outlaw the use of nuclear weapons is necessary in the short term by way of precaution, while serious multilateral negotiations are launched for nuclear disarmament, the objective being a nuclear free world.

Indo-US relations are on the threshold of a bold new era. We have seen unprecedented cooperation in a number of areas. Most recently Indian forces patrolled alongside the US and the UN forces in Somalia. We share common interests in addressing global environmental crises, combating international terrorism and stemming the tide of international narcotics trafficking. In these areas, the US and India have worked closely together.

Yet there remains area where further cooperation is warranted. Export controls on technology, while once a useful means for controlling weapons technology, now hinder developing countries in their efforts to improve the lives of their people. Much of what is termed as weapons technology in fact has vital applications in a modern civilian society. Many special materials and complicated computer processors found in missile control systems are also found in hospital intensive care units and global telecommunications systems.

In October 1949, India's first Prime Minister Jawaharlal Nehru stated, "It was necessary, even desirable and perhaps inevitable that India and the US should know each other more and cooperate with each other more". Late that year, Prime Minister Nehru predicated that the next hundred years are going to be the century of America. The Prime Minister was right. The 20th century will be known as the American century.

As India stands poised to contribute to global prosperity and peace in the next century, we look forward to continuing our partnership with America and with the American people[17].

So Prime Minister Narasimha Rao stressed a whole new relationship with the USA in his speech. On 19th May 1994 President Clinton and Prime Minister Rao called for a new partnership between India and the US.

1. The two leaders agreed that democracy, respect for human rights and economic liberalization provide the best foundation for global stability and prosperity in the Post-Cold War era. They promised to cooperate in the search for solutions to global challenges posed by weapons of mass destruction, AIDS, environmental degradation, population growth, poverty, international terrorism and narcotics trafficking.
2. The President and the Prime Minister agreed to expand the pace and scope of high level exchanges on the full range of political, economic, commercial, scientific, technological and social issues.
3. Both leaders noted with satisfaction their cooperation in support of the UN peacekeeping operations, in particular in countries where forces of both countries have served. The leaders agreed to seek ways to expand their cooperation at the UN. They welcomed the progress in the Middle East Peace Process and hailed the recent elections in South Africa.
4. The two leaders agreed on the need for bilateral negotiations between India and Pakistan to resolve outstanding issues including Jammu and Kashmir, as envisaged in the Shimla Agreement.
5. President Clinton and Prime Minister Rao offered their strong support for efforts towards the non-proliferation of weapons of mass destruction and

their means of delivery and towards their progressive reduction, with the goal of elimination of such weapons, which are among the most pressing challenges to the security of states in the Post-Cold War era. They discussed these challenges in both the global and regional contexts.

6. The two leaders welcomed the successful conclusion of the Uruguay Round and pledged their governments would work to help the new World Trade Organisation continue the process of expanding trade. President Clinton praised Prime Minister Rao's courageous economic reforms and noted that the enthusiastic response of the business communities in both countries has produced record levels of bilateral trade and investment. Prime Minister Rao welcomed the investing response to India's new policies. Recognizing the potential to build a strong and positive economic relationship, both leaders agreed to work to remove impediments that exist to bilateral commerce. Commerce Secretary Brown will lead a Presidential trade and investment mission to India in November 1994 and Energy Secretary O'Leavy is to visit India in July 1994.

7. President Clinton and Prime Minister Rao expressed satisfaction with the accomplishment of thirty-five years of exchange between scientists and researchers in the US and India. They noted the discussion that have taken place with respect to a new framework Science and Technology Agreement that will carry the world's most extensive bilateral science and technology collaboration programme in to the 21st century. They welcomed the signing of two other agreements on cooperation in the areas of narcotics awareness and preservation of cultural heritage sites. They further noted that the US and

India have begun negotiations on a new extradition treaty and on an agreement on renewable energy resources, which they hope to complete in the near future. They are also exploring a treaty on protecting bilateral investment[18].

At a joint news conference with Indian Prime Minister P.V. Narsimha Rao on May 19, 1994, the US President Bill Clinton said, "Today we began what I hope will be a very close working relationship as our two countries forge stronger partnership. Our nations share many common values. And speaking as friend, we explored ways to deepen our ties and to expand cooperation. I express my appreciation to the Prime Minister for India's contributions to peacekeeping in Somalia, Cambodia, Mozambique and elsewhere.

I told the Prime Minister that we heartily support his ambitious programme of economic reform that brings India's economy into the global marketplace. This important reform plan will be the engine of growth in our relationship.

Our Commerce Department has identified India as one of the 10 biggest emerging markets around the world. We are pleased at the rapid expansion of trade and investment between out two countries. We are now the largest bilateral partner and investor with India. We are proud of that and we want that relationship to grow.

We talked about security issues that affect India in the Post-Cold War era. We discussed common efforts to curb weapons of mass destruction and their means of delivery. We pledged to intensify our efforts to achieve a comprehensive test ban treaty and a variable global ban on the production of fissile materials for nuclear weapons.

I told the Prime Minister that I hoped that India and Pakistan would continue their constructive dialogue on ways to resolve their differences, including their differences over Kashmir.

In our talks today, we also agreed to increase the frequency of high level visits and exchanges between our two countries. I have asked our Secretary of Energy, Hazel O'Leary to visit India in July to further our talks on renewable energy. And I have asked the Secretary of Commerce, Ron Brown to go to India in November to continue our important discussions on trade and to promote further growth in trade and investment.

Today's visit was the first between Indian and the US leaders since Rajiv Gandhi came to the White House in 1987. I hope that the promising future in our relations will permit more frequent exchanges.

India's freedom was born out of a remarkable struggle led by Mahatma Gandhi and others whose courage and vision still inspires us and people all around the world".

Prime Minister Rao replied saying India and the US has unprecedented opportunity to free Indo-US bilateral relations from the distortions induced by the Cold War, to look for areas of converging interest in the changed international situation, and work together for our mutual benefit.

We reviewed the tremendous economic opportunities thrown up by the sweeping economic reforms in India. He thanked the President for his administration's strong support in this endeavour. He said, "The US is India's largest trading partner. India is one of the big, emerging economics of the world, offering vast opportunities for trade and investment. Corporate America too is attracted by the prospects that have opened up in India. We will continue steadily along this path of economic liberalization. There will be no turning back".

Prime Minister Rao said on the occasion – The US

has a crucial position in promoting international cooperation. As the first Post-Cold War President of the US you, Mr. President, have a special role to play in this regard. I am happy to note in this context that Indo-US cooperation flourishes in many areas, bilateral and multilateral, ranging from cooperation in the UN peacekeeping and our joint advocacy of the nuclear test ban treaty to our rapidly expanding economic ties.

He also said - The US and India are the world's largest democracies. We share many cherished ideals and values. None are more important than democracy, individual liberty and rule of law. My discussions with President Clinton have strengthened my conviction that our two nations can work together closely for international peace[19].

References

1. P.G. Salvi, "Aid to Collaboration", Bombay, Popular Prakashan, 1978, pp.11-12.
2. Prem Arora, "International Relations", Bookhive, New Delhi-28, p.210.
3. Chintamani Mahapatra, "Indo-US Relation in the 21st Century", by Knowledge World in Association with IDSA, New Delhi, September 1998, p.103.
4. *Ibid*, p.104.
5. Srinivas Mudumbai, "US Foreign Policy towards India", 1947-1954, New Delhi, Manohar Publication, 1980, p.22.
6. Selig S. Harrison and Geoffrey kemp, India and America after the Cold War, Washington D.C.: Carnegie Endowment for International Peace, 1993.
7. "Raphel: South Asia Continues Towards Open markets, Dmocracy", Official Text, USIS, February 5, 1994.
8. Robin Raphel, "India-US Relations: On the Road to an Enduring Partnership", speech at American Centre, New Delhi, March 25, 1994. Official Text, USIS March 25, 1994.
9. "Hamilton Stresses Need for Better Ties with India", Wireless File, USIS, April 30, 1994.

10. Chintamani Mahapatra, "Indo-US Relations in the 21st Century" by Knowledge World in Association with IDSA New Delhi, September 1998, p.21.
11. South Asia Policy, September 21, 1994, p.32.
12. Verinder Grover, edited, "International Relations and Foreign Policy of India-USA", Deep & Deep Publication, New Delhi, 1992, p.365.
13. *Ibid*, p.368.
14. Deepa Ollapally. and Raja Ramanna, "Foreign Affairs", Vol.74, January/February 1995, p.13.
15. *Ibid*, p.16.
16. Documents on Prime Minister visit to USA, Strategic Digest, July 1994, Vol. XXIV, No.7, p.941.
17. *Ibid*, p.944.
18. *Ibid*, pp.946-947.
19. *Ibid*, pp.947-949.

3

The US Administration Under George Bush and India

The year 1989 proved to be a watershed, in terms of the transformation of the global scene. The Soviet Union completed the withdrawal of its forces from Afghanistan in February. By the middle of the year, the Eastern Europe was in ferment, with Communist regimes tottering and collapsing in the Warsaw Pact countries as the democracy movement gained a hold on countries no longer afraid of Soviet-backed repression. The collapse of the Berlin Wall became a milestone in European history and the reunification of Germany which had looked a distant dream, materialized in 1990 with the acquiescence of Moscow. The effects of the democratic movement were also felt in China, where demonstrations by students and young workers were tolerated in major cities till they became violent and destructive and were suppressed in June 1989 in the Tienanmen Square of Beijing in a manner that attracted western sanctions.

So in this critical juncture of world events George

Bush became the American President. From his tenure of Presidentship a new change occurred in the world, one can say the triumph of democracy and the defeat of Communism. All the Communist countries like Poland, Hungary, East Germany, Czechoslovakia, Bulgaria and Romania had ousted their Communist leaders and adhered to democracy and market economy.

Towards the end of the year 1989 a Bush-Gorbachev summit took place which proclaimed the end of Cold War. This December 1989 Malta summit between Mikhail Gorbachev and George Bush opened an unexpected, and thus far unreported note. Gorbachev urged Bush to end his public suggestions that the East is now adopting western ideas. He argued that most of the ideals behind the East's reform efforts are not western but universal[1].

Following the collapse of the Warsaw pact, the relevance and purpose of the NATO alliance came into question. However, it was felt by all the members that the plans and structures achieved over four decades should not be abandoned, particularly as the world order was in a state of flux and possible future threats to peace and stability could not be ignored.

With the Communist bloc in disarray and the Soviet model of political and economic management discredited, western analysts and policy makers saw the need to reassess future threats to the interests of the capitalist world. Islamic fundamentalism was identified as the main ideological challenge taking the cue from the rhetoric used in Iran after the Islamic revolution of 1979.

A second line of thought concerning potential threats centred on the spread of military technology to developing countries notably those in the West and South Asia. When this strand of thinking is linked to the first one, concerning the Islamic fundamentalist threat, the Muslim countries are perceived as being the greater potential menace. This explains why the pressure was built up against Pakistan to conform to nuclear safeguard while India, which had demonstrated its nuclear capability in 1974 began to be seen as a potential partner. A suspicion persisted among influential segments of the US and European intelligentsia that the Islamic countries might pass high technology secrets to each other, whereas such a risk hardly existed in the case of India. So that it had to be viewed as an aspiring regional hegemony whose perceptions could be harmonized with those of the US.

At the Indio-US strategic symposium held in India in December prior to the Gulf war of January-February 1991, which attracted high level participants from both countries, the senior military participant, Rear Admiral W. Pendley of the US Pacific Command called the Asia-Pacific region "the epicentre of the evolving multipolar world" in which India will play a significant role and set the course for stability in the Indian Ocean region. After referring to India as the world's democracy and without question the dominant power in South Asia he identified three challenges facing the US in Asia.

(1) Search for regional peace and stability
(2) Reducing proliferation of weapons of mass destruction
(3) Maintaining and advancing democracy in the region.

To this end, he specified four areas in which the US should concentrate its activities.

(1) Promoting regional security
(2) Combating narcotics traffic
(3) Stemming Islamic extremism
(4) Preventing nuclear, chemical and missile proliferation[2].

When George Bush was the American President, the Gulf war erupted in January 1991. As Iraqi President Saddam Hussain sent his troops to occupy the oil rich Kuwait in August 1990 and created a crisis that threatened to affect practically all corners of the globe, President George Bush, faced with the realization that the crisis in the Persian Gulf could be solved only with the help and cooperation of the traditional allies as well as former adversaries announced his vision of a new world order in September 1990. He said: "We stand today at a unique and extra ordinary moment .... Out of these troubled times ... a new world order can emerge. Today the new world order is struggling to be born, a world quite different from the one we have known, a world where the rule of law supplants the rule of the jungle, a world in which nations recognize the shared responsibility for freedom and justice, a world where the strong respect the weak[3].

In this Gulf war India chose to render significant services to the US, well aware of the opportunity to draw closer to Washington. Though Iraq was India's leading trade partner in the Gulf, the Indian Government provided refuelling facilities to the US aircrafts transiting from the Far East to the Gulf through India. As a consequence, two major benefits accrued to India during January 1991 alone. First, the US President George Bush approved in principle the sale of Cray super computer to the Indian Institute of Science in Bangalore. Second, on 19th January the IMF approved US$1.8 billion in credits in near record time to tide India over a severe external payment crisis.

The super computer sale is particularly sensitive because of its potential use in military programmes opposed by the US, in particular the development of long range missiles with which the scientific establishment in Bangalore is closely involved. The sale, therefore, demonstrates a great deal of trust on the part of Americans, and on the Indian side a willingness to let the US periodically check what has been run on the powerful machine. The only previous export of a Cray computer to India was in 1987 to the Meteorological office in New Delhi, right under the nose of the US embassy, where it is used to help track the annual monsoon.

The IMF credits have been advanced despite considerable doubts about the willingness and ability of India's weak coalition government to put its house in order. Indian officials are highly skilled in 'aid diplomacy', but the speed and lack of fuss with which the loans were arranged was noteworthy. "Certainly the loans could not have come through so quickly if the Americans had opposed it", a senior Indian official admitted.

The US is now the preferred source of technology for Indian industry, which officials attribute to low costs and greater familiarity deriving from the common language and presence of many Indians in the US high-tech companies. Only about 2% of export applications had been turned down and no cases of diversion had been detected. The recent decision by Washington to clear two highly sensitive items - the GE404 jet aircraft engine and fly-by-wire avionics - for use in India's indigenous light combat aircraft project showed the extent of US trust.

The rapid break-up of the Soviet Bloc in the late 1980s enabled the US, as one of its diplomats put it, "to look at the relationship with India in intrinsic terms, outside the Soviet-American relationship". An Indian diplomat said, "differences remained on several issues, but these would not be allowed to exercise a veto (over the whole relationship) as in the past".

India's gradual acquisition of the components of a nuclear strike force - its reputed stockpiling of fissionable material, if not assembly of bombs, and its testing of a 800 km-range missile – is the major subject of the US pressure. However, since there is no military or civilian aid programme to India, the legislation requiring the president's 'certification' against acquisition of nuclear weapons is not activated as in the case of Pakistan. The general US objective is to encourage a regional arms limitation agreement, but India's perception of a nuclear threat from China is a possibly fatal complication to this. China refuses to discuss any theatre nuclear issues with India[4].

Let us examine the refuelling facility given by India to the US warplanes in the Gulf war. It was definitely a tactical move by India. At this time, the Soviet Union no longer existed. India was banking upon the Soviet Union for any type of assistance particularly defence. So a wise decision was taken by the then Indian leadership. Even though it was a minority government, it took a bold decision. But the government could not stick to its decision for longer period. When this secret arrangement of the Indian government came out in the open, there was uproar in and outside the Parliament. Because of this the government was forced to withdraw the facility. But the Bush administration was grateful for the cooperation it received.

These developments led to suggestions for a revised Indian policy towards the US, Including expansion of India's economic and trade ties in tandem with the dominant power the US. Further, massive and unprecedented loans from both the IMF and the World Bank followed as a reflection of Washington's benign attitude. The IMF granted loans of $5 billion in 1991 and in 1992 India was the second largest recipient of World Bank loans that totaled $2192 million. As a result of India's economic reforms, backed by massive external loans and investment, the IMF Chief M. Camdessus expected India to be another tiger. India's external debt which had totaled $62.5 billion in 1989, rose to $74 billion in 1992 and was expected to reach $93 billion in 1996-97, according to the World Bank estimates. India's sovereignty in economic decision-making was naturally affected and it was generally expected that Washington's clout with India with regard to political issues would also increase.

At a conference of American and Indian scholars held in California two months later, after the outbreak of the Gulf war, a noted US scholar on South Asia, Dr. Stephen Cohen identified the following the US post war objectives which were duly highlighted in the Indian press:

(1) Containment of Islamic fundamentalism.

(2) Control of arms flow to developing countries in politically sensitive areas.

(3) Preventing weapons of mass destruction from falling into "irresponsible" hands.

The Indian participants at the conference including retired diplomats agreed on these objectives though they claimed to differ on how they were to be achieved.

During the period of Bush both India and the US became closer and closer. The Soviet withdrawal from Afghanistan late in the 1980s reduced the importance of Pakistan in the US strategic thinking. No longer needing Pakistan for containing the influence of the Soviet Union, the US distanced itself from Pakistan and moved to the position of an independent and impartial mediator. It stressed that the goal of its policy in South Asia was promotion of peace and stability in the region. It claimed that it wanted to prevent the outbreak of a war between the two countries that might escalate into a nuclear war. It thus moved nuclear non-proliferation to the top of its list of priorities in South Asia.

Pakistan was confident that the US would do nothing about its clandestine programme to build a nuclear arsenal, so much so that it began to boast of its achievement in the field. In 1990, for the first time, the US President George Bush refused to certify as required by the Pressler Amendment, that Pakistan be not in possession of nuclear weapons. All assistance to Pakistan, economic and military was consequently suspended. Of course this did not prevent the Bush administration from authorizing commercial arms sales to Pakistan. The Unites States exerted greater pressure upon Pakistan than upon India. It did so because Pakistan had admitted to having an ongoing programme whereas India had denied having such a programme. The US wants both the countries to sign the Nuclear Non-Proliferation Treaty (NPT). Pakistan has declared that it would sign only after India does. And India has refused to sign because it regards the NPT discriminatory. India has also argued that three countries in its neighbourhood have nuclear weapons and that it cannot for that reason agree to give up its nuclear option unilaterally. The US is therefore, engaged in an effort to bring India and Pakistan to the negotiating table. It has not succeeded so far – as India regards the problem as global rather than regional[5].

Actually, the reluctance of the Bush administration to certify that Pakistan is not having any clandestine nuclear programme is a major achievement for India. India got mileage over it. India considered the US as a true partner and the trust between the two became many folded.

The changed American perceptions and collapse of the Soviet Union led Indian analysts and experts to stress the need for a pragmatic approach in dealings with the US, now the only super power, particularly as it was seen as turning to New Delhi as a potential partner in South Asia to realise its revised goals. The former Indian Foreign Secretary Muchkund Dubey said at the end of 1991 that one of the major challenges of the Indian foreign policy would be "to continue to keep on the path of the new basis of our relationship with US". Around this time, Senator Larry Pressler, author of the Pressler Amendment under which aid to Pakistan was suspended, visited South Asia and went even further by warning Indian leaders about the danger of Islamic fundamentalist nations.

In fact the US appeared to move in the direction of military cooperation with India at a fast clip. The Chiefs of Army, Navy and Air force exchanged visits over the year following the Gulf war. General Gordon R. Sullivan, the Chief of Staff, the US Army also visited the Siachen Glacier, a disputed area between India and Pakistan, in what was manifestly an unprecedented gesture. His expression of a keen desire to learn from the experience of the Indian army in defence preparedness at high altitudes was highlighted in the Indian Press. However the foundations in this direction were laid by the then Defence Minister Krishna C. Pant who visited the US in June 1989. It marked the first official visit to the US by an Indian Minister of Defence. Apart from holding serious discussions with the US Secretary of Defence, Dick Cheney, Pant visited the US Space Command Headquarters in Colorado Springs, the US Air Force Aeronautical Systems Division, Wright-Patterson Air Force Base, Ohio and the US Atlantic Command Headquarters in Norfolk, Virginia[6].

While there was no structured proposal for Indo-US defence cooperation from either side, Defence Minister Pant reportedly sought American submarine technology systems and a wide range of warfare technology, such as sea-launched missiles and deep-sea sensors. The US official's response to Indian requests appeared quite encouraging. Washington, on its part, offered at that time to co-produce an advanced jet engine with India[7].

Such high level visits during the Bush period carry more political significance and the real groundwork is done at other levels of official interactions for substantial improvement in any type of relations. In the case of military relations between the US and India, the step-by-step improvement could take place on account of frequent interactions between the military officers of the two countries since 1989.

If we examine the visits of the US flag officers to India and the visits of Indian flag officers to the USA, we can come to the conclusion that military to military contact was at its height during the period of Bush presidency.

Table 1: Visits by US Flag Officers to India

Sl. #	*Visitors*	*Title*	*Date*
1.	Gen McPeak	HQ PACAF	Jan. 89
2.	General Kickleighter	CDE WESTOM	March 89
3.	Admiral Jeremiah	CINCPACFLT	Sept. 89
4.	General Kickleighter	CDRUSARPAC	Nov. 90
5.	Admiral Hardisty	CINCPAC	Dec. 90
6.	General Kickleighter	CDRUSARPAC	April 91
7.	Major Gen. Hyman	DIA/DA-XO	Aug. 91
8.	Admiral Larson	CINCPAC	Oct. 91
9.	Brigadier Gen. Kehoe	HQ USAF	Oct. 91
10.	Admiral Kelso	CNO	Jan. 92

Source: US Embassy in India.

The two tables clearly indicate the intense desire on both sides to improve strategic relations, but the US side appeared to have shown more interest in Army-to-Army and Navy-to-Navy cooperation, while India was equally interested in cooperation between Air Forces of the two countries. However, the key person among the military visitors who came out with a structural and detailed proposal for enhancing security cooperation between India and the US was Lt. General Claude Kickleighter, the former Commander of the US Pacific Army. His first visit to India was in March 1989 when he

Table 2 : Visits by Indian Flag Officers to USA

Sl.	*Visitors*	*Title*	*Date*
1.	Admiral Nadakarni	CNS	Mid 89
2.	Vice Admiral Chopra	VCNS	July 89
3.	Air Marshal Keelov	Inspector General	Sept 89
4.	Air Vice-Marshal Jayakumar	Director, Air Staff Inspection Team	Sept. 89
5.	General Sharma	CSA	Oct. 89
6.	Air Marshal J.K. Seth	CNC Training	Aug. 90
7.	Air Vice-Marshal Sadanand	Commandant IAF Academy	Aug. 90
8.	Admiral Nadkarni	CNS	Oct. 90
9.	Real Admiral Chopra	Eastern Command CNS	Oct. 90
10.	Air Chief Marshal Mehra	CSAF	Nov. 90
11.	Air Marshal B.D. Jayal	DCAS	Nov. 90
12.	Air Vice-Marshal Nadkarni	Air Secy. to the Chief of Staff	Nov. 90
13.	Lt. General V.K. Sood	VCSA	May 91
14.	General S.F. Rodrigues	CSA	July 91

Source: US Embassy in India.

was the Commander of the US Western Command. Later, in his capacity as the Commander of the US Army Pacific, General Kickleighter paid two more visits to India in November 1990 and then in April 1991. The importance of his visits may be gauged from the fact that the US Pacific Command is the largest of the American Unified Commands and it extends from "the West coast of the US to the East coast of Africa, from the Arctic to the Antarctic"[8].

After his three visits to India, General Kickleighter

submitted a proposal before the Pentagon for an "enhanced level of service to service contacts and exchanges" between the military establishments of the US and India. This proposal was made known to the public in the month of September, after General Kickleighter's retirement, to study the general reactions in both India and the US. The disclosure was of course timed to minimize adverse reactions, especially in India, where defence cooperation with the US was almost a taboo in the recent past. Not surprisingly, there was no major opposition to the Kickleighter proposal in Indian academic and defence analyst circles. In fact, the Press coverage of the Kickleighter proposal, days after Indian Army Chief General S.F. Rodrigues' arrival in Delhi after a fortnight's trip to the US helped create favourable reactions to the proposal in the public debates on the issue in India[9]. The US pressure on Pakistan on nuclear issues and on China over the human rights and missile sales issues, moreover, cast a positive impact on the Indian people's mind about the emerging American role in this part of the world.

In the wake of a propitious political climate, India and the US went ahead and signed an agreement the following month to "dramatically step up cooperation in the field of defence" with a substantial rise in the number of Army officers from India to be trained in the American military training institutions. The areas of training were to range from war games and logistics support to communications and nuclear concepts. In a couple of months General Rodrigues could confidently speak out that Indo-American defence ties were based on a shared strategic perception, which will evolve into a mutual arrangement that benefits both equally and then went on to disclose that India would get some force multipliers from the US for augmentation of India's combat power[10].

It was a clear indication that India was exploring

the possibilities of military equipment purchases from the US besides forging ties with the US military establishments. The exploration was understandable in view of the difficulties India started to face when the Soviet Union, a major arms and spare parts supplier, cracked up, and dozens of new political entities appeared. Following the collapse of the Central authority in the erstwhile Soviet Union, India had difficulties in locating the "estimated 3,500 suppliers scattered around the newly independent republics" which manufacture spares and equipment required by the Indian military[11]. There appeared a clear-cut necessity to look for sources of equipment and spares elsewhere. According to reports in the Indian Press, Indian defence planners were looking at the feasibility of purchasing Early Warning Systems and F-5E aircrafts from the US for the use of the Indian Navy and Air Force respectively[12].

In the backdrop of such developments two important military missions were scheduled to arrive in New Delhi in the second half of January. One was to be led by Lieutenant General Johnnie Corns, US Army Chief of the Pacific Command, and the other by Admiral Frank Kelso II, Chief of US Naval Operations. Shortly before their arrival, Defence Minister Sharad Pawar gave an exclusive interview to the Press Trust of India on January 17 and said that "India and the US are moving towards opening each other's forces and defence activities as well as having tie-ups in ambitious defence projects like the Light Combat Aircraft (LCA)"[13].

A few days after Sharad Pawar, the Defence Minister of India made this announcement, Lieutenant General Johnnie Corns and Admiral Frank B. Kelso II landed up in India. General Corns headed a team that included Col. Jimmy Ashworth, Executive Officer, Lt. Col. Lawrence R. Welti, Deputy Chief of Staff Operations, Kenneth R. Bailey, Assistant Deputy Chief of Staff Operations and Kenneth C. Brill and Col. R.J. Crites of the US Embassy in India. This team of the US officers held detailed discussions with the Indian team led by Lt. General V.K. Sood, Vice Chief of the Army Staff. Besides, General Corns also met and held wide-ranging talks centred around defence cooperation and strategic perceptions with Army Chief General Rodrigues, Defence Secretary N.N. Vohra, Foreign Secretary J.N. Dixit, Naval Chief Admiral L. Ramdas and Air Chief Marshal N.C. Suri.

It is pertinent to note here that all these developments in strategic relations between the US and India happened during the tenure of George Bush. After the collapse of the Soviet Union, the pragmatic Americans decided to have defence cooperation with India. The Indian side also looked forward for a good harmonious relations with the US in defence matters.

An upswing in strategic understanding between India and the US was evident when a joint steering committee of the two Armies met and reached some major understandings. The steering committee worked out the number of Army officers from the Indian Army Training Command (ARTRAC) and US Training and Doctrinal Command (TRADOC) who would jointly study and exchange information about their respective tactical, doctrinal, operational and logistical concepts.

Again the mission led by Admiral Frank Kelso, the second high-ranking US Naval official to visit India in the last few months, was equally important. Kelso's visit was preceded by US Pacific Fleet Commander Admiral Chuck Larson's visit to India. Larson had come to India with a clear-cut objective: to identify areas of mutual interest between the Indian and American Navies. The US had for long desired to forge a cooperative relationship with the Indian Navy, the largest among the Indian Ocean littoral, keeping in mind the strategic importance of the Indian Ocean. Writing in the Washington Times on 17 November 1989, two former

US Naval officers Elmo Zumwalt Jr. and Worth Bagley, pointed out: "For decades to come, the Indian Ocean will be a critical arena ... Clearly, in the absence of an effective United Nations Force, the Navies of the Free World are going to have to provide protection for their sea-lanes and power to prevent terrorism and revolutionary excesses for the foreseeable future .... In a decade or two, the US is going to need the support of democratically ruled India to maintain adequate free world control in the Indian Ocean[14].

In a rapidly changing world, the US could not have waited for a decade or two. Frank Kelso had arrived at New Delhi with this delicate mission. The timing of his arrival coincided with Indian Naval Headquarters' request to the Union Cabinet to consider a proposal for holding joint naval exercises with the US Navy. Before putting forth this proposal, the Indian Navy had already broken its isolationist policy by holding joint exercises with the Australian, Malaysian and Indonesian Navies. But still the idea of holding such exercises with the US Navy was a sensitive one in view of India's traditional support for keeping the Indian Ocean free of external naval presence. The times, however, have changed. Frank Kelso met with several Indian officials and political leaders to drive home the US point of view. His mission succeeded and first of all, the Indian and US Navies agreed to setup a joint steering committee, like the one established by the Armies, for concretizing relations between the two Navies. And less than two months after his departure, the Indian Government gave the green signal to the Indian Navy to hold joint exercises with the US Navy in the waters of the Indian Ocean, though outside the Indian coastal waters[15].

So, these were the defence-to-defence cooperation which was a major achievement in the US-India strategic relation during George Bush period. But there were some other areas where the Indian views and the US perception could not coincide. One of them is the NPT. India has been persistently opposed to the Nuclear Non-Proliferation Treaty of 1968. In India's view, it is highly discriminatory document that legalizes the nuclear weapons of the five big powers, seeks to perpetuate the status quo and speaks absolutely nothing about the control of vertical proliferation of nuclear weapons. The US, on the other hand, devotedly champions the NPT's cause and has been going around putting pressure on the non-signatories to sign the treaty.

It was easy for India to withstand the US pressure during the Cold War years when even China and France - two nuclear powers were opposed, though on a different logic to the NPT and a host of US allies such as Pakistan, Israel and South Africa were pursuing clandestine nuclear weapon programmes. The Post-Cold War era has witnessed a lot of changes in this field with China, France and South Africa having decided to sign the NPT and Argentina and Brazil having opened their nuclear facilities for international inspection under IAEA (International Atomic Energy Agency).

In fact, George Bush had put non-proliferation in the priority list of his Foreign policy. The first target of his became Pakistan. The US cut off its military and economic assistance to Pakistan since December 1990 under the Pressler Amendment. The next target is India because India is the only country outside the five power nuclear clubs to have demonstrated its capability to detonate a nuclear device. Many high level military delegations, the US State Department officials and the US Legislators visited India at that time. Two important State Department officials who visited India as well as Pakistan last year to discuss the regional proliferation issue were Deputy Assistant Secretary of State for South Asian Affairs, Terestia Schaffer and Under Secretary of State for International Security Affairs, Reginald Bartholomew.

Schaffer made it quite clear that the focus of the US policy for the region (South Asia) ... is the effort to encourage and develop a regional understanding on nuclear proliferation[16]. She openly supported Pakistan Prime Minister Nawaz Sharif's proposal for a five-nation meet to discuss the proliferation issue in South Asia. Bartholomew informed the Pakistanis that their compliance with the Pressler Amendment alone could remove the strains in US-Pak relations. He tried to convince New Delhi that the Nawaz Sharif proposal would be a sound step towards solving the proliferation issue in South Asia.

In the year 1992, two US legislators visited the Indian subcontinent. One was Senator Larry Pressler, the author of the Pressler Amendment and the other was Senator Daniel Moynihan, who was the US Ambassador to India during 1973-75. Both these Senators tried to convince India that it should change its global approach to nuclear disarmament and rather discuss with Pakistan to find out a regional solution to the nuclear proliferation problem in the South Asian region. Pressler even went ahead to suggest a "US sponsored" Camp David type summit between India and Pakistan to resolve the nuclear issue[17]. A couple of weeks later, when Prime Minister Narasimha Rao met the US President George Bush during the Security Council summit at New York, the latter played a similar tune by suggesting that India should cooperate in the five-nation discussions for a regional agreement on checking the spread of nuclear weapons in South Asia.

In the first half of March 1992, Indian Foreign Secretary J.N. Dixit had made a visit to Washington. When J.N. Dixit made a statement that India would not hesitate to hold bilateral discussions with the US on the South Asian proliferation issue, it was misinterpreted in certain circles and even noises were made in the Indian Parliament. Dixit's position definitely indicated a new Indian approach to nuclear proliferation. But it in no way compromised India's principled stand on the NPT or the Nawaz Sharif proposal. It was new in the sense that India was practically prepared to hold discussions with an extra regional power on regional nuclear issues.

Dixit's new approach was definitely an innovative way of trying to resolve the Indo-US differences over the nuclear issue. Although the US is an extra-regional power, Dixit suggested holding bilateral discussions with it on the grounds that it was the US which is in the forefront of the movement to stop horizontal proliferation of nuclear weapons and it was the US which can persuade Pakistan, China, Israel and Kazakhstan to come to the negotiable table to resolve the nuclear issues in this part of the world.

Some Indian defence analysts such as Jasjit Singh, Director of the Institute of Defence Studies and Analyses and K. Subramanyam, former Director of the same institute say that nuclear issues in South Asia cannot be an India-Pakistan problem alone. The Government of India has now taken up the issue at the official level. Some of the Congressmen and Senators have begun to understand India's point of view, but the US administration does not seem to be showing any interest in it yet. Here lies the relevance of the suggestion made by the Foreign Secretary for holding of Indo-US bilateral dialogue as the beginning of a process towards resolution of the nuclear proliferation issues in this part of the world. To the extent that Washington has accepted India's proposal for a bilateral dialogue, the Dixit mission can be called a success. However, there is a long-way before this issue gets resolved.

The US-India relation in the George Bush period would become incomplete without a reference to Pakistan. During the 1980s Pakistan's relations with its major external patron, the US dominated its foreign policy. After the Soviet invasion of Afghanistan the US ignored proliferation concerns and supplied Islamabad with aid worth $3.2 billion over six years. In 1986, it agreed to another aid package for Pakistan worth $4.02 billion. Almost half of this was used to purchase 40 F-16 fighter aircrafts and other state-of-the-art weapons. In return, Pakistan acted as the 'front-line state' - a conduit for US weapons sent to Afghan guerrillas. Pakistan was able play an international role quite disproportionate to its size and capabilities.

In late 1980s a series of international and regional developments took place. Improved US-Soviet relations and the end of the Cold War had a direct impact on the conflict in Afghanistan. On 14 April 1988 the US and the USSR acted as guarantors as Pakistan and Afghanistan signed agreements for Soviet troops withdrawal from Afghanistan on 15 May. The withdrawal was to be completed by 15 February 1989. It was obvious that Afghanistan had lost its centrality in super power relations and by implications, Pakistan had lost its role as a 'front-line state'.

During the 1980s, the exigencies of the New Cold War had prompted Washington to disregard its nuclear non-proliferation concerns and establish a close relationship with Islamabad. Such was the need to use Pakistan as a 'front-line state' that Washington undermined moves by the US Congressmen to scuttle the aid relationship and forced through the Pressler Amendment in 1984. The amendment required the US President to certify annually to Congress, before aid was approved, that Pakistan did not possess 'a nuclear explosive device'. For the next five years the US administration provided this certification despite its knowledge that Pakistan had developed the capability to produce at least one nuclear bomb by the mid 1980s. With the Soviet withdrawal from Afghanistan, however, the US administration revived interest in the control of nuclear proliferation in South Asia. By 1990 the US was convinced that Pakistan had converted enriched uranium gas into material for a nuclear bomb[18]. The Bush administration, no longer interested in Pakistan as a 'front-line state', therefore, refused to provide the annual certification for Congress. The US aid to Pakistan was suspended on 1 October 1990.

The end of the US-Pakistan aid relationship occurred only two months after Saddam Hussein's invasion of Kuwait in August 1990. The ensuing Gulf crisis and war created numerous economic problems for Pakistan. The oil import bill increased by $1 billion and Islamabad suffered a 30% loss in exports to the Gulf region. The remittances from migrant workers stationed in the Gulf region also declined from $1.8 billion in 1989-90 to $700 million in 1990-91. It posed problems for a government which had increasingly relied on the income from these remittances. There was also the added expenditure of repatriating and settling almost 100,000 Pakistani migrant workers who had fled to Jordan from Kuwait and Iraq. The net result was that Pakistan's foreign exchange reserves dwindled to $100 million - barely enough for two weeks imports. Islamabad had to ask the UN Security Council for $2.9 billion to cover the economic consequences of the Gulf crisis[19].

With the end of Cold War also the close Indo-Soviet relationship came to an end. Though Russia took on the mantle of the former Soviet Union, Moscow's relationship with New Delhi failed to regain the intimacy of the 1970s and 1980s. The 1991 agreement to replace the 20 years Indo-Soviet Treaty of friendship did not refer to Russian military or political support when India is involved in armed conflicts[20]. The Indian armed forces, which relied heavily on Soviet military supplies, also lost access to weapons on concessional terms. Not only did Russia demand market prices, but continuity of supply was no longer assured. Significantly its need for American assistance prompted Russia to renege in July 1993 on its agreement with India for transferring cryogenic rocket technology[21].

During the George Bush period, however, India's relations with the US have improved as their interests converge in the Post-Cold War era. India needs alternative source of military and economic assistance and America needs the Indian Navy to help keep the sea-lanes open. There is also the added attraction of the huge Indian market for the US goods. The two states India and America are expanding the scope of their interaction. The US has emerged as the largest foreign investor in India, accounting for 41.6% of total foreign direct investments between January 1991 and August 1993. The US-Indian military relations have also improved during the Bush period. As mentioned earlier, the two navies held their first joint exercise in 1992 and by early 1993 the US Army was expressing interest in holding joint exercises in a high altitude environment[22]. Although some irritants remain in Indo-US relations, such as the reluctance of the former to enforce intellectual property rights, human rights abuses in India and nuclear non-proliferation, the two states are likely to continue to improve relations.

During the George Bush period, the US-Pakistan relationship has come to a virtual halt. While Washington is unlikely to entirely abandon Islamabad, the latter's usefulness to American strategic policy has clearly diminished. The end of Afghanistan war, at least in terms of Soviet involvement has reduced the importance of Pakistan as a bulwark against further Soviet southward expansion or as a conduit for the US arms supplies to the Mujahadeen. While there was some thought that the Gulf war would serve to promote reconciliation between Washington and Islamabad, this did not materialize. The short duration of the war and Pakistan's unwillingness to actually join the coalition in battling Iraqi troops partially explains the failure of more substantive US-Pakistani ties to develop from the episode.

The US-Pakistani military relationship was a key cause of US-Indian discord during the 1980s and its virtual end has already had palliative effects on US-Indian relations. Two issues of regional discord which have withered have been the US-Pakistani military relationship and the Afghanistan war. Though less central to US-Indian relations, India's establishment of diplomatic relations with Israel and vote in favour of repealing the "Zionism is racism" resolution in the United Nations have also removed an important irritant in relatins[23]. Speaking in mid-1991, Indian Ambassador Abid Hussain suggested that the move towards ties with Israel reflected not only an appreciation of the benefits it would bring in Washington, especially Congress, but a new assessment of India's Middle East policy.

The main focus of the US-India relation is to minimize bilateral disputes as well as strengthening existing and building new areas of cooperation. Resolution of disputes over Tarapur and intellectual property protection and the development of even more constructive economic and defence ties is likely to grow in the US-India bilateral relations. Indeed, President Bush described his hope for bilateral relations very much along these lines, saying:

"During the decade of the eighties, our two governments have worked hard to get off this roller-coaster and establish a solid, steady base of relations capable of absorbing occasional shocks while moving steadily forward. We will need this resilience in order to deal with the challenges that confront your region and the world in the years ahead. We have, to be sure, some difficult issues to deal with. The strength of our times will be demonstrated by our ability to negotiate and resolve our differences without allowing them to obscure the friendship between us"[24].

India's Ambassador Karan Singh also responded by noting that "divergences would probably remain, but expressing a hope that the two countries could work within and through them. The strength of our relationship lies in the capacity to recognize areas of differences and, while attempting to narrow them down, to continue working together harmoniously in the areas of mutual interes"[25].

The trend established in the 1980s, towards treating Pakistan as a less critical issue in the US-Indian relations also continued in the 1990s. The US has ceased its military relationship with Pakistan in the light of Soviet withdrawal from Afghanistan, end of the Cold War, the retreat from involvement in the Afghan civil war, and Pakistan's pursuit of a nuclear weapons option. All these things eases a major Indian concern about the US-Pakistani ties.

Now the US has been less adamant about a plebiscite in Kashmir – a subtle shift in policy which has been appreciated in New Delhi. The Bush administration has emphasized that a settlement of Indo-Pakistani differences over Kashmir should be pursued in the framework of the 1972 Shimla Agreement. Some members of the American Congress attempted to undercut administration policy by introducing legislation that would require the holding of plebiscite. But these efforts were defeated by pro-India forces in Congress and administration. During the Bush administration, Washington has been less hesitant to recognize Pakistan's involvement in Kashmir and Punjab turbulence, implicitly supporting New Delhi's claim that much of the violence, especially in Kashmir, is being spurred by Pakistani activities. In 1990 the US Ambassador to Pakistan Robert Oakley, in a letter to the President of Pakistan-occupied Kashmir Sardar

Mohammed Abdul Qayyum Khan, wrote that "(such support is a violation of the UN charter and makes a political solution more difficult)"[26]. However, the US administration has also criticized India's human rights record in dealing with Kashmir and Punjab and its unwillingness to fully cooperate with international human rights organizations. But the Indian policy makers must have the reason enough to expect a categorical statement from the White House that Kashmir is a part of India and not a disputed territory. They cannot simply brush aside the concerns shown by the American Congress about human rights issues.

India's willingness to be accommodative to Washington's concerns has not been without limits. This was evident in a biff in mid-1992 over the purchase by India of booster rocket engines from Russia. India claimed that the engines were to be used for launching commercial satellites, but the US insisted that the sale would violate the 1987 Missile Technology Control Regime (MTCR) to which Moscow was a signatory. While the dispute reflected long standing US concerns about missile proliferation, especially those capable of carrying nuclear warheads, the US opposition to this particular deal was odd for several reasons. First, the Indians had apparently approached the American Companies General Dynamics and McDonnel Douglas for similar technology without the US government objection. India seems to have turned to Russia due to a better offer. Second, during the 1980s the US had promised, as part of the improving US-Indian relationship, to assist India's peaceful space programme. Finally, Russian officials were willing to allow independent experts to examine the deal, an offer the US refused to accept. In the end, as Russia and India consummated the deal, the US imposed sanctions on both countries' space organizations. It is noteworthy, however, that the Bush administration apparently imposed sanctions only reluctantly, having no choice because of a Congressional law. Whether it would have imposed sanctions in the absence of the Congressional legislation remains a matter of speculation. Nevertheless, the episode illustrated once again the fragility of the US-Indian relations in certain areas[27].

So missile as well as nuclear issues (bilateral, regional and global) confront the US-India relations with their most significant challenge in the Post-Cold War era. While Pakistan's nuclear programme no longer plays a negative role in the US-Indian relations as it did in the 1980s (the US having now cut off military and economic aid to Islamabad) in some sense the pressure of nuclear issues in the bilateral relationship is even more compelling. How these pressures and issues are to be handled which could well affect the future course of the US-Indian relations in other spheres remains to be seen.

There have been no dramatic departures in the economic sphere of the US-India relations since the end of 1980s, despite the bold restructuring of the Indian economy which has occurred during the same period. Several features of the US-Indian economic relations are, however, worth noting.

The US Import - Export Bank has recently doubled its lending profile in India to over $500 million and expects India to be its fastest growing portfolio. This reflects the growing investment interest of American companies in India. American investment in India remains small, especially when compared with other Asian countries. However, it does represent the largest amount of foreign investment in India at just about $630 million. There have not yet been major increases in investment in the wake of the recent changes in India's foreign investment policies though some significant increases are likely to occur soon. The US direct investment in 1990 was only $19 million or half of the $38 million invested in 1989. However, the Indian Government, in less than one year, has approved investment projects proposed by the US companies such as IBM, Kellog's Ford, and General Electric totaling over $200 million.

The US has also retained its position as India's largest trading partner. According to the US Embassy in New Delhi: "US exports to India reached a record $2,486 million in 1990, but fell to $2,003 million in 1991. India's 1991 exports to the US were flat at $3,197 million, increasing the persistent US trade deficit with India to just over $1 billion". It is noteworthy that the US exports to India consist of sophisticated machinery and high tech products and components. One of the key areas of improvement in the US-Indian economic relations over the past decade has been the composition of trade, and not simply its dollar value. In December 1991, India and the US concluded negotiations to extend their bilateral textile agreement. They agreed on a package that would increase India's access to textile and garment exports to the US.

The US has been quite supportive of India's requests for international lending, especially in the aftermath of the Gulf war when India was facing an acute foreign exchange crisis. In 1990, the Bush administration played an important role in the approval of the major IMF loan for India. This constricted sharply with the Reagan administrations hesitations to approve an IMF loan for India in 1981.

Despite some improvement in current and prospective US-Indian economic relations, there remain some serious problems to be addressed. During the George Bush period, the US, in early 1992, suspended duty-free treatment to chemicals and pharmaceutical worth some $60 million imported from India. And India remained on the US's super 301 list of 'unfair traders'. What is noteworthy, however, is the relatively mild response of Indian officials to such US actions, indicating the new tone which has been established in bilateral relations. When in 1991 India was retained on a watch list under the super 301 legislation, the Indian Commerce Minister Subramaniam Swamy said merely that "we are certainly not happy with the US decision but I do not think we need to over react because doors are still open for conciliation and negotiation". While the government of India attempted to play down the dispute, it has been under considerable pressure at home to reject American 'arm twisting'. On May 4, 1992, 50 members of India's parliament had issued a letter to President Bush criticizing the US action[23].

Now the challenge for the US-Indian relations in the economic sphere as in other areas is to minimize frictions and concentrate on taking advantage of the opportunities which are now emerging for substantive cooperation in the changed Indian economic climate.

References

1. Cherles William Maynes, "America without the Cold War", Foreign Policy, Vol.78, Spring 1990, p.3.
2. "Changing US perceptions in South Asia", Spot light on Regional Affairs, Vol.XI, No.12, December 1992, p.20.
3. Quoted in John Dumbrell, American Foreign Policy: Carter to Clinton, London: Macmillan, 1997, p.163.
4. Hamish McDonald, "Technically Friends", Far Eastern Economic Review, Vol.151, Jan. 31, 1991, p.13.
5. B.K. Shrivastava, "Indo-American Relations: Search for a New Equation". International Studies, 30, 2(1993), p.127.
6. USIS Press Release, New Delhi, 1 July 1989.
7. Chintamani Mahapatra, "Indo-US Defence Cooperation: Problems and Prospects", Strategic Analysis, November 1991.
8. USIS Press Release, 10 April 1989.
9. Financial Express, 27 August 1991.
10. Times of India, 1 December 1991.

11. Statesman, 7 January 1992.
12. Hindu, 2 January 1992.
13. Hindustan Times, 18 January 1992.
14. Washington Times, 17 November 1989.
15. Times of India, 17 March 1992.
16. Hindu, 20 January 1992.
17. Hindustan Times, 12 January 1992.
18. William Burrows and Robert Windrem, Critical Mass (Simon and Schuster, 1994), excerpts in, 'The Most Dangerous Place on Earth', India Today, Vol.19, No.3, 15 February 1994, pp.23-34.
19. Jonathan S. Addleton, Understanding the Centre: The Gulf Migration and Pakistan (Karachi: Oxford University Press, 1992), pp.113-119.
20. J.Mohan Malik, 'India Copes with the Kremlin's Fall', Orbis, Vol.37, No.1, Winter 1993, p.69.
21. M.R. Kurup, 'The Cryogenic Imbroglio', The Hindu, 12 August 1993.
22. Times of India, 16 February 1993.
23. Steve Coll, "India to Extend Full Diplomatic Ties to Israel", January 30, 1992 A 17 and Shekhar Gupta, "Indo-Israel Relations: A Pragmatic Peace", India Today, February 29, 1992, pp.67-68.
24. Vasantha Arora, "Bush Urges Dialogue on Trade Differences", India West, August 18, 1989, p.18.
25. *Ibid.*, p.18.
26. "US Envoy Wants Pak to Stop Backing Terrorism", India West, December 21-28, 1990, p.20.
27. Satu P. Limaye, "US-Indian Relations: The Pursuit of Accommodation", Westview Press, boulder, Sanfrancisco, Oxford 1993, p.246.
28. *Ibid*, pp.246-247.

4
Clinton's Policy Towards India : Security Perspective – Nuclear Issue, CTBT, Missiles

While the end of the Cold War transformed the political landscape of Europe, it did little to ameliorate India's security concerns. The rise of China and continued strains with Pakistan made the 1980s and 1990s a greatly troubling period for India. At the global level, the nuclear weapons states showed no signs of moving decisively towards a world free of atomic danger. Instead, the nuclear non-proliferation treaty (NPT) was extended indefinitely and unconditionally in 1995, perpetuating the existence of nuclear weapons in the hands of five countries busily modernizing their nuclear arsenals. In 1996, after they had conducted over 2,000 tests, a Comprehensive Test Ban Treaty was opened for signature, following two and a half years of negotiations in which India participated actively. This treaty alas, was neither comprehensive nor related to disarmament but rather devoted to ratifying the nuclear statuesque. India's options had narrowed critically.

India had to ensure that its nuclear option, developed and safeguarded over decades was not eroded by self-imposed restraint. Such a loss would place the country at risk. Faced with a difficult decision, New Delhi realized that its lone touchstone remained national security. The nuclear test it conducted on May 11 and 13, 1998 were by then not only inevitable but a continuation of policies from almost the earliest years of independence. India's nuclear policy remains firmly committed to a basic tenet: that the country's national security in a world of nuclear proliferation lies either in global disarmament or in exercise of the principle of equal and legitimate security for all.

In 1947, a free India took its rightful place in the world and followed the path of non-alignment. From the very beginning, India's foreign policy was based on its desire to attain an alternative global balance of power that crucially was structured around universal, non-discriminatory disarmament.

Nuclear technology had already transformed global security. Nuclear weapons, as theorists reasoned, are not actually weapons of war, but in effect, military deterrents and tools of possible diplomatic coercion. The basis of Indian nuclear policy, therefore, remains that a world free of nuclear weapons would enhance not only India's security but the security of all nations. In the absence of universal disarmament, India could scarcely accept a regime that arbitrarily divided nuclear haves from have-nots. India has always insisted that all nations' security interests are equal and legitimate. From the start, therefore, its principles instilled a distaste for the self-identified and closed club of the five permanent members of the UN Security Council.

During the 1950s nuclear weapons were routinely

tested above ground, making the mushroom cloud the age's symbol. Even then when the world had witnessed a few dozen tests, India took the lead in calling for an end to all nuclear weapons testing, but the call of India's first Prime Minister, Jawaharlal Nehru, went unheeded.

In the 1960s, India's security concerns deepened. In 1962, China attacked India on its Himalayan boarder. The nuclear age entered India's neighbourhood when China became a nuclear power in October 1964. From then on, no responsible Indian leader could rule out the option of following suit.

With no international guarantees of Indian security forthcoming, nuclear abstinence by India alone seemed increasingly worrisome. With the 1962 war with China very much on his mind, India's Prime Minister Lal Bahadur Shastri began tentatively investigating a subterranean nuclear explosion project. A series of Indian non-proliferation initiatives had scant impact. In 1965, to make matters worse, the second war between India and Pakistan broke out. Shastri died in 1966 and was succeed by Indira Gandhi, who continued the fruitless search for international guarantees. In 1968, India reaffirmed its commitment to disarmament, but decided not to sign the NPT[1].

India demonstrated its nuclear capability on May 18 1974, when it conducted the first nuclear test in Pokhran – a desert area in Rajasthan, some 350 miles away from New Delhi. Technically, India then became the world's sixth nuclear power[2]. However, because of international pressure, particularly from the US and Canada, Mrs. Indira Gandhi was then believed to have bitten off more than she could chew regarding nuclear weapons. The Central Intelligence Agency was caught unawares of the Indian tests. The test was then described as a Peaceful Nuclear Explosion (PNE) by India. But few were willing to buy this explanation. It was also considered as being against the spirit of Nuclear

Non-proliferation (NPT), but since India had not signed the NPT, it was not strictly in violation of any international treaties.

The first 50 years of Indian independence reveal that the country's moralistic nuclear policy and restraint paid no measurable dividends, except resentment that India was being discriminated against. Disarmament seemed increasingly unrealistic politics. If the permanent five's possession of nuclear weapons increases security, why would India's possession of nuclear weapons be dangerous? If the permanent five continue to employ nuclear weapons as an international currency of force and power, why should India voluntarily devalue its own state of power and national security? If deterrence works in the west – as it so obviously appears to, since western nations insist on continuing to possess nuclear weapons – by what reasoning will it not work in India? Nuclear weapons powers continue to have, but preach to the have-nots to have even less. India counters by suggesting either universal, non-discriminatory disarmament or equal security for the entire world.

After 24 years, India surprised the world once again by conducting three nuclear tests on Buddha Poornima Day – May 11, 1998. One was a plutonium type similar to the 1974 test. Another was a thermonuclear or hydrogen bomb, and the third one was a low yield device with a wider application – primarily a tactical weapon. All three devices were triggered by one pull.

Two days later, on May 13, 1998, other two weapons were tested at Pokhran. These tests gave Indian scientists up-to-date knowledge on the latest developments in weaponisation of nuclear technology including an ability to conduct sub-critical tests or testing by computer simulation in the laboratory.

Prime Minister Atal Behari Vajpayee later said: "India now is a nuclear weapon state"[3]. Brijesh Mishra, the Prime Minister's special secretary, also said after the May 11 tests: "These tests have established that India has a proven capability for a weaponised nuclear programme"[4]. R. Chidambaram, Chairman, Atomic Energy Commission stated: "The bombs tested at Pokhran were purely for defensive purposes". This time there was absolutely no reference to any peaceful nature of the nuclear tests.

A fortnight later, on May 28 and 30, neighbouring Pakistan predictably carried out its own tests in the bleak fastness of the Chagai Hills in Baluchistan, near the Afghan border. Suddenly the strategic equipoise of the Post-Cold War world was rattled. The entire non-proliferation regime and the future of the disarmament were at the forefront of international agendas.

Countries around the world joined the US in expressing dismay and condemnation of India and Pakistan's nuclear tests, although the strength of their concrete actions varied greatly. On May 13, President Clinton imposed wide-ranging sanctions on India, remarking that its surprise nuclear testing "recalls the very worst events of the 20th century". Noting that 149 nations have already signed the Comprehensive Test Ban Treaty (CTBT), the President called on India to define its greatness "in 21st century terms, not in terms that everybody else has already decided to reject". On May 13, the US Senate Subcommittee on Near Eastern and South Asian Affairs held hearings on India that had been originally intended to focus on growing ties and economic cooperation between the US and India but instead became a forum for bipartisan condemnation of India's nuclear tests[5].

A number of nations joined the US in imposing economic sanctions on India. On May 14, 1998, Japan announced it was suspending aid loans, reportedly $1 billion, in addition to suspending $26 million in grant aid. Germany, Australia, the Netherlands, Sweden and Denmark also announced economic sanctions on India on varying degrees of severity. The Europeans and Japanese also supported the US in postponing consideration of pending World Bank loans for India.

Amid fears by non-proliferation experts that India's tests would prompt testing by Pakistan and other countries, President Clinton dispatched a high level team headed by Deputy Secretary of State Strobe Talbott, to Pakistan to try to dissuade Islamabad from responding in kind. Acknowledging the pressures on the Pakistani government to test, President Clinton stated that refraining from testing, "would be a great act of statesmanship and restraint on their part". It was not clear what incentives the US officials intended to offer Pakistan, but settlement of the longstanding dispute over the non-delivery of F-16 fighter planes as a result of the cutoff of aid to Pakistan in 1990 was widely cited as one possibility. In any event, whatever incentives the Administration may have offered, Paksitan tested on May 28.

Both countries have long possessed the technology and materials to build nuclear weapons. India conducted its first and only previous nuclear test in May 1974 and since then maintained ambiguity about the status of its nuclear programme. Pakistan probably gained a nuclear weapon capability sometime in the 1980s. Prime Minister Nawaz Sharif declared that Pakistan could have tested years ago has it chosen to do so. India has consistently rejected as discriminatory the Nuclear Non-proliferation Treaty (NPT) and the Comprehensive Test Ban Treaty (CTBT), calling instead for a global nuclear disarmament regime. Pakistan traditionally has maintained that it will only sign the CTBT and NPT when India does so.

Now let us examine what is the motivation behind India going nuclear. The original impetus for New Delhi's development of its nuclear option appears to have been its sense of strategic rivalry with China dramatized by India's 1962 defeat in a short border war, followed by China's first nuclear explosion in 1964. Three decades of chilly relations across a disputed border and China's expanding nuclear and missile capability reportedly served to confirm India's perception of a Chinese threat. Yet until the mid-1990s, India showed no urgency of intent to follow up on its 1974 explosion of a plutonium device underground. India's concerns about China have been further fueled by China's longtime support for Pakistan, including the supply of arms and nuclear and missile technology. India and Pakistan have fought three wars in the half-century since their independence[6].

In a May 12, 1998 letter to President Clinton and other world leaders, Indian Prime Minister Atal Behari Vajpayee listed concerns about the "deteriorating security and nuclear environment" – with oblique references to China and Pakistan – as the impetus for India's conducting the May 1998 nuclear tests[7]. Since 1993, India-China relations had been improving as a result of a agreement that called for a reduction of troops along their common border, talks on border demarcation and an expansion of economic and cultural ties. In late April 1998, however, Indian Defence Minister George Fernandes made several statements in which he referred to China as "India's greatest threat". Fernandes alleged among other things, that China had supplied Pakistan with technology for a medium-range missile tested by Pakistan in early April and that China had extended its military airfields in Tibet and established a "massive electronic surveillance system" in Burma's Coco Islands.

India's emphasis on the China threat as a rationale for its nuclear tests became diluted somewhat after Pakistan's blast. Prime Minister Vajpayee told reporters on May 28, that rather than India forcing Pakistan's hand, it was Pakistan that "forced us to take the path of nuclear deterrence"[8]. In his letter to Clinton, Vajpayee also alleged Pakistan's sponsorship of insurgencies in India's Punjab and Jammu and Kashmir states over the past decade saying, "We have been the victim of unremitting terrorism and militancy".

Despite the rationale offered by the Indian government officials for testing at this time, many analysts point to domestic political factors as a more likely immediate impetus, as Prime Minister Vajpayee was leading an un-widely minority coalition government.

In conducting nuclear tests, the BJP government clearly played the popular national prestige card - long standing aspirations for major power status, which to many Indians means acceptance into the elite club of nations with recognized nuclear programmes. Former Indian Secretary, Muchukund Dubey, stated the Indian case in 1994: "The bomb option is a currency of power that is critical to our survival as a strong nation"[9]. The Congress party, which ruled India for 45 years, also backed the BJP decision to conduct nuclear tests.

Let us know the Pakistan motivation. Pakistan's motivations were largely self-evident. In announcing the May 28 series of tests, Prime Minister Nawaz Sharif described his decision as "inevitable" and declared "we have settled the account of the nuclear blasts by India". Pakistan lived with a demonstrated Indian nuclear capability for more than twenty years and was aware since at least late 1995 that India's nuclear establishment was prepared to test within a short time after receiving 'the political go ahead'. Apart from concerns about the political costs of not testing, Pakistan may have been anxious to test in order to reassure itself that its weapons worked and to impress upon India and others the reality of Pakistan's nuclear capability.

The US President Bill Clinton found the nuclear tests by India an affront to the US efforts to prevent nuclear proliferation. He stated that he was "deeply disturbed by the nuclear tests", that he did not believe that such tests contributed to "building a safer 21st century", and added that "this action by India not only threatens the stability of the region. It directly challenges the firm international consensus to stop the proliferation of weapons of mass destruction[10]. And then he went on to announce on May 13, imposition of sanctions against India under Section 102 of the US Arms Export Control Act, also known as the Glenn Amendment. The US Deputy Secretary of State, Strobe Talbott, characterized the tests by India and subsequently by Pakistan as a path leading to a "dead end", and advised others not to "follow down that path"[11]. Henry Sokolski, a former senior pentagon official for non-proliferation policy commented: "India has just dug a big hole for itself by doing this test – a military, political and economic hole. Its banking system is in a world of hurt now. It is about to get a deathblow. This is not just a nuclear test for India. It is a political test for the US[12].

The nuclear tests by India were criticized by friends and foes alike in the US Congress as well, with some seeking quick action to punish India. Florida Republican Bill McCollum, Co-Chairman of the Congressional India caucus and a longtime advocate of better relations with New Delhi, felt that the tests were "certainly going to strain our relations, which had been better in the past two or three years than at any time in history". Senator John Glenn, Ohio Democrat and former astronaut, whose own Glenn Amendment is a legislative weapon against proliferation, described India's tests as "the triumph of fear over prudence, a monumental setback for efforts to half the global spread of nuclear weapons". Senator Sam Brownback, Kansas Republican and head of the Senate Foreign Relations sub-committee on Near Eastern and South Asian Affairs, urged the Clinton administration to punish India, by saying that the nuclear tests were "a terrible action on the part of the Indian Government". According to Senator Joseph Biden, Delaware Democrat, "It is an enormous negative blow to our relationship with India. It will destabilize the region"[13].

The Americans felt that they have been deceived by India, as the Indians did not disclose its nuclear tests earlier despite the close relations between the two countries. Secretary of State Madeleine Albright once told the US Congress that the Indians had deceived the US by conducting the nuclear tests[14]. Now the question comes, how many countries in the world, including the US, have informed others in advance regarding their respective nuclear weapons programme. The US State Department officials and the American diplomats appear to be under the impression that India should have spelled out its nuclear programme to them, since the two countries were in the process of conducting "strategic dialogue" in the new context of the Post-Cold War era. The US Ambassador to the United Nations, Bill Richardson, was in Delhi not long before the Pokhran II explosions and he felt deceived that his Indian counterparts had said nothing about their plans.

The fact remains that the remaining super power of the Post-Cold War world, the US did feel hurt over the Indian action. On May 12, President Clinton gave a public warning that Indian's defiance won't go unpunished. "As most of you know our laws have very strong provisions signed in them by me in 1994, in response to nuclear tests by non-nuclear states", he said. "And I intend to implement them fully"[15]. In the American perception, India took a step which was bound to hamper the rising security understanding and economic cooperation between US and India. Since 1994, a new American law, known as the Nuclear Proliferation Prevention Act, has been in place. This Act combines all major previous legislations on proliferation issues to facilitate a clearer position of the US on the subject. One of the key parts of the legislation was incorporation of the Glenn Amendment, which authorised sanctions against countries detonating one or more nuclear devices. Acting under this law, President Bill Clinton imposed the following sanctions on May 13, 1998:

* termination of assistance under the Foreign Assistance Act of 1961, except for humanitarian assistance for food and other agricultural commodities:
* termination of sales of defence articles, defence services or design and construction services under the Arms Export Control Act and termination of licences for the export of any item on the US munition list:
* termination of all foreign military financing under the Arms Export Control Act:
* denial of any credit guarantees or other financial assistance by any department agency or instrumentality of the US government:
* the US opposition to the extension of any loan for financial or technical assistance by any international financial institution like the World Bank and IMF:
* prohibition of US banks from making any loan or providing any credit to the Government of India, except for the purposes of purchasing food or other agricultural commodities: and
* prohibition of export of specific goods and technology subject to export licensing by the Commerce Department.

If we go to the genesis of the bomb, let us examine chronological event that produced it. Actually the rivalry between India, Pakistan and China is the main reason behind it.

1947 : British colonial rule ends, and the subcontinent is partitioned into mostly Hindu India and mostly Muslim Pakistan. Both claim the border regions of Jammu and Kashmir. Widespread interethnic violence follows partition; over a million people are killed and some 10 million refuges flee from their homes.

1957 : India constitutionally incorporates its portions of Jammu and Kashmir as a separate Indian State.

1962 : India and China go to war over disputed border territory.

Oct.1964 : China successfully tests an atomic bomb.

1965 : India and Pakistan fight their second major war, but neither gains much territory.

1971 : A flood of some 10 million refuges from East Pakistan into India sparks a third India-Pakistan war, which India wins. Bangladesh is born.

May 1974 : India explodes an underground nuclear device.

Feb. 1984 : Pakistan announces success in producing enriched uranium.

Nov. 1986 : The US reports, Pakistan has produced weapons-grade uranium.

March 1987 : Pakistani scientists say country possesses a nuclear weapon.

Feb. 1988 : India tests short range Prithvi missile.

Jan. 1989 : Pakistan tests short range Hataf missile.

May 1989 : India tests mid range Agni missile.

1989-91 : The Soviet Union, India's ally collapses.

Oct. 1989 : Pakistan loses US military and

economic aid because of its nuclear programme.

1995 : The Nuclear Non-proliferation Treaty is renewed. Neither India nor Pakistan signed.

July 1996 : China stages 45th nuclear test, then signs test ban treaty.

1996 : Both India and Pakistan refuse to sign the Comprehensive Test Ban Treaty.

April 1998 : Pakistan tests mid range Ghauri missile.

May 1998 : India tests a series of nuclear devices. Pakistan sets off its first ever tests two weeks later[16].

Clinton Administration Initiative

In late 1997, the Clinton administration had begun a "strategic dialogue" with India and Pakistan on a range of issues – particularly nuclear and economic. President Clinton met both Pakistan Prime Minister Nawaz Sharif and India's then Prime Minister I.K. Gujral at the United Nations in New York. The meetings were followed by a series of visits to the subcontinent by US cabinet and other high level officials, including Secretary of State Madeleine Albright, who visited India and Pakistan in November 1997. In the aftermath of the nuclear tests, Deputy Secretary of State Strobe Talbott began a series of meetings with high-level Indian and Pakistani officials between July and November 1998. The closely held and ongoing discussions reportedly cover nuclear proliferation, the Comprehensive Test Ban Treaty (CTBT), the Fissile Material Cut Off Treaty (FMCT), Confidence-building measures, Kashmir, and sanctions resulting from the Indian and Pakistani nuclear tests.

Sanctions imposed on both India and Pakistan are a major issue in the US talks with both countries. On June 18, 1998, the State Department released a fact sheet outlining US sanctions on India and Pakistan, as well as goals of sanctions, stating: "In imposing these sanctions, we seek: to send a strong message to would-be nuclear testers; to have maximum influence on Indian and Pakistani behaviour; to target the governments, rather than the people; and to minimize the damage to other US interests. Our goals are that India and Pakistan: halt further nuclear testing; sign the Comprehensive Test Ban Treaty (CTBT) immediately and without conditions; not deploy or test missiles or nuclear weapons, cooperate in fissile material cut-off treaty (FMCT) negotiations in Geneva; maintain and formalize restraints on sharing sensitive goods and technologies with other countries; and reduce bilateral tensions, including Kashmir"[17].

There have been indications of progress toward realization of some of these goals, including cooperation on FMCT and CTBT. Both India and Pakistan agreed in late July to participate in negotiations on the FMCT. Pakistan's decision reportedly was tied to a Clinton Administration announcement, on July 21, that it would abstain from blocking aid to Pakistan by International Monetary Fund (IMF)[18]. On August 11, the conference on Disarmament in Geneva announced that it had reached a consensus on establishment of an adhoc committee to negotiate the final form of the treaty to ban production of fissile materials - highly - enriched uranium and plutonium - for military purposes. Although Pakistan has agreed to take part in the FMCT negotiations, it is reluctant to sign in treaty that freezes the size of fissile material stockpiles at current levels. Pakistan's stockpile is estimated at about one-eighth the size of India's.

Bill Clinton's efforts to mobilize international pressure following the South Asian nuclear tests resulted in strong resolutions by the UN Security Council and the Group of Eight (G-8) urging India and Pakistan to sign the CTBT. Also, in a joint statement on July 23, the Russian and Chinese foreign ministers agreed to press

India and Pakistan to sign CTBT and NPT[19]. On August 6 Japan announced that it will vote to ease economic sanctions against Pakistan by the IMF – in return for assurances not to transfer nuclear technology or materials to any other country. Tokyo reportedly required Islamabad's signature on the CTBT as a precondition for resuming aid[20]. The Pakistan parliament debated the issue in mid-September and the Pakistani cabinet and defence leaders stated that the country would not sign CTBT "under coercion"[21].

In speeches before the September meeting of the UN General Assembly, India and Pakistan announced that they intend to sign the Comprehensive Test Ban Treaty (CTBT) before September 1999. Pakistani Prime Minister Nawaz Sharif states on September 23 that "Pakistan will adhere to the CTBT", but note that he expected that sanctions and other economic restrictions imposed after the nuclear tests would be removed. Indian Prime Minister Atal Behari Vajpayee told the General Assembly on September 24 that India was prepared to bring the CTBT "discussion to the successful conclusion" and sign the treaty. Vijpayee also noted that, following India's nuclear tests, it had announced a voluntary moratorium on testing, and that in doing so, "India has already accepted the basic obligation of the CTBT"[22].

On November 7, 1998, the White House announced that President Clinton had decided to ease sanctions against India and Pakistan "in response to positive steps both countries have taken to address our nonproliferation concerns following their nuclear tests in May. "Congress gave the President authority to waive some nuclear sanctions of India and Pakistan under the Brownback amendment (sponsored by Senator Sam Brownback), which was signed into law on October 21, as part of the Omnibus Appropriations Act. The President's action restored the Export-Import Bank,

Overseas Private Investment Corporation (OPIC), and Trade and Development Agency (TDA) programmes in India and Pakistan, and lifted restrictions on the activities of US banks in India and Pakistan. Also restored were International Military Education and Training (IMET) programmes with both countries. Taking note of the precarious state of the Pakistan economy the President also "decided that the US would work closely with our allies to permit lending from the multilateral development banks as necessary to support an agreement between Pakistan and the IMF". Pakistan Prime Minister Nawaz Sharif was also invited to the White House in early December for further bilateral discussions.

In a speech at the Brookings Institution on November 12, 1998, Deputy Secretary of State Strobe Talbott rounds of talks he has held since July both with India's Deputy Chairman of the Planning Commission Jaswant Singh and with Pakistan's Foreign Secretary Shamsad Ahmed. Talbott stated that the three goals of these talks were (1) preventing an escalation of nuclear and missile competition in the region (2) strengthening the global nonproliferation regime and (3) promoting a dialogue between India and Pakistan on the long term improvement of their relations, including on the subject of Kashmir[23].

Talbott further noted the continuing US commitment to the long-range goal of universal adherence to the Nuclear Nonproliferation Treaty, stating: "We do not, and will not, concede, even by implication, that India and Pakistan have established themselves as nuclear weapon states under NPT". He noted, however, the US recognition that progress towards that goal "must be based on India's and Pakistan's conceptions of their own national interests". Talbott outlined five steps the US is urging India and Pakistan to take to avoid "a destabilizing nuclear and missile competition" and reduce tensions in South Asia:

1. Sign and ratify CTBT.
2. Halt all production of fissile materials.
3. Adopt a package of constraints on development, flight-testing, and storage of missiles and basing of nuclear capable aircraft.
4. Tighten export controls on sensitive materials and technologies that could be used in the development of weapons of mass destruction.
5. Conduct "direct, high-level, frequent and above all, productive" bilateral dialogue.

Talbott stated the strong US interest in returning to the task of "developing the kind of broad-gauge, forward-looking bilateral relationships with these two countries" that had been underway prior to the May nuclear blast.

The Indo-US differences over the nuclear issues constitute a core-limiting factor in their efforts to establish long-term cooperation in defence and security matters. India like the US also champions the cause of nonproliferation as part of an overall goal of nuclear disarmament, but the US espouses a doctrine of nuclear deterrence for itself and four other nuclear weapon powers, simultaneously denying the same to the rest of the world. This fundamental difference in policy and attitude puts India and the US on opposite sides on the issue of the NPT and similarly on the issue of the CTBT. While there is a growing realization, including in certain circles in the US, China, Australia and Japan of the need to establish a nuclear-free world", it is not formally recognized by the nations that have nuclear weapons.

India has all along maintained that the NPT is a discriminatory document and that it perpetuates not only nuclear asymmetry but also legitimizes the possession of nuclear weapons by only five countries in the world. Now the question comes why only five countries of the world will possess nuclear weapons and the rest will not be allowed to keep it. It is illogical. Let the world be free from nuclear weapons. The nuclear weapons from any where in the world be destroyed. If it happens, India will be a party to it, there is no doubt in it. The US, on the other hand, has been incessantly backing the NPT as a good step towards halting nuclear proliferation. During the Cold War, the US itself disregarded the substance and spirit of the NPT and indirectly assisted and encouraged Pakistan in its quest for a nuclear capability. The Regan and Bush administration looked the other way when Pakistan sought to acquire nuclear weapons capability by violating US laws and regulations in the 1980s in view of the latter's participation in the US war against the Soviet Union in Afghanistan.

However, once the Cold War was over, the US priorities changed drastically. It sought to give the NPT indefinite duration, as the defence planners and strategic thinkers in the US began to articulate nuclear proliferation as one of the most serious dangers in the Post-Cold War environment. The Bottom-up Review undertaken by the US Department of Defence in 1993, argued for a three-pronged approach to deal with the nuclear danger – nonproliferation efforts, cooperative threat reduction and counter-proliferation. The first approach aimed at "preventing the spread of weapons of mass destruction to additional countries through the strengthening of existing controls of WMD technologies and materials and the improvement and expansion of international mechanism and agreements for limiting and eliminating nuclear, biological and chemical weapons". The American assessment emphasized that the end of super power arms race increased the relative importance of smaller nuclear threats just as the nonproliferation discipline which the super powers had imposed on their client states was evaporating.

As part of this first approach Washington went on a diplomatic offensive to back the indefinite extension of the NPT at the 1995 Review and Extension Conference. For the Western countries in general and the five members of the exclusive nuclear club in particular, May 11, 1995 would remain a memorable day in the modern history of the world. On this day, the NPT initially signed in 1968 and effective from 1970 was accorded unconditional and indefinite extension at the NPT Review and Extension Conference in New York.

While very few international treaties and agreements are really just, fair, equitable and non-discriminatory, the NPT is the quintessence of an international discriminatory document which has now legitimized the existing nuclear arsenals of the US, Russia, Britain, France and that of the People's Republic of China. Moreover, the permanence of the NPT also means that for all practical purposes any effort by the massive majority of non-nuclear member states of the NPT to acquire, possess, develop or manufacture a nuclear device would be considered an illegal act and violative of treaty commitments. In addition, the nuclear hegemony and superiority of the Big Five has been willy-nilly accepted by a vast majority of nations which are also members of the United Nation Organisations – the world body that in letter, if not in spirit, believes in the principle of the sovereign equality of nations.

However, the twelve odd countries, which stayed away from becoming party to the NPT, would not be strictly considered as indulging in illegal activities if they decide to acquire, develop or manufacture one or more nuclear explosive devices. Out of these twelve, three prominent countries are Israel, India and Pakistan, which have been known as the nuclear capable countries or threshold nuclear powers for quite sometime.

As far as the Israeli nuclear capabilities are concerned, there is little doubt in anybody's mind that Tel Aviv is way ahead of the rest of the West Asian and Middle Eastern countries in its nuclear programme. But the US and its allies have never raised any serious concerns about the Israeli nuclear weapon programme nor have they taken any concrete steps to dissuade Israel from indulging in nuclear weapon activities.

The NPT extension, nonetheless, has to be seen in the backdrop of India's inability to affect the proceedings in the New York conference, since India has never been a member of the treaty. It may not be an exaggeration to say that the history of the NPT since 1968 has been a tussle between India's one nation crusade against the NPT regime and the US mission to expand the regime. In the midst of this struggle, India's strategic environment got nuclerised, China went on modernizing its nuclear arsenals and Pakistan somehow managed to acquire nuclear capability through fair or foul means. Sino-Pakistan nuclear collaboration went on increasing, as we were moralsing and finally the nuclear powers, particularly the US, succeeded by cajoling, bribing, bulldozing or convincing 173 countries to support the indefinite extension of the NPT at the NPT Review and Extension Conference at New York.

Now let us analyse what happened since the indefinite extension of the NPT? China and France went on conducting a series of nuclear tests in order to modernize, refine and update their nuclear arsenals. Secondly, Pakistan succeeded in wriggling out of the US sanctions in place since the imposition of the Pressler Amendment in October 1990. After the passage of the Hank Brown Amendment in the US Congress, the Clinton administration got the authority to supply certain military equipments to Islamabad. Finally, when the CIA revealed that China had supplied 5,000 ring magnets to Pakistan that would assist the latter's nuclear weapon programme, it had only a temporary effect in the US. Apart from shedding crocodile tears over the violation of American nonproliferation law by China and Pakistan and instituting an investigation into this case, Washington did little that affected either Pakistan's or China's nuclear weapon programme.

It is important to note that indefinite extension of the NPT became a reality a few months after the US Defence Secretary William Perry's trip to New Delhi and the signing of the Indo-US Agreed Minutes on defence cooperation. Even when the debates over the future of the NPT were going on in various capitals of the world, including in New Delhi, the efforts to improve Indo-US security understanding were being made by both the US and Indian Governments. The bilateral differences over the NPT were not allowed to adversely affect the overall Indo-US relations. Soon after the NPT extension, the Indian Foreign Minister visited Washington to indicate that the NPT would not be allowed to undo the efforts to improve ties between the two countries.

However, the indefinite extension of the NPT had significant implications for India and or Indo-US relations. Before the extension, Washington was floating proposals for regional arrangements to tackle the nuclear issues in the region. Publicly the US government officials kept on repeating their preference for Indian membership of the NPT. Washington did hold several rounds of talks with India to find out ways and means to resolve the nuclear tangle in Southern Asia. Particularly significant was growing understanding of the Indian concern about the Chinese nuclear capabilities in certain sections of the policy-making community in the US. The State Department, the Pentagon and analysts in several think tanks made no secret of their understanding that China's participation in regional non-proliferation measures only could bring about a lasting solution to the problem.

However, the legitimization of the Chinese nuclear weapons along with those of other nuclear powers, through an indefinite extension of the NPT would make it very difficult to bring the Chinese to the negotiating table, unless other nuclear powers also take similar steps in their respective regions. China in fact conducted a nuclear test days after the NPT extension. Not that earlier it had been easy to bring China to the negotiating table to resolve the nuclear tangle in Southern Asia. But the Chinese membership in the NPT and the indefinite extension of the treaty have bestowed a different status on China. As a result, the US would now more forcefully seek to make the nuclear issue in the region an issue between India and Pakistan.

In fact, Pakistan cares little about international disarmament efforts, refuses to sing the NPT on the ground that India has not done so and occasionally comes out with narrow bilateral or sub-regional arms control proposals. Pakistan has no problem in accepting a regional solution - in fact a bilateral solution - since Islamabad's strategic thinking and threat perception begins and ends with India.

Pakistan has over the years proposed the establishment of a nuclear-free zone in South Asia, joint signing of the NPT with India, joint agreement on full-scope safeguards and bilateral inspections and five power disarmament talks to mediate between India and Pakistan. All these proposals, if they had materialized, would have served the Pakistani interests very well. And all these Pakistani proposals found ready acceptance in Washington. But they were not in keeping with Indian interests. And India's consistent advocacy of global rather than regional disarmament did not find favour either in Islamabad or in Washington.

Despite India's goal and efforts for global disarmament, India did not violate the principles and spirit of the NPT. At the same time, India concluded with Pakistan an agreement not to attack each other's nuclear facilities. These Indian steps, however, did not make a much positive effect upon the American attitude towards India on the nuclear issue. Had it been so, the Clinton administration would not have outlined a policy of "cap, reduce and rollback" to deal with the South Asian nuclear realities. A National Security Strategy of Engagement and Enlargement, mentioned that the US "seeks to cap, reduce and ultimately eliminate the nuclear and missile capabilities of India and Pakistan".

Pakistani nuclear scientists and former military officials have made it clear more than once that they would not accept the policy of rolling back their nuclear capability. In the midst of debate over indefinitely extending the NPT in 1995, the father of Pakistani nuclear weapons programme, Abdul Qadeer Khan, proudly announced in an interview to a Pakistani newspaper that Pakistan's nuclear programme has neither been capped nor rolled back. The following year contrary to the impression of Washington, Pakistan's former Chief of Army Staff, General Aslam Beg, told a seminar in Karachi, that Pakistan has never frozen or rolled back its nuclear programme and that it only reduced the enrichment of uranium below weapon's grade[24].

Actually the bid of the Clinton administration to do away with the Pressler Amendment - the only nonproliferation measure that showed some success - since the very year Bill Clinton entered the White House and its subsequent success in doing so, exposed the hollowness of the US policy of containing Pakistan's nuclear weapon programme. As long as the Cold War was on, administration after administration in Washington turned a blind eye to a series of reports by the US intelligence community about Islamabad clandestine nuclear weapon programme. The reason was simple: Pakistan's role in America's Cold War strategy against the former Soviet Union was crucial.

After the end of Cold War, with the withdrawal of Soviet troops from Afghanistan in 1989, Pakistan's nuclear weapon programme came under serious scrutiny. Then only the Bush administration imposed Pressler Amendment on Pakistan. When it was known to the US that Pakistan is having serious economic consequences because of the Pressler Amendment, the Clinton administration endorsed the Brown Amendment in October 1995. When this happened the left parties in India demanded that India should immediately end its defence cooperation with the US. The right wing BJP described the US decision as an unfriendly act.

The US Government sought to justify the supply of $368 million worth of weapons and military equipment to Pakistan on the ground that it would enhance the US influence in Pakistan and would strengthen its hands to achieve its nonproliferation objectives. How far the Clinton administration's claim that the Brown Amendment would enhance the nonproliferation goal soon came for a test when the US intelligence reports on the Chinese supply of 5,000 ring magnets to Pakistan were made public. The State Department officials were questioned by the Congressmen as to why they had kept Congress in the dark about the Central Intelligence Agency (CIA) report on the ring magnets issue when the Brown Amendment was under discussion. According to published reports, the officials, including those in the South Asian Bureau of the State Department, had known about the Chinese transfer of ring magnets, but the State Department had exerted so much effort for the passage of the Brown Amendment that it had decided against volunteering the CIA report to Congress for fear of jeopardizing its own efforts. Why has the US been so kind to Pakistan? It is because Pakistan was a reliable ally of US. The US does not want to punish Pakistan by imposing sanctions which have in any case not prevented Islamabad from acquiring the nuclear capability.

Clinton on the Comprehensive Test Ban Treaty

President Bill Clinton announced in August 11, 1995 that the US would support an international treaty banning all nuclear weapon tests. Clinton's announcement appeared to break an impasse that had held up agreement on such a treaty, which had been in negotiation for years in Geneva under United Nations sponsorship. Negotiations hoped to conclude the treaty in 1996.

The President's announcement came almost exactly fifty years after the US dropped the first atom bomb on Hiroshima. A senior White House aide insisted, however, that the timing was coincidental.

In a related development, the 1995 Nobel Peace Prize was awarded on October 13 to Joseph Rotblat, a British Physicist who helped develop nuclear disarmament. He shared the prize with the Pugwash Conference on science and World affairs, an antinuclear organization he formed with Albert Einstein and Bertrand Russel.

The Norwegian Noble Committee said it awarded the prize to Rotblat to recognize his efforts to "diminish the part played by nuclear arms in international politics and in the longer run to eliminate such arms". Nobel officials also said that they hoped, with the prize, to pressure France and China into halting their nuclear testing.

Actually, the US and the Soviet Union agreed to a limited ban on nuclear testing in 1963. It was the first arms control agreement of the nuclear age and it was a major step towards reducing tension between the two superpowers. That treaty barred nuclear tests in the atmosphere.

In 1974, the Nixon administration negotiated a treaty with the Soviet Union prohibiting underground nuclear tests with an explosive power greater than 150,000 tons of TNT called the Threshold Test Ban Treaty. It went unratified until 1990, when the US and Soviet negotiators tightened some of the provisions and the Senate gave its approval.

In the meantime, the United Nations convened negotiations to broaden those agreements into a comprehensive treaty banning all nuclear weapons tests worldwide. Those negotiations produced agreement on numerous non-controversial items but bogged down on the basic issue of banning all nuclear tests, no matter what size.

Discussions of a test ban treaty picked up in late 1994 and early 1995 during the concluding stages of the UN sponsored negotiations on extending a related treaty – the Treaty of Non-Proliferation of Nuclear Weapons. That treaty aimed at reducing the spread of nuclear weapons, was due to expire in 1995 unless it was extended.

The US and other nuclear weapon states wanted a permanent extension of the nonproliferation treaty, but other countries were reluctant to take such a step unless the nuclear weapon states agreed to a ban on weapons testing. Bowing to that pressure, the nuclear powers agreed to complete negotiations on the weapons testing treaty in 1996. That step cleared the way for final agreement on extending the nonproliferation treaty.

Clinton's announcement brought praise from groups that had advocated completion of the test ban treaty. Spurgeon Keeny Jr. President of the Arms Control Association, said the move would "help break the deadlock" in the Geneva treaty negotiations.

But the conservative interest groups and their Republican allies in Congress objected strongly to the President's action, saying it would make it more difficult for the US to ensure the reliability of its nuclear weapons – and thus to defer on enemy nuclear attack. "If there's any doubt about the credibility of our system, it can serve to be an inducement for an enemy to use theirs", said Sen. John Warner (R-Va), a senior spokesman on military issues.

Following is the test of President Bill Clinton's announcement on August 11, 1995.

"Good afternoon. Today I am announcing my decision to negotiate a true zero yield comprehensive test ban. This is an historic milestone in our efforts to reduce the nuclear threat to build a safer world. The US will now insist on a test ban that prohibits any nuclear test explosion or any other nuclear explosion. I am convinced this decision will speed the negotiations so that we can achieve our goal of signing a comprehensive test ban next year.

As a central part of this decision, I am establishing concrete, specific safeguards that define the conditions under which the US will enter into a comprehensive test ban. These safeguards will strengthen our commitments in the areas of intelligence, monitoring and verification, stockpile stewardship, maintenance of our nuclear laboratories, and test readiness.

They also specify the circumstances under which I would be prepared in consultation with Congress, to exercise our supreme national interest rights under a comprehensive test ban to conduct necessary testing if the safety or reliability of our nuclear deterrent could no longer be certified.

As a part of this arrangement I am today directing the establishment of a new annual reporting and certification requirement that will ensure that our nuclear weapons remain safe and reliable under a comprehensive test ban ......

American leaders since Presidents Eisenhower and Kennedy have believed that a comprehensive test ban would be a major stride towards stopping the proliferation of nuclear weapons. Now, as then, such a treaty would greatly strengthen the security of the US and nations throughout the world. But now, unlike them, such a treaty is within our reach.

It would build upon the successes we have achieved so far: Securing a permanent extension of the Nuclear Nonproliferation Treaty, freezing North Korea's nuclear programme, cutting existing nuclear arsenals by putting the START I Treaty into force, persuading Ukraine, Belarus, Kazakhstan to give up their nuclear weapons and to reach agreements with Russia that now mean that both our nations no longer target our missiles at each other.

A comprehensive test ban is the right step as we continue pulling back from the nuclear precipice, a precipice when we began to live with 50 years ago this week. It moves us one step closer to the day when no nuclear weapons are detonated anywhere on the face of the earth. Thank you very much"[25].

In September 1996 the UN General Assembly adopted the Comprehensive Test Ban Treaty. A statement was released by the office of the State Department on September 11, 1996. It reads – The UN General Assembly's vote yesterday to adopt the Comprehensive Nuclear Test Ban Treaty (CTBT) was a landmark decision that will strengthen the security of the US and that of every nation in the world. It moves us towards the fulfillment of a decade old dream that there will be no nuclear explosions anywhere. This dream has been shared by world leaders beginning with Presidents Eisenhower and Kennedy.

The CTBT will prohibit any nuclear explosion whether for military or peaceful purposes. It will effectively constrain the development and improvement of nuclear weapons and contribute to the prevention of nuclear proliferation and our ultimate goal of nuclear disarmament.

President Clinton's personal leadership played a key role in the success of the CTBT negotiations. The President's decision in July 1993 to extend the moratorium on US nuclear testing laid the groundwork for the negotiations, and his announcement in August 1995 that the US would support a zero-yield CTBT paved the way for resolution of one of the treaty's central issues.

Of course, this success would not have been possible without the strong and unstinting efforts of so many of our allies and friends around the world. I want especially to acknowledge the role played by the Government of Australia, which led the effort to bring the CTBT to the UN. This treaty demonstrates the power of the international community to unite around a great goal and to act together to improve the security of all its members. The US calls upon all nations, especially those with historic commitment to the CTBT, to sign and ratify it without delay.

What is the purpose of the Comprehensive Test Ban Treaty?

1. Constrain the development and qualitative improvement of nuclear weapons.
2. End the development of advanced new types of nuclear weapons.
3. Contribute to the prevention of nuclear proliferation and the process of nuclear disarmament, and
4. Strengthen international peace and security.

The CTBT thus marks a historic milestone in the

efforts to reduce the nuclear threat and build a safer world. This treaty itself includes a protocol in three parts. Part I dealing the International Monitoring System (IMS), Part II on On-Site Inspections (OSI) and Part III on Confidence-building Measures[26].

India and Pakistan stand as major obstacles to the entry-into-force of the CTBT. Because all 61 nations in the conference on disarmament had to agree to forward the treaty to the General Assembly. India was able to block the needed consensus at Geneva. India failed to prevent its adoption by the UN General Assembly in September, but the treaty still requires the signature of 44 nations, including the threshold states, to enter-into-force. Pakistan voted for the treaty but has indicated that it will not sign unless India does. India remains adamantly opposed. Because India took the lead in laying down conditions that were unacceptable to the nuclear weapons states and other countries with a strong interest in the negotiations, Pakistan largely avoided the opprobrium directed at its regional rival.

The CTBT is an important element of the US policy towards nuclear proliferation in South Asia because the absence of nuclear weapons tests would seriously handicap efforts by India and Pakistan to acquire more advanced technologies or designs for their nuclear programmes. Even though the treaty has been approved by the UN General Assembly, its value as a non-proliferation tool is doubtful because two key proliferant nations have refused to participate. Some believe that India insisted on its longstanding demand for general nuclear disarmament timetable in part to delay completion of the CTBT and preserve its option to test and thereby continue with its nuclear programme unimpeded. After India vetoed the treaty it complained that the nuclear powers had been more ready to compromise to meet China's concerns about the treaty than they had been to consider India's. Many participants in the negotiations believe the treaty would be weakened without India's participation[27].

We have already analysed the US views on CTBT. Let us now examine the Indian views on CTBT. India's decision not to sign the Comprehensive Nuclear Test Ban Treaty (CTBT) in 1996 was based both on its traditional approach to nuclear disarmament and its national security concerns. Yet, this decision has often, somewhat reproachfully, been viewed by Western critics as a reversal of India's traditional stand on nuclear disarmament, particularly former Prime Minister Jawaharlal Nehru's 1954 call for a halt to all nuclear testing. Let us review the historical context of India's approach.

India's promotion of the goal of total nuclear disarmament predates the nuclearization of China and even the emergence of the US-USSR nuclear rivalry. For example, as early as 1948, India tabled a resolution in the UN General Assembly "for the control of atomic energy ...... for peaceful purposes and for the elimination from national armaments of atomic weapons[28].

The bombing of Hiroshima and Nagasaki not only provoked moral outrage, it also gave rise to a particular political perception that such a weapon was a new means by which the country's hard-won independence might be threatened[29]. This concern led Nehru to write in 1954, that, "fear would grow and grip nations and peoples and each would try frantically to get this new weapon or some adequate protection from it". Nehru recognized that "a dominating factor in the modern world is this prospect of these terrible weapons suddenly coming into use before which our normal weapons are completely useless"[30].

This was the context in which Nehru first called for a "standstill" to nuclear testing, one of the steps he proposed to halt, rollback and eliminate nuclear weapons development – a development that India found not only morally repugnant but one whose power could possibly pose a threat to its security and its independence.

In 1978, India once again proposed a ban on nuclear weapon testing, this time as part of a defined program of nuclear disarmament. The proposal was made at the special session of the UN General Assembly on 9 June 1978 by the then Prime Minister Morarji Desai. The first step of the proposal contained four elements: (1) A declaration that utilization of nuclear technology for military purposes, including research in weapon technology should be outlawed. (2) Qualitative and quantitative limitations on nuclear weapons and an immediate freeze under international inspection. (3) Formulation of a time bound programme – not exceeding a decade – for gradual reduction of the stockpile with a view to achieving total elimination of all nuclear weapons, and (4) A comprehensive Test Ban Treaty[31].

This proposal was reiterated when Mrs. Gandhi became Prime Minister for the second time. In 1982, India proposed another program, which included a proposal for a convention on no use or threat of use of nuclear weapons, a freeze on the manufacture of nuclear weapons combined with a cut-off in the production of fissionable material for weapons purposes and a test ban treaty.

Thus, India's approach has been global and the objective, both from the moral and security point of view, has been the total elimination of nuclear weapons. All steps, including a test ban treaty, a convention on no-use, a fissile material cut-off treaty – even the Nonproliferation Treaty – made no strategic or political sense unless they led to total nuclear disarmament.

India also identified that the CTBT should prevent horizontal and vertical proliferation and should not perpetuate a division of the world into two categories of nations – the nuclear haves and have-nots. Second, no test should be carried out under the pretext of safety purposes and nuclear weapon test sites should be closed.

In April/May 1995 the NPT Review and Extension Conference took place. India did not participate in the NPT Review and Extension Conference. To everybody's surprise China and France resumed their programmes of nuclear testing within weeks of the conclusion of the NPT Review conference. The official spokesman of the Ministry of External Affairs stated: We are dismayed by the recent nuclear tests carried out by some Nuclear weapon states. That these steps are being taken by states which are parties to the NPT, soon after its indefinite extension, highlights the inherent defects of the Treaty[32].

So, clearly India's basic concerns were not to be met and it was inevitable that on 20 June 1996, the Indian representative rejected the "clean" text presented by the Chairman, stating in the conference on Disarmament Plenary:

The CTBT that we are emerging ... is not the CTBT India envisaged in 1954. This cannot be the CTBT that India can be expected to accept ... Our capability is demonstrated but as a matter of policy, we exercise restraint. Countries around us continue their weapon programme, either openly or in a clandestine manner. In such an environment, India cannot accept any restraints on its capability, if other countries remain unwilling to accept the obligation to eliminate their nuclear weapons ... Such a Treaty is not conceived as a measure towards universal nuclear disarmament and is not in India's national security interest. India, therefore, cannot subscribe to it in its present form[33].

This position commanded consensus in the Indian

Parliament and in a majority of Indian public opinion. India's position was not only consistent with its traditional stand on the issue but also a logical outcome of the process set in motion in 1993. There was no sudden reversal of its stand.

India's proposal was that the Treaty would not enter into force unless the Nuclear Weapon States made a commitment to eliminate their nuclear weapons in a specific, though negotiated time frame. The proposal was rejected by the Nuclear Weapons States and no effort was made to find an alternative formulation that might have met this concern. The Chairman's text merely dropped India's proposal without explanation.

Secondly, India considered the Treaty to be against its national interest. According to the 1969 Vienna Convention on Law of Treaties, no state can be coerced into signing a treaty, nor can a treaty's entry into force be made conditional on the signature of any country, without that country's consent.

Israel, one of the two so called threshold states, signed the treaty and Pakistan, the other, signalled that it would sign if India did. Pakistan's Indo-Centric foreign policy determined its stand: Paksitan would sign only if India signed.

India's policics towards nuclear disarmament have not changed. Addressing the Indian Parliament on 11 September 1996, India's Foreign Minister emphasized that "... our position for the last 40 years has been to abolish and destroy both nuclear tests and nuclear weapons ... we shall sustain the glorious path laid by Gandhi and Nehru"[34].

Again the CTBT is also defective, because under the treaty the nuclear weapon states can:

1. Design nuclear weapons by using a variety of laboratory testing programmes.

2. Maintain nuclear test sites in states of constant readiness.
3. Withdraw from the treaty without penalty under a standard "Supreme national interest" clause, which would enable nearly complete designs to be fully tested.
4. Conduct sub-critical tests underground, which would make it extremely difficult or impossible to verify whether small nuclear yields are actually being produced.
5. Maintain huge weapons – design teams as well as archives that preserve the designs of nuclear weapons no longer in arsenals[35].

India rejected both the CTBT and the NPT extension. The vote on the Comprehensive Nuclear Test Ban Treaty at the UN General Assembly in September 1996 was 158 in favour and three against, with five abstentions. The only countries voting with India against the resolution were Bhutan, a country whose foreign policy India strongly influences and Libya.

Previously in May 1995, the near-universal membership of the Nuclear Nonproliferation Treaty (NPT) extended that treaty indefinitely. Today there are 185 parties to that Treaty, which India has long rejected.

India stands for total elimination of all nuclear weapons within a specific time period. But the big five do not agree with this proposal. The ultimate elimination of nuclear weapons depends on many factors. Chief among them are create conditions allowing states with nuclear weapons to reduce their reliance on them over time. Such steps can be taken at all levels – unilaterally, bilaterally, regionally and globally. Of course, 40 years of nuclear arms race cannot be cancelled over night. That's why India has put forth the proposal for elimination of all types of nuclear weapons within a specific time period. The CTBT has no meaning if a country goes on producing nuclear weapons and becomes a member of CTBT. Therefore, India says that we abide by the principle of CTBT and NPT, even though we have not signed it. In 1991 India and Pakistan ratified an agreement not to attack each other's nuclear facilities. India has also advocated for no first use of nuclear weapons. The US stands for nuclear nonproliferation, there is no doubt in it. India is also not a proliferator as propounded by our President A.P.J. Abdul Kalam. But the US is silent on elimination of nuclear weapons. Let the US eliminate all nuclear weapons and then tell others to follow the footsteps. Then only all countries in the world including India will definitely follow the footsteps of USA and the whole world will become free of nuclear weapons. Thereby USA will become example for others and the whole world will stand by the US.

Even though India took the moralistic view of complete elimination of nuclear weapons, it exploded the bomb in 1998. The reasons given by India for the bomb explosion was the threat perception from China and to some extent Pakistan as it was known to the Indians that Pakistan is developing a bomb with the help of China.

Clinton had made the achievement of a CTBT a top priority for his administration and before the treaty was opened for signature on September 24, 1996, was involved in three years of multilateral negotiations[36]. On the day he signed the Treaty he had called it "the longest-sought, hardest-fought prize in nuclear arms control".

The CTBT, the overall accord of which contains a preamble, 17 treaty articles, two treaty annexes, and a protocol with two annexes detailing verification procedures, seeks to prohibit all nuclear weapon test explosions or other nuclear explosions anywhere in the world. By the Treaty's provisions, a global network of monitoring facilities is sought to be established and allowance is made for onsite inspections of suspicious events in order to verify compliance.

While the preamble lists disarmament principles and objectives and sets the overall political context of the treaty, it states that a CTBT will constitute an effective measure of nuclear disarmament and nonproliferation by "constraining development and qualitative improvement of nuclear weapons and ending the development of advanced new types of nuclear weapons. The scope of the treaty, is contained in Article I which establishes that all states – parties are prohibited from conducting "any nuclear weapon test explosion or any other nuclear explosion, which on the basis of negotiating history, is understood to include all nuclear explosions with yields greater than zero.

The overall governing body of the organization is the conference of the States Parties, which is to meet once a year unless otherwise decided and will handle treaty-related policy issues and oversee the Treaty's implementation. The treaty's principal decision-making body is the Executive Council which will consist of 51 members.

The primary body responsible for implementing the treaty's verification procedures is the Technical Secretariat and it is in this capacity that it will supervise the operation of the International Monitoring system (IMS) as well as receive, process, analyse and report on the systems' data apart from managing the International Data Centre (IDC) and performing a series of procedural tasks related to conducting on-site inspections.

An important article that establishes the Treaty's verification regime is Article IV along with the verification protocol, The regime will consist of four basic elements: the IMS, consultation and clarification, on-site inspections and confidence building measures (CBMs). Until the Treaty enters into Force (EIF), the verification regime will not be completely operational[37].

The Clinton administration transmitted the CTBT to the Senate on September 23, 1997. The US Senate on October 13 rejected ratification of the Comprehensive Test Ban Treaty (CTBT), which would prohibit nuclear weapons testing, in a 48-51 vote. The largely partisan vote was seen as a major policy defeat for President Clinton, who had made passage of the treaty a top policy priority and had personally lobbied for its ratification in the week before the vote.

The vote marked the first time since 1920 - when the Senate failed to ratify the Treaty of Versailles, creating the League of Nations - that, the US Senate had defeated a major international security agreement supported by the President. The US's rejection of the pact also raised concern that the treaty would never be implemented.

The 48 votes in favour of the treaty were well short of the two-third majority, or 67 votes, needed to ratify it. Clinton had been the first leader to sign the CTBT after it was approved by the United Nations General Assembly in 1996. Since then, 153 other nations had signed the treaty, which was aimed at preventing countries from developing new warheads and other more sophisticated arms. The ban would take effect after all of the 44 countries with nuclear capability who had signed the treaty also ratified it. Currently 26 of those countries had done so.

Clinton, following the vote and in a Press Conference on October 14, criticized Republican Legislators for what he called their "reckless partisanship" in the defeat of the treaty.

Senate Majority Leader Trent Lott (R. Miss.) Oct. 13 defended the Senate's rejection of the treaty. "The

Founding Fathers never envisioned that the Senate would be a rubber stamp for a flawed treaty", he said. Lott denied that the rejection of the treaty was politically motivated.

A number of Republican Senators had expressed opposition to the CTBT because they said it was impossible to verify other countries' compliance with the ban. Others said that it would freeze in place the US's nuclear stockpile while nations that did not ratify the treaty or that violated the ban, continued to develop their weapons programs. Some say that there is a flaw in the treaty that on-site inspections could not be conducted without the approval of 30 members of the treaty's 51-member executive council.

Clinton on October 14 said, "By this vote, the Senate majority has turned its back on 50 years of American leadership against the spread of weapons of mass destruction". Clinton also said that the US would continue to adhere to its policy of not testing nuclear weapons – which the country had maintained since 1992 – despite the Senate's rejection of the CTBT. Clinton urged other countries to continue refraining from testing, and urged those that had not yet signed or ratified the test ban to do so.

The President singled out India and Pakistan, both of which had not signed the treaty. "Let me say to India and Pakistan, Do not take yesterday's vote as a sign that America does not care whether you resume nuclear testing and build up your nuclear arsenals" he said. He added that if they did it "will hurt your economy and endanger your future". As we know both countries in 1998 had carried out nuclear weapons tests.

On October 7, Clinton had urged the Senate to approve the treaty, saying that its defeat would give a "green light to every other country in the world" to develop nuclear weapons programs. Pakistani diplomat

Shaukat Umer on October 7 said, "If the largest power is out of this, its all over - this treaty is dead". Many world leaders on October 14 expressed dismay over the outcome of the Senate vote. French President Jacques Chirac called it "a setback to the progress of nonproliferation and disarmament"[38].

MISSILES

India and Pakistan both produce ballistic missiles and appear to be involved in an incipient race to produce missiles with nuclear warheads. As in the case of its nuclear programs, the Indian missile program is much more ambitious and less dependent on imported technology than that of Pakistan.

India's military missiles are developed under its Integrated Guided Missile Development Program. In addition to surface-to-air and antitank missiles, this program produces one surface-to-surface ballistic missile the Prithvi-150, and is developing others[39]. All of India's ballistic missile programs have suffered from funding constraints and have encountered suspensions and delays, some possibly induced by American pressure, that periodically have caused domestic critics to question the government's commitment[40].

Missile Programs of India and Pakistan

Designation		***Type***	***Mis-siles***	***Range (kg)***	***Payload pulsion***	***Pro- Status***
INDIA						
Prithvi-150	Ballistic	75	150	1,000	Liquid	In-service
Prithvi-250	Ballistic	25	250	500	Liquid	
Prithvi-350	Ballistic		350		Liquid	
Agni	Ballistic		1,500-2,500	1,000+	Solid/ Liquid	In development
Koral (SS-N-22	Anti-ship		110		Solid	To be built in India

version)						
Sagarika	SLBM		300		Solid	In development
Surya	Ballistic				Solid/ liquid	In development
PAKISTAN						
HATF-1	Rocket		80	500	Solid	In-service
HATF-2	SRBM		280	500	Solid	In development
HATF-3	SRBM		600	500	Solid	Unknown
M-11 (CSS-7/DF11) (Chinese)	SRBM	30	300	500	Solid	Unknown
Ghauri			1,500 km	500-750 kg		

The Prithvi-150 is a mobile, liquid fuel, single-stage, ballistic missile capable of delivering 1,000 kilogram (2,200 pound) warhead to a range of 150 kilometer (90 miles). India has completed testing the missile and has begun production. The Indian Army had originally ordered 75 Prithvi-150 missiles and planned to equip four regiments with 16 missiles each but later decided to field only one regiment and suspended production. In October 1995 one source reported that India had delivered Prithvi missile to a new army missile regiment and had resumed production[41], but this has been disputed by Indian officials.

In January 1996, India test-fired the next missile in this series, the Prithvi-250, or known as Prithvi II, a mobile, liquid-fuel missile capable of ranges of about 250 kilometers or somewhat more than 150 miles, with a 500 kilogram (1100 pound) warhead. With that range, Indian missiles could reach Islamabad, the capital of Pakistan, possibly with a nuclear warhead[42].

India has indicated the Prithvi missile may be available for export to other countries. Exports of the

Prithvi-150 and Prithvi-250 may not violate the guidelines of the MTCR, which apply to missiles that can deliver a 500 kg warhead to a range of 300 km. Even the Prithvi-350 may not cross the limits of the MTCR depending on the size of warhead it is able to deliver.

The Agni is a multistage, medium range, ballistic missile. It has been flight-tested. It has an estimated range of 1500-2500 km (930-1550 miles) with a 1,000 kg warhead. After a third test firing of Agni in May 1994, India announced that further trials were indefinitely postponed, apparently due to budgetary constraints but also possibly in response to US pressure. In early August 1996 officials at the Defence Research and Development Organization which was developing the Agni, reportedly called for the resumption of tests[43].

India is also reported to be working on an anti-ship missile, another ballistic missile (the Surya), a submarine-launched ballistic missile (the Sagarika), possibly a cruise missile or unmanned-aerial vehicle, and three space launch vehicles that could be converted to intermediate-range or intercontinental ballistic missiles.

Pakistan's missile programme

Pakistan's most important missile appears to be the Chinese M-11 short-range ballistic missile. China reportedly has provided Pakistan technology for the M-11 solid fuel short-range ballistic missile, some 30 complete M-11 missiles and most recently, a factory that will enable Pakistan to construct some, if not all of the missile's components[44].

The M-11 is a mobile, solid fuel, ballistic missile that has the capability to deliver a 500 kg (1100 pound) warhead, approximately 300 km (190 miles). The export of these missiles or this missile technology violates the guidelines of the Missile Technology Control Regime that China agreed to observe. During the summer of 1996 a number of press reports citing information provided by relevant US officials appeared to confirm Pakistan's possession of M-11s. Reportedly, the intelligence community believes with "high confidence" that Pakistan has obtained M-11 ballistic missiles made by China and that the missiles may be "opreational"[45].

Pakistan also is believed to produce a field artillery rocket, the HATF-1, and to be developing a short-range ballistic missile, the HATF-2. The HATF-1 reportedly can deliver 500 kg (1100 lbs), 80 km (50 miles) and HATF-2 can deliver the same size warhead to 280 km (175 miles). Both weapons programs have received technical assistance, materials and components from China.

The Chinese assistance to Pakistan appears to be motivated by several considerations. First, China and Pakistan have long been allies, based on their mutual adversal relationship with India. Second, support to Pakistan fits into a broad Chinese pattern of cultivating Islamic countries in the Persian Gulf and adjacent regions. Third, the Chinese military is heavily involved in the business side of the armaments industry and actively seeks opportunities for commercial exports, with little evident regard for their diplomatic and international political impact. Last, but by no means least, exports to Pakistan may be viewed by China's leaders as a means of gaining leverage against the US with respect to US sales of military equipment and technology to Taiwan.

The US has put various pressures on China to limit its exports of nuclear materials, technology and missiles, including preventing such assistance to Pakistan, with mixed results, at best.

China is not a member of the 28-nation Missile Technology Control Regime (MTCR), which bars the transfer of certain technologies and missiles with the capability of delivering a 500 kg (1100 lbs) warhead to 300 km (186 miles).

The US has twice sanctioned companies or governmental entities in China and Pakistan (1991 and 1993) in response to the transfer of M-11 technology or components. The Clinton administration on August 25, 1993, imposed a ban on the sale of satellites, satellite technology, and other advanced technology to China and Pakistan as a result of evidence that China has provided M-11 components to Pakistan. The US and China in early October 1994, however, signed a statement in which Washington agreed to waive the sanctions in return for Beijing's agreement not to export ground-to-ground missiles with range/payload characteristics exceeding the MTCR guidelines, in effect accepting the US position that the M-11 missile had the "inherent capability" to exceed the MTCR range limits[46].

The US is against any type of nuclear and missile proliferation. Under the leadership of Bill Clinton the US is stepping up its pressure on India and Pakistan by asking them to take what Talbott calls "five practical steps" to avoid a destabilizing effect of nuclear and missile competition. The aim also is to reduce tensions in the Subcontinent more generally and bolster the global nonproliferation goals. The steps are:

1. To sign and ratify CTBT.
2. To halt all production of weapons-grade fissile materials pending the signing of the Fissile Material Cutoff Treaty (FMCT).
3. To adopt prudent constraints on development and deployment of missiles and aircraft capable of carrying weapons of mass destruction.
4. To tighten export controls on sensitive materials and technologies used to make weapons of mass destruction.
5. To encourage the countries to continue talks to

resolve their long-standing dispute and underlying causes of tension.

What the US is asking may be consistent with the security interests of India and Pakistan in theory, but practical politics is a different matter. Of the five steps, India and Pakistan have already agreed to two – signing the CTBT and preventing the export of technology used for weapons of mass destruction. Of course till this day India and Pakistan have not signed the CTBT. Both India and Pakistan have said they would join the Geneva negotiations on the proposed FMCT, but the US suggestion that they stop producing fissile material pending conclusion is unlikely to be accepted. Washington is concerned that, since the signing of the FMCT is several years away, India and Pakistan will embark on a race to produce more bomb making ingredients in the interim.

Pakistan's Ahmad, however, publicly rejected the idea of undertaking "any unilateral obligation" in that regard. He said that Pakistan needed to have a sufficient stockpile of fissile material before accepting to the demand for a moratorium. India, too would resist suspending fissile-material production since its state goal is to achieve minimum deterrence vis-à-vis Pakistan's powerful friend, China.

The US demands that India and Pakistan should limit the development and deployment of missiles and aircraft capable of carrying weapons of mass destruction will also be hard to sell. Talbott says: "Unless both India and Pakistan exercise genuine restraint and great care, the delivery systems themselves could become a source of tension and could, by their nature and disposition, increase the incentive to attack first in a crisis. There is also the risk that weapons could be used as a result of accident or miscalculation"[47], he adds.

Washington officials privately acknowledge that

the demand that India and Pakistan halt their missile tests is unrealistic. But they want both to adopt certain measures that could reduce tension and the risk of accident. They include restricting the number of flight tests, restricting the type of missiles to be tested to two for both sides - the Prithvi and Agni in India and the Ghauri and Tamruk in Pakistan - and giving prior notice of tests to each other. They also want measures to avoid launching missiles in each other's direction and stationing missiles close to where the warheads are kept.

Stephen Cohen, a senior fellow at the Brookings Institution who follows the subcontinent closely says, Indian scientists are telling politicians not to accept restrictions on missile tests because India is so far behind everybody else, including Pakistan. "The fact is", he says, "India's defence scientists are not bad, but they are in a race not with Pakistani scientists but with the Chinese and North Korean missile industry". (Pakistan's Ghauri missile is actually of North Korean origin)[48].

On January 27, 1996 India test fired a ballistic missile off its eastern coast into the Bay of Bengal. The missile, the Prithvi II, was an improved version of India's Prithvi missile. It had a range of 156 miles (250 km), which made it capable of striking deep into Pakistan. The test, which marked India's 15th missile launch, came in the wake of a January 26 rocket attack in a Pakistani - held area of Kashmir, which Pakistan officials blamed on Indian gunmen in the region.

The Prithvi II missile was one of five ballistic missiles under development in India's Integrated Guided Missile Development Program. India has also developed an Agni missile, which with a range of 1,550 miles, would be capable of striking targets in China.

India's launch of the Prithvi II angered Western countries that had been pressuring India to halt its missile program. India however, contended that it was compelled to pursue further missile development because it was vulnerable to Pakistan's more advanced missiles. Washington reportedly feared that India's test-launch of the Prithvi II, which could be fitted with nuclear warheads, would lead to an arms race between Pakistan and India and further destabilize the region[49].

Enemies since birth, Pakistan and India have been squabbling for more than 50 years. But though the hostility may manifest itself in politics or territorial dispute, religion is its underlying motif. Hardly surprising, then, that Pakistan should plump for religious symbolism in choosing a name for its medium-range, surface-to-surface missile with the potential to carry a nuclear warhead. The missile tested on April 26, is called Ghauri, named after Mohammad Ghouri, an Afghan Muslim king. Significantly, Ghauri defeated Prithviraj Chauhan, a 12th Century Hindu ruler whose name evokes that of Indian Missile the Prithvi, to counter which Ghauri was built.

Islamabad's display of missile muscle has significant political ramifications for itself, India, China and another big player in the region - the US. Most importantly, western pressure, which had worked in the past to contain the missile rivalry, no longer carries the same weight. It seems, domestic political compulsions are now driving India and Pakistan in their missile build-up.

Actually Ghauri is Pakistan's biggest and longest-range missile with a range of 1500 km and a payload of 700 kg. India's Prithvi, Pakistani authorities say, can reach every Pakistani city except northwestern Quetta. Both Prithvi and Ghauri can be carried on mobile launchers. Once they were fired, the other side would have just three minutes to react.

Immediately after the test of Ghauri, the Bharatiya

Janata Party government announced it would launch an indigenous spy satellite to monitor future Pakistani missile test and troop movements. Again after the test of Prithvi, India's Defence Minister, George Fernandes claimed that no part of Pakistan is out of range of Prithvi. Fernandes also accused China, another long time rival, of helping Pakistan to develop the Ghauri. And he also urged the US to investigate his claims. He told this to attract the attention of the anti-China lobby in the American Congress. Washington in 1993 slapped a short-lived arms embargo on Pakistan and China for trading missile technology. China denied the charge that it has supplied Pakistan the missile technology. Jim Foley, a spokesman for the US State Department said on April 10, Privately, US officials say they believe North Korea supplied key missile technology to Pakistan, a charge Islamabad denies. In a bid to play down the Ghauri test, Washington expressed mild regret at the test and urged Pakistan and India to exercise restraint.

Bill Clinton's state department fears that the two countries' extensive missile programmes are being coupled with research in the miniaturization of nuclear warheads, which could give nuclear capability to their conventional surface-to-surface missiles. Pakistan is considered to be ahead of India in acquiring this technology, while India leads in the capability to deliver nuclear warheads by aircrafts. "The missile rivalry is really all about perfecting delivery systems for nuclear weapons", says an Islamabad based Western ambassador[50].

So a new problem related to the proliferation of missile technology has erupted in India-US relations in the Post-Cold War era. The US looks upon India's development of intermediate-range missiles such as Agni and Prithvi as destabilizing the military balance in South Asia, and has exerted pressure on Delhi not to develop its missile programmes further and denying it critical technologies. In 1989 Washington had declined to authorize the sale to India of the Combined Acceleration Vibration Climatic Test System (CAVCTS), but India went ahead and test-fired Agni, declaring it was only a technology demonstrator and that the system was not going to be deployed.

With the collapse of the Soviet Union, the US began to pressure Russia not to transfer missile technology to India. Consequently Boris Yeltsin had to reverse his commitment to the sale, which he had expressed during his New Delhi visit in January 1993, and meekly cancelled a large part of the cryogenic rocket technology deal with India. Earlier the US had imposed sanctions on the Indian Space Research Organization (ISRO) and the Russian space agency, Glaskosmos, for two years to slow down India's space program[51]. Washington has thus chosen to ignore the Indian plea that MTCR is a fundamentally flawed and discriminatory arrangement among the nuclear haves and a few of their allies. The transfer of cryogenic technology would have given India the means to launch vehicles for civilian purposes and perhaps to compete with other space powers in the vehicle-launching business. The Indian policy makers, therefore, feel that they cannot accept any agreement that may result in denying Indian access to modern technology.

That these programs enjoy overwhelming domestic support and are not likely to be reversed by external political and economic pressures is evident by the strong domestic reaction in India against the American pressure for suspension of Indo-Russian cooperation in space technology and against the temporary suspension of the Prithvi test before Rao's US visit. Indeed, India has shown a strong determination to develop a whole range of technologies – from integrated circuits to rocket fuels. Its successful launching of the Augmented Satellite Launch Vehicle (ASLV) in 1992, Polar Satellite Launch

Vehicle (PSLV) in 1993 and the 1994 Prithvi test after Rao's return from Washington clearly underlines Indian resolve in this regard. India is already a missile power and there is no doubt in it.

The Clinton administration is against any type of missile proliferation. But India needs missiles for its own security. So far, India has not exported missile technology to any third party. To cite only one example, it rejected a very lucrative offer by Iraq to import Indian missile technology during the Gulf crisis in 1991[52].

Even though China supplied M-11 missiles to Pakistan, USA showed leniency to China because of several factors. It is a fact that US delayed action against China. Washington was constrained by the powerful lobby that has a strong stake in smooth relations with China because of US $6 billion investment there. Besides should US-China ties break, American firms stand to lose several billion dollars worth of business in the short term. In addition Washington has its eye on the more than $50 billion foreign exchange reserve that China is going to have[53]. So it seems the key to manage US-India tensions lies in India's economic capability and the implications of its economic reform programme.

The US' efforts to stop missile proliferation will become incomplete without reference to MTCR. Actually the seven industrialized countries the USA, the UK, Japan, Italy, France, Canada and Germany produced the Missile Technology Control Regime. The US in particular accelerated the pace of the ballistic missiles proliferation control drive around the world.

During the 60s and 70s very limited member of Third World countries had ballistic missile development programmes. In the early 1980s there was phenomenal growth in international trade in ballistic missiles. Thus, consequent to the proliferation of the ballistic missiles and the missile related technologies among the third world countries (mainly in countries like Argentina, Brazil, Egypt, India, Iran, Iraq, Israel, Pakistan, South Korea, Libya, South Africa and Saudi Arabia), and recognizing the dangers emanating from this development, the seven industrially developed countries, after almost four years of secret negotiations, mainly on the initiative of the US, signed a multilateral agreement on 16 April 1987 and established Missile Technology Control Regime (MTCR). It was thus the most significant multilateral nonproliferation efforts by the seven industrialized countries.

Unlike the nuclear Non-proliferation Treaty (NPT), the Missile Technology Control Regime is neither a treaty nor an executive agreement with no new organization what so ever formed to administer it. It is a voluntary agreement to develop guidelines to control the transfer of equipment and technology that could contribute to nuclear capable missiles[54]. While making a distinction between the military and civilian space programmes, the MTCR signatories declared that it was not "designed to impede national space programmes - as long as such programmes could not contribute to nuclear weapon delivery system"[55].

The MTCR rules works, because US had imposed sanctions on Russia and India for Russia's cryogenic engine sale to India. The US had also imposed sanctions on China and Pakistan for China's supply of M-11 missiles to Pakistan. The Clinton administration's imposition of sanctions on China has been criticized because on the one hand US imposes sanctions on China and on the other hand approves the sale of super computer – a product Beijing has long sought. The Chinese while asking for the super computer have claimed that it is needed for peaceful purposes, though it is no secret that super computers are often used to "target ballistic missiles and to verify without testing whether nuclear warheads will explode. Despite objections from many corners the US did approve sale of super computer to China.

MTCR like the nuclear nonproliferation regime has been opposed by most of the countries of the South. By and large, all its participants, and adherents belong to the industrialized world except Brazil and Argentina who virtually had to be pressurized into becoming its adherents. China is still a reluctant adherent. Most of the third world countries including India have expressed serious concerns and apprehensions about the motives of the missile haves in trying to impose a hegemonic and a highly discriminatory technology denial and control regime on the countries who are trying to develop technologies for their peaceful space programmes.

References

1. Jaswant Sing, "Against Nuclear Apartheid", Foreign Affairs, Vol.77, No.5, Sept/Oct. 1995, pp.42-43.
2. Dennis Kux, "Estranged Democracies": India and the US 1941-1991 (New Delhi: Sage, 1994), p.313.
3. Times of India, May 16, 1998.
4. *Ibid.*
5. CRS Issue Brief 93097, US-India Relations.
6 CRS Report 97-23, India-Pakistan Nuclear and Missile Proliferation: Background, Status and Issues for US Policy.
7. Indian's Letter to Clinton on the Nuclear Testing, New York Times, May 13, 1998: A12.
8. Reuters, May 28, 1998.
9. Raj Chengappa, "Nuclear Dilemma", India Today (New Delhi), April 30, 1994: 51.
10. Karl F. Iderfurth, "Situations in India", Testimony before the Senate Foreign Relations Committees Sub-committee on Near Eastern and South Asian Affairs, May 13, 1998, Washington D.C.
11. Cable News Network (CNN), Internet Website, June 18, 1998.
12. Hindustan Times, May 13, 1998.

13. *Ibid.*
14. Economic Times, June 17, 1998.
15. Far Eastern Economic Review, Vol.161, Issue 21, May 1998.
16. *Ibid*, Vol.161, Issue 21, May 1998.
17. "Fact Sheet: India and Pakistan Sanctions", USIS Washington File, June 18, 1998.
18. "India's decision to talk on FMCT hailed by US", Indian Express, July 22, 1998; "Banning Fissile Material Output: Pakistan Agrees to hold talks on Treaty", Dawn (Karachi), July 31, 1998.
19. "China and Russia underscore pact on South Asia". Dawn, July 24, 1998.
20. "Japan to back Pakistan at IMF", Dawn, August 7, 1998.
21. Andrew Hill, "Pakistan parliament to debate nuke test ban treaty", Reuters, September 9, 1998.
22. Judy Aita, "US Praises Steps by India, Pakistan towards signing CTBT". USIS Washington File, September 24, 1998; John M. Goshko, "India ready to sign nuclear treaty ban", Washington Post, September 25, 1998.
23. "US Diplomacy in South Asia: A Progress Report", Speech given by Deputy Secretary of State strobe Talbott at the Brookings Institution, November 12, 1998.
24. Chintamani Mahapatra, "Indo-US Relations in the 21st Century, pp.119-125 by Knowledge World in association with IDSM, New Delhi, September 1998.
25. Historical Documents of 1995, Congressional Quarterly, pp.553-557.
26. Secretary Christopher, White House Fact Sheets, Dispatch, September 16, 1996, Vol.7, No.38, pp.461-463.
27. CRS Report for Congress, December 16, 1996, p.7.
28. Resolutions Presented by India on 7 October 1948 at the Third Session of UN General Assembly, Document A/C, 1/315.
29. Mohandas K. Gandhi, "Atom Bomb and Ahimsa", Harijan, 7 July 1946.
30. Jawaharlal Nehru, "The Death-Dealer", National Herald, 2 April 1954.
31. Speech by Prime Minister Moraji Desai, UN General

Assembly Special Session, New York, 9 June 1978.

32. Statement made by the official spokesman of the Ministry of External Affairs, New Delhi, 11 September 1995.
33. Statement by Ambassador Arundhati Ghose, Conference on Disarmament Plenary Document CD/PV 740 (Geneva: 20 June 1996).
34. Statement by External Affairs Minister of India, Inder Kumar Gujral, Indian Parliament (New Delhi: 11 September 1996).
35. Arjun Makhijani, "India's Options", The Bulletin of the Atomic Scientists, Vol.53, No.2, March/April 1997, p.51.
36. USIS - Wireless File, "Fact Sheet - White House Chronology on Nuclear Test ban Treaty", September 25, 1996.
37. Kalpana Chittaranjan, "State of the CTBT", Strategic Analysis, June 2000, Vol.XXIV, No.3, pp.476-477.
38. Facts on File, Vol.59, No.3071, October 14, 1999, p.737.
39. Washington Post, January 28, 1996, p.A23.
40. Rahul Bedi, India Pressured to Halt Prithvi Production, Jane's Defence Weekly, April 15, 1995, p.5.
41. *Ibid.*
42. Narayanan Madhavan, Reuters, January 27, 1996; New York Times, January 28, 1996, p.A23.
43. Nelson Graves, Reuters, August 9, 1996.
44. R. Jeffrey Smith, China Linked to Missile Plant, Washington Post, August 23, 1996, pp. A1, A23.
45. *Ibid*, pp. A1, A23.
46. Joint Statement of the US of America and the People's Republic of China on Missile proliferation, October 4, 1994.
47. Nayan Chanda, "Secure Arms", Far Eastern Economic Review, Vol.161, Issue 47, November 19, 1998.
48. *Ibid*, pp.29.
49. Facts on File, Vol.56, No.2878, February 1996, p.57.
50. Faith Keenan, "A missed chance", Far Eastern Economic Review, Vol.161, Issue 17, April 23, 1998.
51. Times of India (Bombay), 15 July 1993: P.M. Kamath, "Short-Sighted American Diplomacy", Observer of Business and Politics, May 20, 1993.
52. N.C. Menon, "The Racket of Rockets", Hindustan Times (Patna), July 26, 1993.

53. Robert E. Hunter, "Strategy at Zero: US Foreign Policy for the 1990s", Washington Quarterly, Winter 1992, p.37.
54. Department of State Bulletin (Washington D.C.), Vol.87, No.21, July 24, 1987, p.68.
55. White House Press Release, April 16, 1987.

5

Clinton's Economic Relations with India

For the last more than four decades, Indo-US economic relations have witnessed ups and downs. Previously America had essentially ignored both economic and strategic issues affecting India. But with the disintegration of former USSR, Indo-US economic relations have started moving in productive manner. But the real break though came when India initiated a policy of "outward looking" in the name of economic liberalization in the middle of 1991. This very fact could be tested from the emergence of the US as India's biggest trade and investment partner.

There was a time when politics was dominating economics. But now it is a fact that economics is determining politics. A new era came when India opened up its economy. The socialist pattern of economy was thrown away and India adopted the free market economy. Indian economy became global. It happened not only in India but in many developing countries of the world. After the collapse of the Soviet Union, the US the only remaining super power in the world took no time to grab the opportunity. Even though there were differences between the two countries on many other issues, both the countries showed genuine desire to improve the commercial relationship. Now let us examine first the trends in Indo-US trade since the initiation of India's New Economic Policy (NEP) since 24th July 1991.

Trends in Indo-US Trade

Since 1988-89, India's trade with the US of America has been almost stagnant and as a result the trade has been ranging between US $5.5 billion and US $5.7 billion till the end of 1992-93 registering a marginal rise of 3.6 per cent during the span of 5 years or 0.7 per cent per annum. But during the year 1993-94, the two-way trade between India and the US has crossed a figure of US $7 billion with over US $ 4.5 billion in India's account witnessing a sharp rise and this has been possible due to the visit of Indian Prime Minister to Washington. Table 1 shows trends in India's trade with the US from 1988-89 to 1993-94.

Table 1: Trends in total volume of trade between India and the US between 1988-89 and 1993-94.

Year	*Total volume of tradeUS $ (billion)*	*Growth rate (in %)*
1988-89	5.5	—
1989-90	5.8	5.0
1990-91	5.8	0.0
1991-92	5.2	–10.0
1992-93	5.7	+9.6
1993-94	7.0	+22.8

Source: The Hindustan Times, New Delhi, August 4, 1993; India Today, New Delhi, July 5, 1994.

It is clear from the data set out the Table 1 that there has been a marked rise in the two-way trade between India and the US during the year 1993-94. The most revealing fact has been that from a negative growth rate of 10% during 1991-92, total bilateral trade has been converted into positive growth rate and the same has been of an appreciable nature i.e. as high as 23 per cent. This shows that India's economic policy has started yielding dividend which has proved to be productive and purposeful.

Trends in India's Exports to the US

India's exports to the USA have been showing almost an upward trend since 1988-89, the last year of the decade of eighties. In the year 1988-89, India's total exports to the US amounted to US $2.9 billion and the same figure reached a record level of US $4.4 billion during the year 1993-94 registering an overall increase of 517 per cent during the span of 6 years. However, yearly data has been showing a fluctuating trend. Table 2 indicates trends in India's exports to the US between 1988-89 and 1993-94.

Table 2 : Trends in India's exports to the US from 1988-89 to 1993-94.

Year	***Total Export US $ (billion)***	***Growth rate (in %)***
1988-89	2.9	—
1989-90	3.3	14.0
1990-91	3.1	-3.0
1991-92	33.1	0.0
1992-93	3.7	19.0
1993-94	4.4	18.9

Source: The Hindustan Times, New Delhi, August 4, 1993; India Today, New Delhi, July 5, 1994.

Statistics given in Table 2 reveals an erratic trend in India's exports to the US and the variations have been ranging between 0.3 and 19%. This means the steady growth with stability has been the missing link.

Major Indian exports to the US are diamond and jewellery including precious and semi-precious stones, garments, fabrics, carpets, floor coverings, coconut, cashew-nut, footwear, travel goods and bags. It is pertinent to point out here that since the initiation of India's economic liberalization policy, the composition of India's exports to the US has witnessed a change. Presently, the major exports of India to the USA are both traditional and non-traditional items. The six major items namely – textiles, clothing, prawns, footwear, leather goods and cashew nuts accounted for nearly 75 per cent of India's total exports in 1992-93.

In 1992-93, the US took action to withdraw benefits under Generalized System of Preferences (GSP) (under which selected goods from the developing world enter the US market duty free) from the entire range of chemicals and chemical goods. This was done due to continuing differences between India and the US on the issue of patents[1].

Very recently the US has been identified as a thrust country particularly after July 24, 1991 (when NEP was announced) for exporting and expanding India's export base. One of the export areas which is likely to be of great importance in the decade of nineties is software exports. India's exports from other sectors of the economy which are also on the priority list of promotion and expansion are engineering goods, gems, jewellery, textiles and clothing. In this respect, steps for promoting exports to the US have been initiated by the concerned ministries and allied agencies.

India's Imports from the US

India's imports from the US are confined to high technology categories which accounted for more than a quarter of all US exports to India. In recent years,

India's imports from the US have been witnessing a continuously decline trend till the end of 1992-93. Table 3 indicates trends in India's imports from the US between 1988-89 and 1993-94.

Table 3 : Trends in India's imports from the US between 1988-89 and 1993-94.

Year	*Total imports US $ (billion)*	*Growth rate (in %)*
1988-89	2.5	—
1989-90	2.5	—
1990-91	2.4	-4.0
1991-92	2.0	-17.0
1992-93	1.9	-5.0
1993-94	2.4	26.3

Source: The Hindustan Times, New Delhi, August 4, 1993; India Today, New Delhi, July 5, 1994.

India's imports to the US in 1993-94 went up to \$2.4 billion from US \$1.9 billion during 1992-93 registering an increase of more than 26 per cent. This is a sharp increase within a span of a year indicating a positive movement in India's trade relations with the US.

India's major imports from the US are confined to aircraft including parts, fertilizer, oil from petrol, bitum, and minerals excluding crude oil, machinery and machine tools, soyabean oil and extracts.

If we throw a glance on India's exports and imports from the US, we find that there has been a negative balance of trade from the US point of view and more positive balance of trade from India's angle. In the year 1988-89, India's trade surplus with the US amounted to US \$0.5 billion. This figure went up to a level of US \$2.0 billion in 1992-93 and thereafter during the last year i.e. 1993-94 India's trade surplus reached a level of 2.2 billion. These trends and situation have been persisting due to higher growth rate in India's exports to the US as compared to India's imports from the US. But during the year 1993-94 the rate of growth in India's imports from the US has improved and this could lead to a higher volume of trade between the two countries in the years to come.

From the above analysis, it is very clear that bilateral trade between India and the US have gained momentum particularly from July 24, 1991. The US and India have become trading partners, on equal footing. India is now not approaching the US for food aid as it happened in the past, on the contrary India is now doing business with the US. Of course full potential to it has not been achieved and both countries have to make efforts to enhance the existing volume of bilateral trade in the years to come.

When India opened its door and adopted the free market economy, the US deepened its commercial relations with India. The US now encourages and reinforces India's commercial reforms. It should also upgrade its efforts to promote exports to India, including heightening awareness on the part of the US firms in regard to commercial opportunities in India.

Clearly, the ongoing reforms create a freer business climate conducive to economic growth in India. This growth and the new openings for trade and foreign investment create new possibilities for the US-India commercial relations[2].

The Clinton administration has identified India as one of 10 "emerging markets" for US exports along with China, Indonesia, South Korea, Turkey, South Africa, Poland, Argentina, Brail and Mexico. The US is viewing these emerging markets to boost its national export strategy.

It is often believed that the US and India has been representing two ends of a "rich-poor spectrum", in the

Post-Cold War era. This would be a vast over-simplification. Today the US and India play a major role in the world economic scenario and have been wrestling to better define it. After a long isolation from market oriented policies leading to "import substitution", India is now seeking to join the international economic mainstream. India has a vast population of one billion and a larger middle class. So now the US has a great opportunity in India in the sphere of consumer goods items.

Although predominantly a rural-based economy, India possesses diverse industrial manufacturing base that ranks as the world's 12th biggest. India's US $250 billion economy is witnessing a growth rate of 4 per cent per year, although a number of sectors of interest to US firms are expanding at a much more rapid rate. It is an undisputed fact that, 1/5th of the world's population produces one-quarter of global economic output. The US has emerged as India's biggest trading partner.

Based on current market shares and some rough estimates of economic trends, the US exports could increase to an annual US $6 billion by the end of 2000. The US exports of aircraft and air traffic control equipment currently averaging US $100-200 million annually will continue to benefit from strong growth in India's air travel sector and programmes to modernize India's aviation infrastructure. Equipment sales and equity investment in the power-generating sector could total several billion dollars during the next six years. The US sales of petroleum exploration and refining equipment and services, which have averaged nearly US $100 million per annum, would provide an extended base for India seeking technology and capital to reduce its dependence on imported oil. It is an undisputed fact that, India has an enormous potential in regard to consumer market. Hence the country's vast consumer market with an annual value of nearly US $200 billion, is slowly being opened to foreign firms. A number of US firms have very recently been permitted to setup consumer goods projects and the Indian Government has started making concerted efforts for eliminating licensing barriers on consumer imports by the end of 1996.

Similar trends and situations have been emerging in regard to the US service industries, especially banking, insurance, brokerage which view India as a critical market. India's liberalization policy should reap full benefit of this new US sector. According to the US point of view, the greatest beneficiary of a more open and less restricted market will be India. The US companies bring high-technology manufacturing capabilities of the kind we see in Bangalore - India's "silicon valley". Strategic alliances with American firms hold the promise of helping India to integrate into the global economy which is the need of the day.

Trends in the US FDI Flows to India

The nature, magnitude and scope of Indo-US investment relations have undergone a sea change especially after 24 July 1991, when India's New Economic Policy was announced. The US has emerged as India's largest source of foreign collaborator. The largest source of foreign development assistance to India comes from the US. This new economic relationship reflects the longstanding policy of both the nations to build the economic relationship on an even and constantly expanding base.

Now the US of America has emerged as the largest investing country in India, having committed over an investment amounted to US $2 billion in the last three years and it is hoped in the future too. India needs the US with its green-bucks, technology and markets and the Government realizes that it needs to push hard if it wants to capitalize on them. The US is driven by the necessity to look increasingly outward for profits and has identified India among the list of "Big emerging Market"[3].

The most interesting and highly revealing fact has been that the USA is much ahead of others in regard to total investment approvals. While in 1991 the US FDI approval was at Rs.186 crore, they went up to Rs.1232 crore i.e. an increase of 562 per cent in 1992 and the first half of 1993. The total figure amounted to Rs.2098 crore and the same has crossed the total FDI approvals figure of the entire year of 1992. A comparative figure in regard to FDI flows to India from major investing countries between 1991 and 1994 (January - April) could be seen from Table 4.

Table 4 : Major investors in India : The US tops (1991-94).

Country	***US $ Million* 1991**	***1992***	***1993***	***1994 (Jan.-April)***
US	75.8	426.1	1100	182.9
Japan	21.5	211.2	350	6.0
UK	13.1	40.7	200	41.9
Germany	17.0	29.9	125	19.3

Source : India Today, New Delhi.

It is seen from table 4 that there has been a tremendous increase in FDI approvals of the US and since 1991 there has been a continuous increase. The US companies have shown greater interest in India's economic liberalization policy and accordingly the US has emerged as the single largest investing nation as well as biggest trade partner of India. The need of the day is to continue economic and financial reforms, as the continued progress is very essential if bilateral trade and investment are to grow[4].

To make the US-India commercial relations more vigorous, certain steps are to be taken:

1. Bureaucratic delays should be stopped which makes delays and hinders implementation.
2. Adequate legal protection should be given to the foreign companies.
3. Regular exchange of visits should be done at the government level to remove misunderstanding.

If all these steps are taken up seriously, the US-India commercial relations will grow horizontally as well as vertically.

To boost Indo-American commercial relations, President Clinton visited India in the year 2000. The main focus of President Clinton's five-day visit to India was on forging a long-term business and economic relationship between the world's two largest democracies. It has also underlined India's standing as an important political and economic ally of the US. In the Post-Cold War scenario, the US has perhaps belatedly recognized India's strategic importance as a counterweight to China's growing shadow in Asia.

While the synergy of economic interests is expected to give a boost to the knowledge-based sector, there is better understanding between thetwo nations on political issues. The signing of business agreements between India and US companies totally $3 billion - over $2 billion in commercial ventures and $1 billion in US export-import bank financing - indicate that more such ventures may come in the future.

More significant is the move to institutionalize the ongoing dialogue between the two countries as part of intensifying and regularizing their bilateral exchange efforts on a host of economic issues ranging from trade, investment, energy and environment to those pertaining to foreign policy, regional and international security and nonproliferation concerns.

The economic dialogue for a "qualitatively new" relationship will be initiated by a high-level coordinating group led by officials in the Prime Minister's office and the External Affairs Minister on the Indian side and by the White House assisted by the State Department on the US side. Its prime focus would be to leverage on the enormous potential for enrichment of economic and business relations between the two countries in the knowledge age.

The vision document outlining the contours of the Indo-US relations for the 21st century states: "Together we represent a fifth of world's people, more than a quarter of the world's economy. We have built creative, entrepreneurial societies. We are leaders in the information age. The currents of commerce and culture that link our societies run strong and deep. In many ways, the character of the 21st century will depend on the success of our cooperation for peace, prosperity, democracy and freedom".

With broad inter-agency and inter-ministerial representations at the senior official level, the coordinating group will develop a common economic agenda and regularly convene to ensure that discussions therein complement and reinforce broad economic objectives, particularly the deepening of bilateral cooperation on high technology and information technology issues.

During Clinton's visit to India, it was resolved that India's Finance Minister and the US Treasury Secretary would host a separate forum on finance and investment issues, macro-economic policy and international economic development at regular intervals. This will be supplemented by sub-cabinet meetings, which also involve the participation of official from the US Securities and Exchange Commission and Securities and Exchange Board of India, the US Federal Reserve, the Reserve bank of India and other agencies.

Simultaneously, the Minister of Commerce and industry and the US Secretary of Commerce will have a 'commercial dialogue' mechanism to deepen ties between the business communities. The dialogue will encompass regular government-to-government meetings to be held in conjunction with private sector interactions. The aim would be to facilitate trade and maximize investment opportunities across a broad range of sectors, including information technology, infrastructure, biotechnology and services. More than 400 businessmen from both countries who attended a business meeting in Mumbai where the US President described India as an I.T. Superpower were in a buoyant mood as all the senior business and industry leaders underlined the immense possibility of forging an alliance, particularly to exploit opportunities in the knowledge-based sector.

Further, the two sides will establish an independent Indo-US Working Group on Trade "which will serve as a locus of consultation on a broad range of trade related issues, including those pertaining to world Trade Organization". Here individual trade issues would be examined in 'greater depth' with inputs received from the private sector.

Apart from the regular trade, finance and investment issues, India and the US will extend their cooperation in the fields of energy, environment and science and technology. Accordingly, there would be a Joint Consultative Group on Clean Energy and Environment. Emphasis will be on collaborative projects focussing on developing and deploying clean energy technologies, climate change and other environmental issues. The India-US science and technology forum would seek to promote R&D, transfer of technology and creation of a comprehensive electronic reference source for information dissemination.

The US overtures couldn't have come at a more opportune time. India is the second largest economy in Asia and also one of the 10 fastest growing economies in the world. To modernize its infrastructure, it needs foreign investments which it can pay back by exporting its software products. Two-thirds of India's total export of software is used by US companies. However, India gets only one-third of the visas. There is also a double levy faced by Indian InfoTech companies.

The US would need to review its approach as in the past it had adopted a negative attitude on exporting high technology to India as it could be used for defence purpose also. India was denied a super computer by the US but India built it through its indigenous R&D efforts. This is one area of concern to India. The US is the most powerful country with about 28 percent share in the world economy and can offer both capital and technology to a variety of industries and services.

There are other concerns as well. The US has pressurized India into removing QRs before the end of next year although we had another three years to do that. But the textile quota by which the US industry is protected will be phased out only at the fag end of the ten-year period. Many export products attract anti-dumping duties in the US. And also India is still on the watch list of the dreaded section 301 of the US Trade Act.

But the most significant aspect of Mr. Clinton's visit is India's emergence as an economic and strategic powerhouse in Asia paving the way for macro-level Indo-US cooperation and investment by US companies in Indian ventures. And it is a matter of time before the US sanctions are removed to strengthen economic and technological cooperation between the two countries[5].

India's economy has been attracting attention from the Western press, diplomats and businesses since

1991. This is when Prime Minister Mr. P.V. Narasimha Rao inherited the mantle of the Congress Party following the tragic assassination of Prime Minister Rajiv Gandhi.

Mr. Rao is consolidating all the strengths of the Indian economic system to integrate India's economy with that of the rest of the world through policies boldly enunciated since 1991. The new economic policy is bold in the sense that it effects an apparently significant departure from a certain philosophy and pragmatism that had served India during the Cold War between the West and the Soviet Union from 1945 to 1991. During these decades, India was labelled a socialist economy and society, a perception that makes the current focus on liberalization and competition, both internally and externally, bold and almost revolutionary.

Soon after coming to power Mr. Rao and his finance minister, today's Prime Minister Dr. Manmohan Singh, announced a programmme of economic liberalization. Dr. Singh had faithfully served Mrs. Gandhi's Governments as economic adviser and in Mr. Rajiv Gandhi's government as head of the Planning Commission which is responsible for Five Year Plans. An economist trained in neoclassical economics with specialization in international trade, Dr. Singh has proven himself to be flexible in adapting to ideas and practices of market economics as well as regimes which include economic planning. He changed and shifted his policies to suit his new Prime Minister and new economic situation at home and abroad.

The new policy and programmes announced in 1991 included a significant reduction in import tariffs and elimination of import quotas except for consumer goods, elimination or reduction of restrictions on foreign ownership, currency convertibility on the trade account, reduction in licensing requirements, reduction in domestic excise taxes, among others.

As a result of these reforms foreign direct investment poured in from companies such as Pepsi, General Motors, General Electric, International Business machines, Coca-cola, McDonald's, Enron etc. and similar companies from Great Britain, Japan, and Germany. Now the Indian economy is ready for a take-off because investment is growing, foreign capital and technologies are coming in, competition is at work and state intervention is less[6].

The US-India Relations in the 1990s

George Washington, the founding father of the US of America had laid down a foundation principle for the American Foreign Policy. He had said, "The great rule of conduct for US, in regard to foreign nations, is in extending our commercial relations[7]. Almost two centuries later, President Bill Clinton echoed the same principle. He declared, "In this new era, our first foreign priority and domestic priority are one and the same: reviving our economy ... I will elevate economics in foreign policy, create an Economic Security Council ... and change the State Department's culture so that economics is no longer a poor cousin to old school diplomacy"[8]. Economic factors will dominate the political relations between nations of the world in the 21st century. The US-India relations will be guided by this.

Today's bilateral relationship is mainly based on economic interests. India's Economic Reform Programme is a point of great attention to the whole world and the US in particular. With the liberalization policies of the Government of India, the interest of the American business to invest in India has enormously increased. President Clinton has said that it is the economic reform of India that has become the engine of growth in the bilateral relationship. India's economic programme has unleashed the expanding trade and investment ties of the US[9].

Ambassador Frank G. Wisnor opined that the trade and economic ties that are growing between the two countries provide the basis for a new era of engagement[10]. The US is India's largest investor, with proposals from American companies accounting for nearly half of all investment approvals issued by the Government of India in 1993. India has received massive infusion of private capital through both direct investment in joint ventures and portfolio investment in stock markets.

The approvals of direct foreign investment proposals have risen from $73 million in 1990 to $1,318 million (Rs.3,888 crore) in 1992 to $2,381 million in 1993. The actual flow of foreign investment in India exceeded $3 billion in 1993-94 since August 1991 and by mid 1994-95 the accumulated foreign investment stands at $5.9 billion out of which actual inflow of foreign direct invest stands at $1.2 billion. Foreign Institutional Investors (FIIs) have invested US $2.2 billion and inflow through Euro Issues and Global Depository Receipt came to US $2.5 billion[11].

Indo-US collaborations have shown a dramatic rise since 1991. The number of Indo-US collaborations approved has risen from 177 in 1991 to nearly 300 in 1993. In 1993, US investment worth US $1,103.56 million accounting for 40 per cent of the total was approved. The US is not only a major source of foreign direct investment but also an important source of technology for India.

In the past, a total of 2,168 technical collaborations and 1,892 financial collaborations have been approved. Out of these, the US accounts for 442 technical collaboration approvals and 389 financial collaboration approvals. Hence, in terms of number of collaboration approvals also, the US occupies a leading position accounting for over 20 per cent collaboration approvals.

Also, the US is India's largest trading partner, buying 20 per cent of the merchandise India exports, according to Robin Raphael[12]. During Prime Minister Rao's visit to the US in May 1994, the late Commerce Secretary Ronald H. Brown said that the previous years' 44 per cent increase in American exports to India and the 20 per cent in Indian exports to the US were both a result of Rao's economic reform programme. With the ongoing reform package, the Clinton administration has designated India as one of the ten Big Emerging Markets (BEMs) that will account for nearly three-fourths of the growth in world trade in the next two decades and have extraordinary influence on global affairs in the Post-Cold War era[13].

The 1996 "National Trade Estimate Report on Foreign Trade Barriers (NTE) lists a wide range of trade barriers which restrict US exports as well as those of other nations. The US trade representative, Mickey Kantor, emphasized that last year, the US experienced "largest dollar volume increase in exports in history".

According to the report, India was the US' 30th largest export market in 1995 and the US imports from India totalled $5.7 billion last year or about 8 per cent more than in 1994. The stock of US direct investment in India was $818 million in 1994, 33.9 per cent higher than in 1993 and much of these investments were largely concentrated in banking, manufacturing and wholesaling.

The report acknowledges that as part of India's economic reform process, there has been a more open and transparent trade regime.

Under a purely bilateral set-up, economic relations between India and the US have been remarkable, evolving a fruitful partnership in the last five decades. From the viewpoint of India's balance of payments and external earnings, the US market is crucial. But much more important is the US interest to invest in India. There has been a great improvement in this direction. The new policy of liberalization is a point of great attraction to the US. One basic reality about India is that India, with all its frailties, is a large continental economy with a great deal of opportunities within the country itself. Now America has acknowledged India as a BEM. The US Under Secretary of Commerce for International Trade, Jeffrey E. Garten has said that as economic reforms gather momentum, India may be in a position to provide significant commercial opportunities for the US firms throughout the 1990s[14]. Although Japan and Western Europe are likely to remain the biggest markets for the US, Garten suggests that the BEMs hold far more promise for large incremental gains in exports. He estimates that nearly three-fourths of the growth in the world trade in the next two decades is likely to take place in the developing world, much of it in the BEMs. By the year 2010, according to Garten, the share of the BEMs in world imports is likely to exceed that of Japan and the European Union combined[15].

The Carnegie Report advises the US to follow a more liberal policy towards India and support the Special Drawing Rights of India[16]. The same view about the BEMs has been expressed by John F. Cogan Jr., President of one of the oldest mutual funds in the US. He stresses that there is certainly much to get excited about China, but India may be a very large yet hidden jewel among the emerging equity markets[17]. India, out of 21 emerging markets along with Indonesia, Pakistan and Malaysia, is projected to have the second highest Gross Domestic Product (GDP) growth of 7 per cent in the next five years, only next to Hong Kong with 8 per cent. Similarly, in respect of expected earnings per share growth rates for 1993, India ranks second among 21 markets with 33.3 per cent.

Since the beginning of the decade, the trade

between the US and India has been gaining strong momentum. In the past three years since 1990-91, the overall trade with the US has risen by 20 per cent. The exports during the same period had a phenomenal spurt of 50 per cent. The imports during the same period have risen by 7.1 per cent. The trade balance of India which stood at negative US $253 billion, has now risen to US $1.2 billion, which is greater than its export levels of 1980-81. The bilateral trade between India and the US, on the whole, has expanded considerably in the last five-six years, rising from $4 billion in 1994.

In the sphere of foreign trade, after India has opened herself:

1. There is a great decline in trade deficit, both in terms of dollars and rupees.
2. Imports have increased in rupee terms while in dollar terms they have increased much more.
3. Imports have increased by 28 per cent in rupee terms, but declined by 5 per cent in dollar terms.

The composition of India's exports over the years has undergone a change: crude oil which was the second largest item in 1985 has been virtually phased out. In spite of this, India's exports to the US have been rising mainly on account of significant increases in exports of gems and jewellery, readymade garments, carpets, yearns, handicrafts, drugs and pharmaceuticals, electronic goods and transport items.

Over the past decade, the US share in India's exports has hovered around 18 per cent, and for imports at nearly 11 per cent. On the other hand, India accounts for a miniscule portion of the US's exports and imports at nearly 0.6 per cent.

Thus, today's evolving bilateral relationship between India and the US is mainly based on economic interests. The US has become India's largest trading partner and the largest source of investment. India's economic reform programme has been well appreciated and responded to by the US. Ambassador Wisnor's remark at the Senate Foreign Relations Committee highlighted the economic sphere as having the most dramatic potential in future Indo-US relations. The progress of India's liberalized economy is literally breathtaking and is building a fundamentally new dimension for Indian and American interaction.

Here one must analyse as to why India has assumed so much importance in the global market. First of all, India is viewed as one of the "hottest and hugest emerging markets" in the world today[18]. The important advantages of India are:

1. One of the largest economies in the world, the sixth largest in terms of Purchasing Power Parity.
2. A large and rapidly growing consumer market with up to 300 million people who constitute the market for branded consumer goods – estimated to be growing at 8 per cent annum, demand for consumer products growing at over 12 per cent per annum.
3. One of the largest manufacturing sectors of the world, spanning almost all areas of manufacturing activities.
4. One of the largest pools of scientists, engineers, technicians and managers in the world.
5. Long history of market economy infrastructure, along with sophisticated financial sector.
6. Vibrant capital market with over 6,500 listed companies and market capitalization of US $140 billion.
7. Policy environment that provides freedom of entry, investment, location choice of technology, production, import and export.
8. A long history of stable parliamentary democracy.

However, the US-India economic relationship has not always been a smooth one. There have been many irritants in the past like imposition of certain types of control of super 301 etc. But when two nations get into a mutual relationship, everything need not be smooth between them. President Bill Clinton explained: "When two nations are friends, it does not mean that they agree on every thing or that they should. But in the context of their friendly relationship, they are then able to discuss differences, problems or issues between them". During the confirmation hearing, the then Ambassador designate Frank G. Wisner touched on the same thing saying, "We cannot let our differences define our relationship". So by all accounts, economic links will form one of the strongest pillars of the relationship, and there is going to be a strong, mature partnership in peace and progress between the US and India in the future and this relation will encompass all fields including economic, political and cultural interests of both the countries.

India's economic reforms have created an immense demand for foreign direct investment (FDI) in practically all major sectors of US competitive strength. These include power, telecommunication, environmental protection, automobiles, oil refining, food processing, biotechnology and computer software and services. As mentioned earlier, in 1994, the Commerce Department identified India as a Big Emerging Market.

During most of Prime Minister Narasimha Rao's government (1991-96) differences between the US and India on security issues were deliberately ignored. Both countries found it more convenient to accentuate the positive. There was, in fact, significant justification for optimism, as long as attention focused on the unprecedented opportunities for economic cooperation arising out of the dramatic shift in India to market-based economic policies. The US and Indian policymakers alike publicly emphasized mutual beneficial economic relations as the driving force of the whole relationship. These opportunities were created by a drastic cutback in the number of Indian industries reserved to the public sector, the removal of compulsory licensing of investments in all but 15 low priority industries, primarily consumer durables, and the lifting of restrictions on foreign investment up to 51 per cent equity in 127 major industries.

The Government approved licenses for foreign collaboration in consumer durables and for wholly owned subsidiaries. Foreign companies received permission to borrow funds in India, raise public deposits and expand their operations by creating new businesses and taking over exiting businesses. Foreign financial institutions could also make direct portfolio investments in India's two stock markets. In addition, the government removed quantitative quotas on imports, steadily reduced tariff levels on imports and made the rupee convertible to pay balances on the current export and import (trade) account.

A major selling point is India's great market potential. A 1994-95 national sample survey of Indian market demographics in urban and rural areas estimated that 28 million households or about 150 million persons, belong to the consumer classes. Consumer demand is growing most rapidly for higher price items. A significant proportion of the country's 90 million low-income households, which constitute 500 million persons or 57 per cent of the total population, are also entering the market to buy at least some inexpensive consumer durables – especially bicycles, radios and watches – as well as low-priced consumables like detergents, cooking oil and tea. Altogether, an astounding 780 million people bought some products at least once during 1994-95[19]. The large consumer market, along with less expensive skilled personnel, and opportunities for manufacturing products for export at lower costs, persuaded American CEOs of large multinationals that India offered key long-term growth opportunities, comparable to those in China. By including in their equations the fact that India follows a stable democratic political process, has a developed legal system and a long established private business sector and can offer English speaking technical and managerial talent, these executives also had reason to consider India a lower-risk opportunity than China.

During 1991-95 American MNCs were India's largest source for foreign direct investment, providing 26 per cent of the country's total[20]. The largest share of US investment, hovering around 50 per cent, went to manufacturing, with the consumer sub-sector accounting for a little more than half of that total. Other major investments were made in banking (28 per cent), energy (9 per cent) and computer/ software (9 per cent)[21].

Altogether, by the end of 1994, some 426 US companies had Indian operations. Most MNCs, however, had done little more than testing the waters. The absolute amount they actually invested was $981 million. Nevertheless, when one takes into account new investments projected at $712 million during 1995, planned investments of $1.8 billion during 1996-200, and several anticipated major infrastructure projects, American investment by 2000 is expected to reach more than $5 billion. Such figures contributed to the dominant view held by US officials in New Delhi on the eve of 1996 national election that the economic relationship, with its immense potential, had taken on a life of its own.

India's needs for massive foreign investment in infrastructural sectors alone provided confirmation of the opportunities that could open up. By the end of 1996-97, Indian power shortage reached 15 per cent of total installed capacity, with peak levels of shortages as high as 30 per cent. This leads to the immediate necessity of installing new projects on the ground to generate an additional 12-24 gigawatts of power, with long-term requirements much higher. The Central Government cannot mobilize more than about 60 per cent of the expenditure needed to bridge this gap. State Governments are virtually bankrupt. Their State Electricity Boards (SEBs), which control the transmission and distribution of power, set prices considerably below cost and are unable to meet the modest minimum rates of return which, under state law, are fixed at 3 per cent. On the contrary, deficits have been steadily rising and losses are projected at 18.2 per cent in 1996-97[22]. My point here to mention all these is that power sector needs private investment because private investment can only provide the additional resources required in the power sector.

Similarly, the need to build a national network of basic telephone services, as well as to meet global standards in more sophisticated telecommunications – such as cellular phones, pages, video conferencing and commercial data transmission links – is beyond the capacity of government funding and internal generation of resources[23]. One estimate by the CII, based on reaching levels of 8 per cent growth in gross domestic product (GDP) per annum by 1991, puts the requirement for private sector investment in infrastructure at $55 billion between 1995-96 and 1999-2000, and $171.5 billion in the subsequent five years. Overall, the Ministry of Finance in its 1995-96 Economic Survey asserted that India has to be prepared to encourage a rapid increase in FBI to levels comparable to China's $30 billion or more per year[24].

There are certain American projects, whose progress has been halted because of party differences. In August 1995, soon after it came to power the BJP announced unilateral termination of the agreement signed between the previous Congress(I) government and the Dhabol Power Company, a subsidiary of Enron, the largest natural gas company in the US. The project to construct a $2.8 billion, 2,015 megawatt power plant had been cleared by the Power Ministry, the Finance Ministry, the Central Electricity authority and the Maharashtra SEB. Nevertheless, the BJP claimed that the deal had been negotiated in secret, without competitive bids, on the basis of inflated costs (implying corruption) and that the price of electricity placed too great a burden on the people of the state. In one swoop, the BJP cast doubt on the fairness of all eight 'fast-track' power projects in Maharastra, Gujarat, Andhra Pradesh, Karnatak, Orissa and Rajasthan negotiated by the Congress(I) Government with foreign investors and involving three American companies[25].

The US Under Secretary, Joan E. Spero remarked about Indo-US economic relations in the Post-Cold War era. He commented that our economic relationship must be founded on the mutual benefit, which the Indian and the US companies derive from working together. According to him India has not fully participated in or benefited from the global economy in the past. The desire to shield Indian industry from international economic competition for more than four decades steadily diminished India's role in the international trading system. While it provided some protection to Indian companies in their home market, it also made them less competitive internationally. India's share of world trade declined from 3.6 per cent in 1950 to 1.2 per cent in 1970 and was only 0.58 per cent in 1992.

Now India's leaders have had the wisdom and vision to take a new path. They have began the process of making India one of the great economic powers in the world, not by turning inward, but by releasing India's energy and talent to participate fully in the world economy. The people of India have already begun to reap the benefits of these decisions. America and India must promote their own interests – But we cannot do this by turning our backs on the world, he said. President Clinton has told the American people that we must compete not retreat – that our national security in the Post-Cold War period depends on our economic strength at home and abroad. The President also has said repeatedly that change is never easy, but we must make change our ally. The President is pursuing a new economic strategy which is strengthening our nation's ability to compete in the global marketplace.

He said, "Likewise, I believe that the Government of India has made a fundamental and wise decision – that India's well-being, its national security and its social progress can best be pursued through economic freedom and by developing India's economic strength at home and abroad.

In India, four years of economic reforms have proven conclusively what many had long believed: that Indian businesses, entrepreneurs, scientists and workers can thrive in an open marketplace. Growth and exports are up, and India is earning a reputation as one of the most important economic players in the world.

He said, "As you know, our department of commerce has identified India as one of the ten big emerging markets in the world. Surely it is in the upper tier of that group. In deed, by some measures, India already has the sixth largest economy in the world, valued at about $1 trillion in purchasing power parity."

About bilateral relationship he said, "The US is also continuing to develop strong bilateral relation with our most important trading partners, including India. The US has been, remains and will make every effort to continue to be India's most important trading partner and its largest single source of foreign investment. Approvals of proposed US investment in India since 1991 are approximately equal to twice the total amount of investment in the prior 40 years.

It has been estimated for instance, that India will require in excess of $100 billion in infrastructure investment between now and the end of the century. Much of that investment will come from outside of India. We believe that the largest share of external direct investment will continue to come from the US. Already more than 200 US firms have equity investments in India. Those firms provide employment for between 60,000 and 70,000 Indians. Although we have long been India's most important partner, today our economic relations have a breadth and depth unimaginable just a few year ago, he said.

Prime Minister Rao and President Clinton personally recognized the vibrant growth in our relationship during the Prime Minister's visit. At that time they pledged to revive the Indo-US economic / commercial sub-commission[26].

The Under Secretary of Commerce for International Trade, Joffrey E. Garten remarked that there is very much in common between India and America.

1. India is world's largest democracy. America is world's oldest democracy.
2. India will, within our lifetime, become one of the world's largest emerging markets. America is the world's largest developed market.
3. English language is common in both America and India.
4. India and the US both achieved independence via civil disobedience and revolt against oppressive authority.

When Prime Minister Rao visited the US earlier, a new spirit was born. President Clinton in his remarks to the Prime Minister and in private remarks within the administration has repeatedly emphasized that he hoped that we were entering a new era in our relationship, one in which we were motivated by our great mutual interests to forge new closer ties.

Paramount among these interests are the commercial opportunities that are increasingly at the heart of the Clinton administration's foreign policy. Economic reforms enable American companies to take advantage of the opportunities within the Indian market and enable Indian companies to better enter the global market place. Economic growth in India is a powerful stabilizing force in a region of the world where stability is of paramount importance. So the end of Cold War has ushered in an opportunity for both India and America to look at the world a new.

America has identified India as the Big Emerging Market (BEM) including China, Hong Kong, Taiwan, South Korea, Indonesia, Turkey, South Africa, Poland, Argentina, Brazil and Mexico. The Big Emerging Markets constitute a category of countries which will have extraordinary influence on global affairs in the new Post-Cold War era. They will become major actors in trade and finance and they will be nations that will make the decisive differences in the kind of global economy that exists in the next century - liberal and open, or protectionist and closed. These are the nations which will be political heavyweights in their geographical regions. Many will have significant influence on military balances. Many hold the key to halting the spread of weapons of mass destruction. Many will have a major impact on the global environment. All strive to move up the ladder of technological sophistication, and some will pioneer new technologies, too. The four Asian BEMs will account for the lion's share of this trade expansion. Already, they constitute 40 per cent of the world's population and half the GDP of all the BEMs. They could account for as much as two-thirds of the total import growth of the BEMs during the next twenty years.

The Clinton administration is mounting a major commercial initiative towards these markets. To each of the BEMs, America will devote more time, money and manpower. America will establish new commercial bilateral mechanism with most such markets to offer a permanent conduit through which it can resolve commercial difficulties and seize business opportunities.

In fact, commercial ties between Washington and New Delhi still reflect patterns fostered by Indian import substitution policies and restrictions on foreign investment. However, recent data show that India's new policies and heightened US business interests have already begun to show results. Indian exports to the US increased by 21 percent in 1993, to a record of $4.6 billion. US exports to India rose by 44 percent in 1993, to a record $2.8 billion. Hence, India enjoyed a $1.8 billion surplus in Indo-American bilateral balance of trade. It was also estimated that surplus would rise again in 1994 to about $2.6 billion.

Much of the US export growth in 1993 represents a rebound in US sales after a 20 per cent plunge in exports during the 1991 and 1992 balance of payment crisis. Still, it is believed that the US export growth to India will continue to be strong, with annual increase of ten per cent through the remainder of the decade - not an unrealistic expectation.

Indian Governments' approval of American investment totalled approximately $1.1 billion in 1993, more than double the previous year's level and roughly equal to the cumulative investment approved during the four decades prior to 1991.

A distinguished economist Jagdish Bhagwati has written in his book, "India in Transition", "Reform by Storm" has replaced "Reform by Stealth" of Mrs. Gandhi's time, and "Reform with Reluctance" under Rajiv

Gandhi. In fact 1995 will be a landmark year in the US-Indian relations in terms of high-level visits alone. India came under the radar screen of the USA in many respects.

1. The Indo-US Joint Economic Sub-commission was formed which would serve as the primary bilateral mechanism for dealing with the commercial issues of mutual interest.

So, India is on the move. By cutting import duties, by promoting exports, by reforming the exchange rate regime, by dismantling the "license raj" (a system of industrial controls), by the growth of joint ventures between Indian and foreign companies, India is breaking the chains of 40 years of attempted self-reliance and entering the mainstream of the world economy in full force.

According to World Bank projections, of the seven largest economies in the world, four will be the Asian BEMs. China will be first. America and Japan will be next. India will be the fourth followed by Indonesia – then Germany – and South Korea[27].

Foreign direct investment is now welcomed and encouraged in India. Between January 1991 and July 1994, the government approved $5.1 billion in foreign investment, more than that which had been approved in the previous four decades. India has also welcomed investment from foreign institutional investors.

The available data indicate that Foreign Direct Investment (FDI) in India increased from $280 million in 1992-93 to, $872 in 1994-95, to $2057 million in 1996-97and further to $2956 million in 1997-98. FDI in India, however, declined to $2000 million in 1998-99. The countries which have significantly contributed to FDI in India include Germany, Japan, Italy, Mauritius, the Netherlands, South Korea, Switzerland, the United Kingdom and the US of America. It may be pointed out that in 1992-93 Switzerland with an FDI of the order of $35.3 million ranked first amongst all the countries which had participated in this process in India. During the year 1993-94 and 1994-95, the US of America was on the top amongst the countries which participated in FDI in India[28].

The Clinton administration has recognized India as a major player in the economic field. South Asia as a whole is increasingly becoming a region of intense growth and development. The economic liberalization policy of the Government of India paved the way for unprecedented trade and investment between India and the US. As mentioned earlier, India is on the US Commerce Department's top ten "big emerging markets". The Clinton administration has recognized India as a major player in the economic field. It may be recalled that during the visit of Commerce Secretary Ron Brown along with a big business delegation to India in January 1995, projects worth $7 billion were signed. Energy Secretary Hazel O' Leary's visit to India was equally successful particularly on the power front.

The US-India commercial alliance has been established to promote greater interaction between the private sectors of the two countries. It may be recalled that during Prime Minister Narasimha Rao's visit to the US in May 1994, it was decided to revive the India-US Economic/Commercial Sub-commission. Hence the former acts as a complement to the work of the latter. The Indo-US commercial alliance has been a success so far, due to the Indian government's commitment to open markets and setup a fair and transparent regulatory system. India is now going through the gigantic task of transforming its economy while maintaining its democratic traditions. It is expected that the economic dimension will have a multiplier effect on bilateral ties between the two countries in the yeas to come.

The US is the largest trading partner with India. The total volume of bilateral trade is now in the range of nine and ten billion dollars. India has a favourable balance of trade with the US, with a trade surplus of nearly $500 million to $1 billion. The US is now the single largest investor in India accounting for almost billion $4 out of a total of about $12 billion worth of foreign investments cleared by the Government of India since 1991. Being the largest foreign investor in India, the US accounts for about half of all foreign equity. Much as exports to the US are important for India, the US also needs the Indian market in a global market that is increasingly becoming competitive. The tremendous increase in Indo-US economic cooperation is the cornerstone of the new relationship between the two countries[29].

In 1999, the US trade deficit with India was $5.4 billion, an increase of $696 million from the US trade deficit of $4.7 billion in 1998. The US merchandise exports to India were $3.7 billion, an increase of $163 million (4.6 per cent) from the level of US exports to India in 1998. India was the United State's 29th largest export market in 1999. The US imports from India were $9.1 billion in 1999, an increase of $859 million (10.4 per cent) from the level of imports in 1998. The stock of the US foreign direct investment (FDI) in India in 1998 was $1.5 billion, a decrease of 5.3 per cent from the level of the US FDI in 1997. The US FDI in India is concentrated largely in the banking, manufacturing and financial service sectors, but a substantial portion of new investment approvals are in infrastructure projects.

Actually in June 1991, the then newly elected Government recognized that India's budget deficit, balance of payments problems, and structural imbalances would require reevaluation of past economic policies and structural adjustment assistance from international financial institutions. As part of its economic reform since that time, the Indian Government has taken consistent steps towards a more open and transparent trade regime, leading to a significant increase in Indo-US trade and investment. With substantial additional liberalization, the US-India trade could become quite significant.

Intellectual Property Rights Protection

Based on past practices, India was identified in April 1991 as a "priority foreign country" under the "Special 301" provision of the 1988 Trade Act, and a Section 301 investigation was initiated on May 26, 1991. In February 1992, following a nine-month investigation under "Special 301", the USTR determined that India's denial of adequate and effective intellectual property protection was unreasonable and burdens or restricts US commerce, especially in the area of patent protection.

In April 1992, the President suspended duty-free privileges under the Generalized System of Preferences (GSP) for $60 million in trade from India. This suspension applied principally to pharmaceuticals, chemicals, and related products. Benefits on certain chemicals added to GSP in June 1992, were withheld from India, increasing the trade for which GSP is suspended to approximately $80 million. Significant revisions to India's copyright law in May 1994 led to the downgrading of India as "priority foreign country" to the "priority watch list", a designation under which India has remained since 1995[30].

Having already taken punitive action against Brazil by raising tariffs, the US first named India in 1989 as one of eight countries on a "priority watch list" of "most egregious violators" of American IPR. As part of its two-track (bilateral-cum-multilateral) strategy, it had earlier that year pressurized India to accept the inclusion of TRIPS in the Uruguay Round. Following its placement on the watch list, India back-pedaled somewhat arguing at the GATT negotiations in Geneva that it had "serious reservations about the relevance and utility of these negotiations as long as the bilateral coercion and threat continue". However, having allowed TRIPS to be placed on the GATT agenda, it was now committed to negotiating for its interests within the expanded framework. Meanwhile, bilateral American pressure continued and after a respite, India was named as an offender of IPR by the USTR in 1991. Although no action was taken then, in 1992 Washington suspended duty-free privileges under GATT's generalized system of preferences for Indian pharmaceuticals and other chemicals to the value of $60 million. This was a relatively small amount, but a strong bargaining chip as an indicator of things to come should India remain recalcitrant at Geneva. In 1993, India was identified once again under Special 301, but no action was taken because India was falling into line at the GATT negotiations.

By mid-June 1994, India became a signatory to the GATT accord of April 1994, which incorporates agreement on TRIPS. American pressure continued. The April 30 deadline for naming India as an IPR violator was pushed back to June 30, before Prime Minister Narasimha Rao's visit to the US in May. But the threat remains. The GATT accord allows India to modify its patent law by 2005[31].

Actually, the new economic policy of Prime Minister P.V. Naramsimha Rao was marvelous. In order to attract foreign investors India reduced restrictions on equity, revised investment-licensing controls, raised limits on repatriation. Import procedures and tariffs were altered in favour of foreign investor. Labour laws were modified to make the business environment more appealing. Under the old policy, foreign direct investment was approved on a case-by-case basis and only up to a maximum of 40% foreign equity participation. Now 51% equity participation is allowed.

The response of the investment community was also immediate. In 1990, prior to the beginning of Prime Minister Rao's policy renovation $60,000,000 in new foreign investment was added to the Indian economy, rising to $210,000,000 in 1991. For 1992, foreign investment surpassed $1,000,000,000.

While the changes in industrial and business policy have brightened prospects for India's future, the implications for the US and the Clinton administration are important as well. The American economy has suffered in part over the last decade from its inability to compete effectively with Asian business power such as Japan, Taiwan and South Korea. Particularly under President George Bush, China came to hold a central role in America's Asian and global policy. But for Clinton, India presented an opportunity to balance that out[32].

References

1. The Hindustan Times, New Delhi, August 4, 1993.
2. Rethinking US – Indian Commercial Relations, Economic News from the US, March-April 1994.
3. Iqbal, B.A. and Khan A.O, TNCs: India in the World Perspective; India Quarterly, Vol.1, No.3, July-September 1994, pp.95-102.
4. Badar Alam Iqbal, "Are Indo-US Economic Relations Really Improving", India Quarterly, Vol.LI, No.1, Jan-March 1995.
5. Girish Chandra, "Indo-US economic ties, National Herald, 2nd April, 2000.
6. Surendra K. Kaushik, "India's Evolving Economic Model", American Journal of Economics and Sociology, Vol.56, No.1, January 1997.
7. Quoted from Span, May 1994.
8. *Ibid.*
9. *Ibid.*
10. Remarks by Frank g. Wisner at the Confederation of Indian

Industry, New Delhi, August 8, 1994.

11. US and India: Forging a New Balance, Published by Indo-US Joint Business Council, New Delhi.
12. Speech by Robin Raphel, Assistant Secretary of State at American Centre, New Delhi, March 25, 1994.
13. Speech by Ronald H. Brown, US Commerce Secretary at Bangalore, January 18, 1995.
14. Raja Mohan, "US sees India an Emerging Market", The Hindu, January 26, 1995.
15. *Ibid.*
16. Selig S. Harrison and Geoffrey Kemp, "India and America after the Cold War", Washington D.C., 1993.
17. Ludwina Joseph, "A Mission to the Indian Market Place", Business World, November 2-15, 1994.
18. Carla Anderson Hills, "India: Land of Opportunities", Seminar, 422, October 1994.
19. S.L. Rao and I. Natarajan, "Indian Market Demographics, The Consumer Classes", New Delhi: National Council of Applied Economic Research, 1996, pp.13, 196, 216-217.
20. US Embassy, Office of the Economic Counselor, New Delhi, SIA Newsletter, December 1995, p.9.
21. US Embassy, Office of the Economic Counselor, New Delhi, "1995 Survey of US Investment in India", December 1995.
22. Government of India, Ministry of Finance, Economic Survey, 1995-96, pp.147-151.
23. Telecom Policy, cited in India News, June 15, 1994.
24. Government of India, Ministry of Finance, Economic Survey, 1995-96, p.15.
25. Francine R. Frankel, "Indo-US Relations: The Future is Now", The Washington Quarterly, Autumn 1996, Vol.19, pp.129-135.
26. USIS Official Text, April 11, 1995.
27. USIS Official Text, November 14, 1994.
28. Foreign Direct Investment in India, P.K. Bhargava, Mainstream, May 20, 2000.
29. India-US Relations in a Changing World, M.J. Vinod, Strategic Analysis, Vol.XX, No.3, July 1997, pp.441-442.

30. 2000 National Trade Estimate Report on Foreign Trade Barriers, pp.159-160.
31. Vinay Kumar Malhotra, "Indo-US Relations in the Nineties", Anmol Publications Pvt. Ltd., 1995, pp.121-122.
32. Liewellyn D. Howell, "India: Rising Asian Economic Superpower", USA Today, Vol.121, ISS.2574, March 1993, p.37.

6

Kashmir and Pakistan as A Factor in the US-India Relations

The Kashmir issue has been a real bone of contention between India and Pakistan and perpetually bedeviled the relations between them. In 1846, the State of Jammu and Kashmir came into existence as a separate entity. Before that, it was in the possession of Maharaja Ranjit Singh who conquered it in 1819. Since the 1819 Sikh conquest, it formed a part of the Sikh empire till 1846, when it was ceded to the British. During the British rule, the Jammu and Kashmir was a semi-independent Princely State ruled by Maharaja Hari Singh. The relations of the Princely States with the British Crown were maintained and regulated on the basis of treaties, which made the Crown the paramount power.

The Indian Independence Act of 1947 created two independent sovereign states – India and Pakistan. This Act also made all the Princely States fully independent and free to accede either to India or Pakistan or to remain independent.

Kashmir did not accede either to India or Pakistan before August 14, 1947. The Maharaja of Kashmir signed a standstill agreement with Pakistan on August 15, 1947. Negotiations went on for the same with India. The Standstill Agreement with Pakistan was confined to the topics of communication and trade and did not include the subjects of foreign affairs and defence.

Pakistan was not satisfied with this standstill Agreement. In order to bring about the accession of Kashmir, Pakistan cut-off essential supplies to Kashmir and incited the tribal people, to invade Kashmir. The Maharaja sought India's help to defend his State from the attack of the tribesmen crossing the North-West Frontier Province of Pakistan. The Government of India replied that unless Kashmir acceded to India, the Indian Government could not give any help to Kashmir. So the Maharaja of Kashmir on October 26, 1947 sent a letter to the Governor-General, requesting him to accept the accession of Kashmir to India.

Accepting the accession of Kashmir, the Governor-General replied that, "as soon as law and order have been restored in Kashmir and its soil cleared of the invaders, the question of the State's accession should be settled by a reference to the people. But the letter did not say anything about a plebiscite. India sent her troops to Kashmir only after the Instrument of Accession was concluded on October 26, 1947.

The tribal people had used Pakistan territory as a base for their operation against India. Pakistan not only refused to accept India's demand that Pakistan Government should not let these raiders pass through her territory, but showed sympathy with the operations. Later, to India's dismay, it was found that Pakistani regulars were also engaged in hostilities along with tribal raiders. In these circumstances, Prime Minister Nehru accepted the suggestion made by the Governor-General,

Lord Mountbatten, to use the good offices of the UN. The Government of India under Article 35 of the Charter referred the matter to the UN on December 31, 1947.

This issue was taken up by the Security Council on January 6 1948. The Security Council passed a resolution on January 17, 1948, which called upon both India and Pakistan to take immediate measures to improve the situation and to refrain from those measures which would aggravate the situation. To settle the dispute, a United Nations Commission for India and Pakistan (UNCIP) was constituted. The Commission visited the Indian subcontinent. After the arrival of the Commission in the Indian subcontinent, Pakistan admitted the presence of its regular troops in Kashmir. Cease-fire became effective from the midnight of January 1, 1949.

The Commission adopted a resolution on 13 August 1948 and another on 5 January 1949 dealing with cease-fire and truce agreement and plebiscite in order to settle the dispute. But the Commission could not secure the agreement of the parties. In March 1949, Admiral Chester Nimitz was appointed as plebiscite administrator by the Secretary-General after consultation with India.

The Commission in its report submitted on December 9, 1949 recommended its own replacement by a UN representative with broad powers. The President of the Security Council, General McNaughten's effort to bring about a settlement failed. Therefore, he submitted a report to the Security Council on February 7, 1950 recommending the appointment of a single mediator. In April 1950, Sir Owen Dixon was appointed as UN representative by the Security Council. Sir Owen Dixon in his report to the Council suggested the partitioning of Kashmir between India and Pakistan and also recommended that the settlement of the issue be left to parties themselves. On the request of Sir Owen Dixon, he was relieved of his post. On April 30, 1951, the

Security Council appointed Dr. Frank P. Graham as the UN representative. In his final report submitted to the Security Council on March 27, 1953, he suggested the leaders of India and Pakistan to solve the impasse.

In February 1954, the constituent Assembly unanimously ratified the accession of Jammu and Kashmir to India. It also adopted a constitution in November 1956, which made Jammu and Kashmir a constituent part of the Indian Union. On January 26, 1957, the constitution of Kashmir formally came into existence. The resolution which the Security Council passed two days before January 26, called for a status quo in Kashmir. On February 20, 1957, the USSR vetoed a resolution sponsored by four powers in the Security Council to send the UN forces to Kashmir to solve the problem. Immediately after the failure to push through the above resolution in the Security Council, the US moved another resolution proposing Gunnar Jarring of Sweden, President of the UN to go to the subcontinent with a view to finding out the possibilities of settling the dispute. Gunnar Jarring in his report submitted on April 30, 1957 admitted his failure to make any concrete proposals.

In spite of the objection of India, the Security Council passed a resolution on December 2, 1957, authorizing Dr. Graham, the UN representative, to proceed to the subcontinent and to make recommendations to the parties concerned and take suitable action to implement the UNCIP resolutions and thus, bring about a peaceful settlement of the issue. Dr. Graham in his report submitted on March 28 1958, made it clear that again he had failed to achieve any significant progress.

In February 1962, Pakistan again revived the Kashmir issue in the Security Council by protesting against certain speeches made by Indians, calling for the liberation of Azad Kashmir. Zafrulla Khan, Pakistan delegate in the UN also announced the failure of direct negotiation between India and Pakistan since Dr. Graham's last report. In Kashmir a crisis occurred which lasted from December 1963 to January 1964 when a sacred Islamic relic, a hair of the prophet Mohommed disappeared from the Hazratbal Shrine near Srinagar. This resulted in civil disturbances in the Kashmir valley. In early 1964, following the above crisis, Pakistan raised the Kashmir issue again in the Security Council. But this time, the Council did not even proceed to draft a resolution and adjourned the debate sine die in the hope that a new climate, of which signs were then found, should produce more fruitful negotiations between India and Pakistan. The debate was still adjourned when war broke out between India and Pakistan over Kashmir in the summer of 1965[1].

So, this is the background to understand the Kashmir problem. The Congress Party maintained that the US was not impartial and it explicitly supported Pakistan in the Kashmir issue. In the circumstances it felt that there was hardly any hope of justice in the case of Kashmir in this Anglo-American dominated Security Council.

Jawaharlal Nehru, while speaking in Rajya Sabha in 1957, hinted that the US was responsible for Pakistan's refusal to vacate the occupied area. He said: "They talk about plebiscite. Again and again we have pointed out that in terms of the Resolutions passed by the United Nations Commission in the Security Council, the first thing to be done was for Pakistan to get out, that Pakistan was there by virtue of invasion, of aggression, and it has been practically admitted, and until it goes out nothing else is going to be done. Instead of going out it has entrenched itself ..."[2].

Nehru was astonished to see England and America keeping "so far out from facts, from truth and from even a fair appraisal of the situation.

In 1962, referring to plebiscite and the US accusation against India that she had refused to have plebiscite, Nehru said: "Now we are reminded of the resolutions passed in 1948 and 1949 by the United Nations Security Council and by the Commissions (UNCIP) they sent, which we accepted, and the very first thing in that resolution was that Pakistan should vacate. Then other question arose. Now it does not strike the distinguished representative of the United States, the distinguished representative of the United Kingdom to lay stress on the fact that Pakistan has not vacated and has not carried out the Security Council resolution for these fourteen years and they always go on saying that India had refused to have a plebiscite. We agreed to a plebiscite and I have no doubt we would have had the plebiscite then and there if Pakistan had withdrawn its forces"[3].

In 1964, Krishna Menon said that India's sovereignty over Kashmir was not to be questioned. In a denouncing tone, he asked the US:

Would the US apply self-determination to Louisiana and let it go back? Or, would they risk applying the idea of self-determination for the return of Alaska which was purchased from the Czar of Russia for 10 million pounds? There can be no self-determination in this way.

Later on, many Congress Party members maintained that "legally, constitutionally, through Constituent Assembly and through elections this matter has been settled and there was no necessity for plebiscite and requested the US which was one of the biggest democracies to take this fact into consideration. In 1957 speaking on the foreign affairs debate, Prime Minister Nehru expressed:

Originally the plebiscite offer was made to the people of Kashmir by us, if I may say so, I do not call them a plebiscite. I am not trying to juggle with words, but in the course of the last few years, we have had two general elections in Jammu and Kashmir State, except that part which is under the illegal and unlawful occupation of Pakistan, I do not call them plebiscite. But anyhow, the people of those territories have been given a chance to elect their representatives[4].

So, the American posture on Kashmir is a very complex phenomenon. When it was first brought to the Security Council, America largely followed the British line which was coloured with sympathy for Pakistan, mainly because the logical implementation of the Mountbatten formula about accession of the Princely States should have brought Hyderabad to the Indian Union and Jammu and Kashmir to Pakistan.

But later American position on the Kashmir issue was largely determined by her Cold War strategy. The main concern of America at that time was containment of Communism and as Pakistan was on the front line of the "ring of deterrence" it involved American security. In its zeal to combat Communism, the Eisenhower Administration, without closely studying the sequence of events that had made the holding of plebiscite difficult for India, aggravated the difficulty by signing a military alliance with Pakistan much to the Chegrin of India. From then on Kashmir became involved in American Cold War policies in South Asia and the Northern Tier of the Middle East. American support for Pakistan brought forth the counterbalancing Soviet support for India. Till the Cold War years, this situation prevailed. An equitable solution of the Kashmir problem, the US thought, could be found on the basis of the principle of self-determination. With this view in mind it endorsed the United Nations resolution on January 5, 1949. Speaking on this occasion the US representative to the UN, Cross said:

In our view it is eminently fair and sound and in

fulfillment of our duty as a member of this Council dedicated to peaceful settlements, to recommend to the parties that they accept a principle which strengthens the concept and value of the cease-fire line and avoids the risk of an extension of military activity[5].

Not only should the plebiscite be free and impartial, according to US, but it was equally important that the interests of India and Pakistan be protected by a plebiscite held under UN auspices, so that the results could not be influenced by coercion or intimidation.

Meanwhile, the Kashmir Government decided to convene the Constituent Assembly to draft a constitution for the State as part of the Indian Union. By February 1954, the Constituent Assembly ratified Kashmir's irrevocable accession to India. From May to December 1963 the process of integration of Kashmir with the Indian Union went on unchecked. And on January 30, 1964 India categorically told the Security Council that, under no circumstances can we agree to the holding of a plebiscite in Kashmir.

The United States was also willing to offer its good offices to help settle the dispute. As Barco, US representative to the UN, said in the Security Council that the US considers the Kashmir issue on the merits of the case and that the US "seeks to assist both India and Pakistan - and I say this with great sincerity in finding a just and equitable solution of the Kashmir problem"[6]. But India has rejected third party negotiation to resolve the Kashmir problem, since then.

So ever since the Kashmir problem was tabled in the UN, the US has been involved in it. However, the US view of this problem can only be comprehended from the perspective of Cold War and the US attempt at containing international Communism. The US main concern and interest by 1947-48 was to prevent the problem from escalating into a general war between the two countries, as this would adversely affect US policies and strategies in Asia generally and might push either or both of the belligerents into the Communist camp. Coincidentally, the Kashmir problem emerged at the peak of Communist expansionism. The US-Pakistan pact took place in 1954[7]. That's why India from the very beginning charged the US with siding with Pakistan.

When the Kashmir problem was erupted, the USA strongly advocated for a plebiscite in Jammu and Kashmir. It sounds O.K. from the US point of view, but this view has few takers in India. Had there been a plebiscite under the UN supervision, it is almost certain that the Hindu-majority Jammu area would have acceded to India and the Muslim region of Kashmir to Pakistan. Had it been happened, the Kashmir problem would have been solved for all time to come. If this would have happened, the people of India would not have forgiven Nehru for given Kashmir to Pakistan. In the naming of Pakistan also P- stands for Punjab, A for Afghan Suba, Ki for Kashmir, S for Sind, tan for Beluchistan or North West Frontier Province.

Once the Kashmir question was taken to the United Nations by Nehru on the advice of Lord Louis Mountbatten, Washington took active interest in the issue. Indian leaders almost always perceived the US policies and approaches towards resolving the Kashmir issue as anti-Indian in character and the US administrations felt the Indian position unhelpful in the resolution of the problem. As a result, Kashmir issue continued to vitiate the political atmosphere preventing India and the US from moving politically closer towards each other. As the UN Security Council Resolution of April 1948, primarily moved by the US and the UK, failed to criticise Islamabad for the aggression and treated the aggressor and the victim of aggression equally, Indian leaders were enraged, Nehru charged that Washington and London played a "dirty role" in the UN on the Kashmir issue[8].

As the US continued to seek a role in the Kashmir issue, it occasionally bounced back to widen the political chasm between New Delhi and Washington. In 1953, as Sheikh Mohammad Abudullah began to change his position on the status of Kashmir and even toyed with the idea of an independent Kashmir, his meeting with the former US Democratic Presidential candidate sparked off a severe political row between India and the US. It was alleged that Abdulalh was conspiring with the Americans for the US support for an independent Kashmir in exchange for military base facilities in the state. When India and Pakistan fought a war over Kashmir in 1965 in the wake of Pakistan launching operation Gibralter the US attitude was clearly pro-Pakistan. Although Washington apparently sought to adopt an even-handed approach by imposing an arms embargo against both India and Pakistan, for the second time it equated the aggressor with the victim of aggression. After all, the US knew that it was Pakistan which initiated the aggression a repeat of 1947-48 and India had to respond. Now, in fact, it has become known that Washington was aware of the Pakistani design even before the war was initiated[9].

"Pakistan attacked India in September 1965", write Harold Gould and Sumit Ganguli, "Precipitating the second Kashmir war. The United States, though quietly acknowledging that Pakistan had initiated the war, imposed an arms embargo on both countries ... From the Indian standpoint, nothing could be less fair. As far as New Delhi was concerned, Pakistan had initiated the conflict, used American arms, and now -- to add insult to proverbial injury - the United States had equated the nations through the imposition of arms embargo". According to another American scholar, Robert J. McMahon, "The war had been precipitated by Ayub's decision in early August (1965) to send Pakistani volunteers into Kashmir. A gradual escalation had ensured, culminating on September 6 with an Indian invasion on Pakistan"[10]. Did the US gain anything by siding with the aggressor? McMahon argues that the end result was that Soviet diplomacy rather than American one that "ultimately facilitated a diplomatic settlement" in the subcontinent. The US did not gain politically or strategically in Pakistan and lost all good will in India generated by its response during the 1962 Sino-Indian war.

Six years later, the US administration would once again side with Pakistan which unleashed a large scale massacre of innocent people in East Pakistan and the end result was the division of Pakistan, and the Simla Agreement that subsequently became the basis for any future solution of the Kashmir problem. The Nixon administration's tilt towards Pakistan during the war for the liberation of Bangladesh in 1971 is now a well-known fact of history. It was ironical that President Nixon, who took a momentous step in charting out a new policy towards China on geopolitical and geostrategic calculations in late 1960s and early 1970s, perceived the developments in Indian subcontinent on the basis of his personal whims and fancies. According to Christopher Van Hollen, former Assistant Secretary of State for NEA: "Nixon's reaction to South Asia was influenced by his long-standing dislike for India and the Indians, and his warm feelings for Pakistan". Despite disclaims, Richard Nixon's contrasting feelings towards the Indian and Pakistani leaders undoubtedly coloured his judgments in 1971[11]... But the war was a thumping victory for India. It brought about a substantial alternation in the geopolitics of the subcontinent. As Simla Accord was signed in 1972 and it was stipulated that issues between India and Pakistan, including Kashmir, would be resolved bilaterally by the two countries without any third party mediation, Washington significantly came around to accept this position[12].

The Kashmir issue became relatively calm thereafter, until December 1989 when terrorism struck the state. As Pakistan was involved in Afghanistan crisis, Kashmir remained calm. So long as Pakistan acted as proxy of the United States in fighting against the Soviet military presence in Afghanistan, Kashmir could remain calm and free from external interference. By the time the Cold War was coming to an end and dialogues between Washington and Moscow had showed signs of conclusion of the Soviet military operation in Afghanistan and Pakistan had begun to realise that its strategic importance to the US might go down. At the same time, the victory of the Mujaheedin forces in Afghanistan with Pakistani help had inculcated a certain confidence in Pakistan that it could try its hand in Kashmir as well. Around this time, secessionist tendencies had begun to appear in Kashmir.

In 1988 restoration of democracy took place and Benazir Bhutto became the Prime Minister of Pakistan. Although Prime Minister Bhutto sought to improve ties with India, her domestic opponents prevented her from going far in this initiative. Some of the agreements signed between New Delhi and Islamabad in the areas of travel, trade, cultural exchange, double taxation, drug trafficking and border smuggling could have given ways for positive improvement in ties in other areas. But Benazir's opponents had other desires in mind, especially taking advantage of the law and order problem in Kashmir. Their aim was to replay Afghanistan in Kashmir by supporting efforts at formation and training of anti-Indian and pro-Pakistani groups in Kashmir. Incidentally, Kashmir got affected by trans-border terrorism and insurgency only after six months of the Tiamanman Square episode in China, about three months after the former Soviet Union pulled back its last batch of military troops from Afghanistan. Benazir soon retreated from her initiative to reshape Pakistan's relations with India. According to strategic survey, 1990-91, "At the turn of the year, she abandoned the Afghan policy to General Beg and his Inter-Services Intelligence Agency (ISI), which had long been managing the mujaheedin on the ground. She yielded to army demands for both a forward thrust in Pakistan's nuclear weapons programme and a 50 per cent increase in the defence budget, in response to threats and opportunities arising from unrest in the Indian part of Kashmir. Bhutto took up the cause of the Kashmiri "freedom fighters" in an attempt to steal her political opponent's thunder with her own fiery nationalistic rhetoric. She left the job of assessing Pakistan's support for the insurgents to the army: this involved providing weapons, training and a sanctuary in Pakistan's part of divided Kashmir ... Kashmir was not a matter of domestic dispute in Pakistan. Generals and politicians shared the objective of putting maximum pressure on India, short of actually provoking a war which Pakistan was certain to lose"[13].

The Kashmir militancy grew at a time when India was facing an economic crisis and political uncertainties of coalition politics after the defeat of the Congress Party in the general election. Communalism in India also threatened to increase instability in the society. The crisis over the Babri Masjid was also gaining momentum. How did Washington view the Kashmir problem at this time? At that time, Washington failed to see the Pakistani involvement in a game of destabilization and the rising menace of cross-border support to terrorism in Kashmir. Instead, it sought to view Kashmir issue in the light of a human rights issue and the nuclear development in the subcontinent. Another round of Indo-US political row thus started.

In May 1990, as Indo-Pak relations deteriorated over the growing incidence of Islamabad-backed militancy in Kashmir, President George Bush sent his

Deputy National Security Advisor, Robert Gates and Assistant Secretary of State, John Kelly to the subcontinent. It was reported in American Press that Gates impressed upon New Delhi and Islamabad that yet another round of war over Kashmir could lead to a nuclear confrontation and that his diplomatic efforts succeeded in averting a possible nuclear confrontation in South Asia[14]. Since then it has become fashionable in the American academic as well as policy-making circles to speak of a nuclear danger in the Indian subcontinent.

In the Press, a new kind of political game was played by linking up the Kashmir and the nuclear issues. The American scholars as well as officials have been seeking to create an impression that one of the best ways to resolve the nuclear issue between India and Pakistan is through the resolution of the Kashmir problem between the two countries. All kinds of rumours were spread that the next nuclear holocaust may occur in the Indian subcontinent where India and Pakistan may resort to a war over the Kashmir issue. In early 1995, the US Secretary of Defence William Perry in his speech at Washington's Foreign Policy Association said: "I would start off by observing that India and Pakistan have long-standing ethnic, religious and territorial differences dating back to their partition in 1947. It is because of these differences, they have fought three wars since partition. Each of them has the capability to build nuclear weapons. Because of this nuclear capability, a fourth Indian-Pakistan war would not just be a tragedy, it could be a catastrophe – so we care a lot about what happens there"[15]. In March 1996, in his annual report to the Congress on the global situation and the role of the US military, Perry wrote: The ongoing dialogue can help all three countries (US, India and Pakistan) to focus on areas of common interest, such as international peace keeping, nuclear proliferation and the long-simmering conflict over Kashmir[16]. The annual report of the US Arms Control and Disarmament agency for the year 1996 mentioned that "while the likelihood of a fourth war between India and Pakistan is small, the possibility of a war in the region going nuclear are perhaps higher than anywhere else in the world. We continue to believe that both nations could assemble nuclear weapons within a short time, and that both have tested missiles and acquired aircraft capable of delivering such weapons. In addition, the past year has witnessed a significant decline in Indo-Pakistani relations ... Regional stability, and therefore proliferation continue to be driven by Indo-Pakistani tensions, particularly over Kashmir"[17].

It is well known to all those who are familiar with the nuclear issues that neither India's nor Pakistan's nuclear programmes were developed with the Kashmir issue in mind. The origin, evolution, target and the nature of the Indian and the Pakistani nuclear programemem are in no way connected with the Kashmir issue. Of course, it serves the Pakistani purpose to link up the Kashmir issue with the nuclear issue, as it seeks to justify its nuclear programme on the basis of India's larger and more sophisticated nuclear capability. It has also, at the same time, taken advantage of the American concerns over the human rights issue around the world by pursuing a diplomatic offensive against the Indian Government's handling of the militancy problem in the Kashmir valley by portraying it as violation of human rights.

While India managed to produce several credible evidences of Pakistani involvement in Kashmir militancy, it failed to prompt the Bush administration to declare Pakistan as a state sponsoring international terrorism. There is little doubt that Jammu and Kashmir Liberation Front (JKLF) was formed in 1989 with the assistance and encouragement of Islamabad. The JKLF has always aimed at achieving independence for Kashmir which include the Pakistan occupied Kashmir (POK) as well. Islamabad thus was looking for an opportunity to encourage groups other than JKLF which would not aim at independence and which would take advice from the Pakistani capital. In a couple of years, Pakistan succeeded in distancing itself from JKLF and in training and equipping pro-Pakistani groups, particularly Hizb-ul-Mujaheedin.

When the United States was undergoing the process of Presidential election in 1992, Indo-Pakistan relations had deteriorated further, as reflected in Islamabad's initial permission to JKLF leader Amanullah Khan to march across the LOC in Kashmir, a sympathetic strike in Pakistan solidarity with the "Islamic brothers" in Kashmir, abduction and torture of an Indian diplomat in Islamabad and clashes in the Siachen glacier. When Bill Clinton won the Presidential election, there were hopes in certain quarters in India that Indo-US relations could take a positive turn. Clinton's emphasis on restoring American economic competitiveness raised hopes that Washington under his leadership would view positively the economic reforms under taken in India since 1991 and that there would be no more US interference in the sub-continental affairs.

Such hopes were, nonetheless, misplaced. President Clinton hinted that his approach to the Kashmir issue may alter a little by referring to the ethnic conflicts "from Caucasus to Kashmir" in a speech before the UN General Assembly in September 1993. Islamabad became very happy over Clinton's remark, whereas there were resentments in India. The following month, Robin Raphel, Assistant Secretary of State for South Asian Affairs, reportedly said in an off-the-record briefing in Washington that the United States did not accept the Instrument of Accession of Kashmir which led to the merger of Kashmir with India. Her statement challenging the legal validity of the Instrument of Accession, in particular, created an uproar in the Indian Parliament as well as among the Indian public. Soon after that Raphel, while speaking at the Asia Society in Washington, linked up the Kashmir issue with Afghanistan.

Such statements not only threatened to create a political divide between New Delhi and Washington but also encouraged the Kashmir terrorists and their supporters from across the border. There was considerable escalation in terrorist activities in Kashmir around this time and one of the worst attempt by the terrorist was to steal a secret religions relic – a single strand of Prophet Mohammad's hair – from the Hazart-Bal Shrine in Kashmir and put the blame on the Indian Security Forces. While the Government of India took timely steps with the help of the Security Forces and foiled the attempt by the terrorists, Islamabad sought to make political capital out of it and even raised the issue at the meeting of the Commonwealth Heads of States.

In late 1993, the political divide between India and the United States widened further, as President Bill Clinton shared Pakistan's concern over the "human rights violation" in Kashmir at the time of accepting the credentials of the new Pakistan Ambassador to the US and had little sympathy for the innocent people who were killed by the terrorists. However, in response to considerable resentment in India, the US position on Kashmir was soon clarified and the US support to the Simla Agreement was reiterated. Nonetheless, a new element was inserted into the US stand, which was that in the resolution of the Kashmir issue, the view of the Kashmiri people should be taken into account. India had taken into account the views of the Kashmiri people, not at the behest of the United States but by releasing some of the extremist elements from jail who wanted to join the political mainstream and abjure the path of violence. Since 1994, the Government of India has taken several measures to facilitate the holding of elections in Kashmir, while dealing sternly with the terrorists. Pakistan nonetheless sought to destabilize Kashmir through consistent support and assistance to the Kashmiri militants and simultaneously trying to tarnish India's image internationally by making false and exaggerated propaganda about the human right violations in Kashmir.

With the improvement in Indo-US relations, particularly since the then Prime Minister Narasimha Rao's trip to the US in 1994, the State Department has refrained from making rhetorical statements on Kashmir issue. Pakistan, however, occasionally succeeded in seeking political issue of human right in Kashmir during various congressional debates. At no point Washington conceded the Government of India's views of the Pakistani hand in Kashmiri militancy to an extent that would have been politically acceptable to India. Washington's overall stand appeared to have been tilted in favour of Pakistan. New Delhi's endeavour to drive home the point that the Kashmir issue had to be seen in the backdrop of rising Islamic extremism, fundamentalism failed to receive adequate political support from the US. In the Post-Cold War era, Islamic fundamentalism has been identified as the growing source of international tension and instability.

More worrisome is the fact that these fundamentalist forces are not isolated cases in diverse societies but are increasingly developing cross-border connections. The fact remains that even without capturing political power, the fundamentalist forces can create tremendous trouble internationally. What is happening in Kashmir may happen elsewhere. Washington has to redesign its stand on the Kashmir issue in the light of this development rather than harp on the old-fashioned theories. Washington should not compartmentalize terrorism as "domestic" and "international". The US State Department's annual report on terrorism, patterns of Global Terrorism 1996, considered terrorism in India, Algeria, Sri Lanka and Pakistan as domestic terrorism. It also says that "Domestic terrorism is probably a more wide spread phenomenon than international terrorism"[18].

It would perhaps be more appropriate if Washington keeps its hands off Kashmir to avoid serious political confrontation with India. There are, unfortunately, no indications that Washington would mind its own business and allow the Kashmir problem to be resolved by the regional countries. The USA reiterates its support to the bilateral concept envisaged in the Simla Agreement. But sometimes-unthoughtful statements of some US officials make confusion which is not helpful in resolving the Kashmir issue. Recently George Pickart, a senior advisor to the South Asian Bureau of the State Department, reportedly said that "the USA believes that Jammu and Kashmir is a disputed territory and is an issue to be resolved between India and Pakistan taking the desires of the Kashmir people into account"[19]. President Bill Clinton, on the other hand, reportedly had stated in the first week of August this year that the US presence should be heavily felt in South Asia and that it was a source of continuing concern to him that "the people of Pakistan and the people of India have not been able to work though their differences". He then went on to say that the US would be a better friend of India and Pakistan in next fifty years and that it would be a "more constructive supporter of resolving these difficulties in the near terms"[20].

The entire spectrum of political and public opinion in India took serious objection to the American statements. Prime Minister I.K. Gujral forcefully remarked that the Indian sovereignty over Kashmir was not negotiable[21]. Several times in the past all kinds of statements have been made in the US and clarifications have been issued in the face of protest in India. This time was no exception. On President Clinton's remark, stressing the need for strong US presence in South Asia, the new State Department Spokesman James Rubin said: "perhaps, he was talking about the fact that Secretary of State Madeleine Albright has said that she hoped to go to the region this year" and that the President was not referring to a physical US presence in the region but was hinting at the importance of the region to the US"[22]. The State Department also issued a statement on Pickart's remark saying that any impression created by his speech of "enunciating a new policy" was wrong[23].

The issue was, however, not enunciation of a new policy. It was a question of the timing of such statements. At a time, when India and Pakistan have been taking positive steps on their own to resolve several bilateral issues, including Kashmir, American activism and unnecessary statements do not appear to be helpful measures. The United States wants to be involved in almost all the disputes around the world and in some form or the other. As far as South Asia is concerned America is suspect in the Indian eye for several valid reasons. First, the US has a long history of close political and strategic ties with Pakistan and seeks to contain its relations with that country. One of the main factors that induced Nehru to alter his earlier stand on plebiscite in Kashmir was the US arming of Pakistan. Till this date, the US arming of Pakistan is a serious issue in the Indian assessment of American role in South Asia. Secondly, the US position on Kashmir throughout history has been tilted in favour of Pakistan. Thirdly, in Indian perception the sub-continental issues can best be sorted out without the external interference. And in this connection, the more Islamabad approaches Washington to play a direct role in Kashmir affairs, more resentment and suspicion are created in India. There is actually no viable alternative to the Simla Agreement as a means of resolving the Kashmir issue. American activism is the problem rather than a solution to the Kashmir question.

The Principal Deputy Assistant Secretary of State for South Asian Affairs, John R. Malott has put forth the America's point of view on India, Pakistan and Kashmir. The Soviet collapse has altered significantly America's relations with the key players in the region, Pakistan and India. The failure of socialism has prompted governments to initiate market-based economic reforms and liberalize foreign investment.

According to John Malott, America's primary interest in South Asia is to reduce tensions and prevent war between India and Pakistan, as it could lead to the employment of nuclear weapons. To address this problem, he says, we will pursue a comprehensive, incremental and long-term approach that seeks: (1) to cap, then reduce over time, and finally eliminate weapons of mass destruction and their means of delivery from the region, (2) to deal with the underlying security concerns that drive the weapons programmes in each country and to help create a climate in which each country's sense of security is enhanced through tension reduction, confidence-building measures and a process of arms control, (3) to encourage direct high level Indo-Pakistani discussion on regional security and nonproliferation, to supplement that with our own bilateral discussions with both countries, to encourage other countries to do likewise, and to work towards broader regional discussions and agreements.

He made a reference to the Kashmir problem. It is clear that the Kashmir dispute is a major source of Indo-Pakistan tensions, he said. We are increasingly concerned by what is happening in Kashmir today. A military stand off continues along the line of control.

Civilians in the Kashmir valley continue to suffer at the hands of both the militants and the Indian security forces. The cycle of violence is achieving a momentum of its own, making a political solution even more difficult. To break that cycle, both India and Pakistan must act. He also mentioned that, "there have been credible reports that Pakistan is providing official support to some of the militants". We have raised this matter continuously at the highest levels of the government of Pakistan and are keeping the situation under active review. For its part, India must take steps to curb the abuses of its security forces, making them strictly accountable for their actions. We also urge genuine access to Kashmir for international human rights groups to help shine greater light on the human rights abuses from all sides. Actually India strongly opposes human rights violation in Kashmir as alleged by the US. It also condemns abuses of the security forces. These are the pro-Pakistan stands taken by the US in relation to Kashmir and Pakistan, in which India does not agree.

Mr. Malott stated, "We believe that India should pursue a meaningful political dialogue with the Kashmiris. Such a dialogue should not be held hostile to the actions of the militants, lest it should give them the upper hand". India does not agree with the American suggestion. Kashmir is an internal, integral part of India. India does not like or need any third party mediation in the Kashmir affairs.

Again he had stated, "As for the question of Kashmir's status, the United States will advocate no particular solution. Our concern is with process. There are three basic principles that govern our position:

1. We consider all the Kashmir to be a disputed territory, on both sides of the line of control.
2. This is an issue to be settled peacefully by India and Pakistan, taking the views of the Kashmiris, both Muslim and non-Muslim into account.

3. The United States is prepared to be helpful in this process, if that is desired by both sides"[24].

India's view is quite different from American perception. India does not consider Kashmir as a disputed territory. There are 28 States in India and Kashmir is one among them. India's former Prime Minister Rajiv Gandhi had once stated "Kashmir is ours".

Pakistan has fought four wars with India - 1947-48, 1965, 1971 and 1999 (Kargil) and failed in all of them. Suddenly in the last week of May 1999, the Pakistani army with the help of Afghan Mujahiddens captured the Kargil, the Drass and the Battalic sector of the Jammu and Kashmir. The Indian army took up offensive action called operation Vijaya against the intruders from 26th May 1999. The world community at large condemned the action of Pakistan. The United States categorically termed Pakistan as intruder in the LOC and asked Pakistan to vacate the Indian area to diffuse tension. The Group of 8, the European Community, Russia, Germany and Japan also condemned the action of Pakistan in escalating tension between two friendly countries.

The talk of Pakistan Prime Minister Nawaz Sharif in this issue was very provocative. He said that many more Kargil-like situation will erupt if Kashmir issue is not resolved. According to him Kargil issue is just a small portion of the bigger issue of Kashmir.

When the USA got indication that Pakistan may not hesitate to use nuclear weapon against India, the US President Bill Clinton sent US Deputy Assistant Secretary of State, Gibson Lanther and General Anthony Jimmy to persuade Pakistan to come out of the occupied territory. A General can convince them better. That's why General Jimmy was sent by the US.

When Indian Prime Minister was asked about his bus trip to Lahore in February last, he commented that, it is unfortunate that the Indo-Pak friendship bus was grounded in Kargil. Then Bajpayee said that there can be no talk with Pakistan on any issue unless Pakistan vacates the occupied territory. The US President also talked over phone with Prime Minister Nawaz Sharif for 15 minutes and persuaded him to call back Pakistani troops from the Indian side of the LOC. There are newspaper reports that Indian Prime Minister A.B. Bajpayee had written a letter to US President Bill Clinton indicating that India would enter Pakistan if Pakistan did not vacate the territory of Indian side of line of control. He also mentioned that there was tremendous pressure in India after seeing the mutilated bodies of Indian soldiers, sent by Pakistan.

On 30.6.1999, Wednesday, a newspaper report came on the Asian Age: "The United States categorically denied that she will not mediate in the Indo-Pak conflict. US also denied that the intention to send Lampher and General Jimmy was not to mediate in the Indo-Pak affairs. US wants that India and Pakistan should resolve the present crisis bilaterally through dialogue".

India wants good, friendly harmonious relation with Pakistan, not only Pakistan but with all neighbours. That is the reason why Lahore declaration occurred followed by the bus trip from Amritsar to Lahore. But if the neighbouring country takes away one's land, occupies one's territory, there is no way but to fight. India fought against Pakistan and drove them away from Kargil sector. The US Congressmen strongly denounced Pakistan saying that it should immediately vacate the occupied territory. They also suggested ways to pressurize Pakistan like blocking of loans. Russia also denounced Pakistani occupation of Kargil and said that Pakistan should come out of the occupied territory.

It becomes meaningful to examine the implications of the Kargil war on Indo-Pak relations. Kargil has to be seen in the context of the proxy war conducted by

Pakistan in the last decade. Kargil was in a sense culmination of the proxy war. The purpose of the Pakistani operation in Kargil is clear. Pakistan wanted to enlarge the conflict in Kashmir, and to bring to the focus of the international community, the danger of another Indo-Pak war, one in which nuclear weapons could be used. By fabricating this kind of danger, Pakistan hoped for international intervention which would succeed in defreezing the Kashmir issue. Pakistan's manifold goals in its offensive in Kargil can be described in the following manner: Firstly, it hoped to cut off the Srinagar-Leh road so that movement of supplies to Leh garrison and Siachen would become impossible. Secondly, it wanted to block Zojila Pass and threaten Kashmir Valley from the north, which would be a new direction to make inroads. Thirdly, it wished to have control over the Himalayan range so that it would have unopposed access for insurgents-terrorists going into the Kashmir valley and Doda district of Jammu. Fourthly, it wanted to outflank the Indian Army deployed on the LOC in northwestern Kashmir and the Siachen glacier through Shyok valley[25]. Pakistan assumed that India would not retaliate because of the threat of nuclear weapons but India fought and recovered its territory.

The roots of the Kargil episode can be traced back to Pakistan's yearning to mastermind a people's revolt in Kashmir. The people of Kashmir, despite being under duress due to terrorist activities, went in for an elected government in 1996. Pakistan realizing the hopelessness of the situation opted for military action in Kargil. Pakistan disregarded the peace initiative offered by India in Lahore. It deceived India by simultaneously planning the Kargil operations in great secrecy. The Kargil conflict was a great setback for the peace process and the confidence building measures initiated in the year preceding the Kargil intrusion. The Pakistani forces were found to be composed of Pakistani army units, mercenaries and Afghan war veterans. The Pakistani troops operating across the LOC were identified to be from the 2nd, 3rd, 4th, 5th and 6th Battalions of the Northern Light Infantry. These battalions were augmented by Afghan war veterans and Islamic militants trained by the Lashkar-e-Taiba and Harkat-ul-Mujahideen, etc.[26].

India got immense international support during the Kargil crisis. A meeting was held between Bill Clinton and Nawaz Sharif on July 4, 1999 where Sharif agreed, that concrete steps would be taken for the restoration of the Line of Control in accordance with the Simla agreement[27]. Nawaz Sharif by agreeing with President Clinton on this point, admitted not only that Kargil constituted a violation of the Line of Control, but that it was a mistake of Pakistan. The implicit suggestion was that he would withdraw his forces from Indian Kashmir, to the position, as it existed before Pakistan's aggression in Kargil sector across the LOC. In a sense, the Pakistani Government accepted the sanctity of the LOC, thereby putting a stamp of approval on it as forming a defacto boundary between India and Pakistan. According to reports, General Zinni, the Chief of US Central Command, during his visit to Islamabad in the last week of June 1999, received a firm commitment from the Pakistani leadership that they were ready to take concrete measures to de-escalate the situation. Faced with a serious economic situation, Pakistan could not afford to antagonise the US which could have withheld the 100 million dollar tranche of the IMF loan due in July. The G-8 countries condemned the infiltration and demanded withdrawal of the intruders from the Indian side of the LOC. China stated that both India and Pakistan must exercise restraint and should solve the Kargil problem peacefully through negotiations. Pakistan, of course, continued to deny that its troops were operating across the LOC, even though a meeting was held between the Indian Director General of Military Operations and Pakistan's Director of Military Operations in the second week of July 1999, to chalk out the time frame for Pakistani forces to withdraw from the Indian Territory. The restraint shown by India in not crossing the LOC, even in the face of severe provocation was widely appreciated by the international community.

All the Pakistani Government had to show for itself at the end was an ignominious retreat, without any quid pro quo on Kashmir and a total loss of credibility, not only among foreign countries but within the country itself. The editor's note in the well-known Pakistani news magazine, Newsline stated, "The Washington agreement confirmed Indian and western allegations that the Mujahideen action was backed by Pakistan. Far from internationalizing the Kashmir issue, the government's mishandling of the Kargil crisis has diplomatically isolated the country[28]. Another article stated, "That the Kargil adventure was ill conceived, if not down right foolish, was becoming clear, albeit slowly, even to the congenitally blind. That consequently Pakistan, swallowing its pride and not a few of its brave and gallant words, would sooner or later have to mount a retreat was also becoming clear, especially after Niaz Naik's secret visit to New Delhi which was a desperate bid to get India to agree to some kind of a deal which would provide a face saving way out[29]. Air Marshal (Retd.) Asghar Khan, admitted that, "in 52 years of its existence, Pakistan has fought four wars with India without a clear objective".

India felt terribly cheated by Pakistan because India had invested a lot of hope and faith in the Lahore process. That something as disastrous as an act of blatant aggression across the LOC in the Kargil sector could have been done by Pakistan so soon after the Lahore Declaration came as a fatal blow to India's hope about improving relations with Pakistan. Disappointment turned into disgust when widespread stories emanated from Pakistan suggesting that the army had specifically sought and obtained Prime Minister Nawaz Sharif's clearance with regard to intrusions in Kargil soon after Nawaz had signed the Lahore declaration[30].

Indo-Pak relation can become incomplete without reference to the Simla agreement. The United States today voices her opinion that the Indo-Pak problem must be resolved through Simla agreement. It is the Simla agreement which defines the basic parameters according to which Indo-Pakistan relations have been conducted in the past and it will hopefully be defining the parameters in the future as well. So it is not out of place to mention here as to what constitutes the Simla agreement.

As per the Simla agreement, the Line of Control, indicating the position of the two armies on the day of the cease fire i.e. December 17, 1971 was delineated by designated military commanders of India and Pakistan. The Simla agreement desired that the sanctity of the Line of Control was to be maintained by both sides and both sides agreed that, "neither side shall seek to alter it unilaterally, irrespective of mutual differences and legal interpretations. Also there was a commitment by both countries to respect each other's territorial integrity and sovereignty as well as to solve problems between the two countries by peaceful means. The two countries also agreed "that in accordance with the Charter of the United Nations they will refrain from the threat or use of force against the territorial integrity or political independence of each other". While talks on Kashmir have been held on and off and India had agreed to the concept of a "composite dialogue", the Pakistani army still preferred to violate the LOC and commit aggression against India, violating the very foundations of the Simla Agreement.

Another important aspect of the Simla Agreement to be borne in mind is that the unwritten part of the Simla understanding between the then Prime Minister Indira Gandhi and the then Pakistani President Zulfiqar Ali Bhutto was that the LOC would be converted into an international border in due course. This in a sense meant that even though such an agreement i.e. converting the LOC into an international border, had not yet been arrived at, the LOC was to have the sanctity of an international border.

In another important clause of the Simla Agreement, both India and Pakistan agreed to "settle their differences by peaceful means through bilateral negotiations or by any other peaceful means mutually agreed upon between them". Pakistan has been resorting to internalization of the Kashmir problem at NAM, OIC, ECO and UN meetings. It has been accusing Indian security forces of violating human rights in Jammu and Kashmir. Pakistan, in contravention of the Simla agreement has urged various countries to mediate between India and Pakistan.

While the Simla agreement can be regarded as having maintained peace between the two countries and in Jammu and Kashmir for a period of nearly two decades, that peace was broken by Pakistan's proxy war which was launched by "Operation Topac" in 1989.

Ever since 1947, Pakistan made several attempts to seize Kashmir from India as Kashmir accession to India remained unacceptable to Pakistan. Pakistan tried to achieve its objective in 1947 by engineering a tribal invasion of Kashmir, which resulted in the Kashmir war of 1947-48. Pakistan tried to achieve the same objective through 'Operation Gibraltar' in 1965 but failed to wrest Kashmir from India. In 1971, when decisive Indian military intervention in the civil war between the two wings of Pakistan helped in the creation of Bangladesh, Pakistan again hoped that Kashmir would be detached from India through the use of force. Pakistan failed to achieve its objective.

As Pakistan did not succeed in wresting Kashmir from India by the use of military fore during the three wars, in the latter half of 1988, Pakistan launched a low intensity operation to create alienation of the valley from the rest of India. Pakistan abetted full-scale subversion, terrorism, insurrection and insurgency in Jammu and Kashmir which is still going on and by which thousands of civilians and security forces have been killed. Between 1990 and 1998, 5,845 civilians were killed in Jammu and Kashmir while the figure of the security forces killed was 1,401. Moreover, large quantities of weapons were found in Jammu and Kashmir from 1988 to 1997. These include 18,378 AK-47s and 2,015 LMGs[31]. The Pakistanis are convinced that such a form of unconventional war would help reinforce and channelise the discontent in the valley and over a period of time lead it in the direction of secession from India.

The obvious involvement of Pakistan in the Kashmir valley, in the form of a methodically planned proxy war, has been a part of Pakistan's scheme to bleed India of its resources without having to get involved in an open conventional military confrontation. In the early years, the most active militant group was the Jammu and Kashmir Liberation Front. However, by 1989-1990, JKLF began to be sidelined by Pakistan as JKLF's favoured "third option", implying independence for the Kashmiris was inconsistent with Pakistan's definition of "self-determination" for the Kashmiris which implied a willingness to join Pakistan. At this time, the Hizb-ul-Mujahideen, which was the military wing of Jamat-e-Islami cam up as a rival to the JKLF. Over the years it became obvious that Pakistan was suffering a setback, due to the fast declining Kashmiri support in the valley to militancy, and things were fast approaching normalcy in Indian Kashmir by 1995-1996. In fact, militant activity gradually shifted to new areas such as Doda, Punch and Rajouri, as the Indian security forces came to have almost complete control of the security situation in the Kashmir valley. After 1995-96 the role and participation of foreign militants of Pakistani, Afghanistani and POK origin increased in the Kashmir valley. In recent years, the Harkatul Mujahideen militants have been involved in fighting in Kashmir. The Harkatul Mujahideen is just a new front for the Harkatula Ansar which was declared a terrorist organization by the US in 1994. The Harkatul militants operate in Afghanistan and Kashmir, and have strong links with the Jamiat-ul-Ulema-Islam (JUI), as well as the Sipahe Sahaba Pakistan (SSP). The Lakshar-e-Taiba another dominant militant group which sends its recruits to battle in Kashmir, is the militant wing of the Markaz Dawa wal Irshad, an Ahle Hadith-Wahabi organization based in Muridke near Lahore. The Hizbul Mujahideen operated in Kashmir and has strong links with the Jamat-e-Islami[32].

India has voiced her concern about Pakistan's cross border terrorism. It is because of Pakistan sponsored terrorism, so much bloodshed took place in Kashmir, so many innocent lives were lost. India demanded that Pakistan be declared a terrorist state. But nobody including the United States paid greater attention to India's terrorist problem. It is when on September 11, 2002 the World Trade Centre was demolished in America, America showed serious concern over terrorist problem not only in America but any where in the world. Till today, terrorism is continuing in Jammu and Kashmir. The militant organizations funded by Pakistan like the Lashkar-e-Taiba, Harkat-ul-Mujahideen and Hizbul Mujahideen are highly active in the Kashmir valley. In fact, the Chief of the Lashkar-e-Taiba, Mohammad Saeed, while addressing a congregation near Muridke in November 1999, declared that the Mujahideen would continue their Jehad in Kashmir till they attained victory.

The Prime Minister A.B. Bajpayee had stated at that time that no talks with Pakistan is possible unless Pakistan stops cross border terrorism.

Kashmir stands at the apex of Pakistan's foreign policy. Whenever there is an internal problem in Pakistan, Kashmir problem has been raised by the Pakistani leadership. In 2004 in Pakistan while giving an Iftihar party to a distinguished gathering, Pakistan's President General Pervez Musharaf said, "There are seven regions in Kashmir. Out of these seven regions, two are in Pakistan and five are in India. First identify the regions, then demilitarize the zones, withdraw the forces from both sides etc.". But there were few takers of Musharf's suggestion in India. In 2005, while in an official visit to India, Musharaf again made a statement that the LOC of Jammu and Kashmir between India and Pakistan should be redrawn. The Indian Prime Minister, Dr. Mahmohan Singh categorically said that there was no question of redrawing the LOC. Then again during that visit the General said that Kashmir problem couldn't be solved on the basis of religion. On the other hand, he said it should be solved on people to people basis. This was in contrast with Pakistan's earlier demand that the problem of Kashmir should be solved on the basis of religion. Very recently, the Hurriyat leaders, a conglomeration of various parties having less followers (who have contested no election in Jammu and Kashmir) visited the POK (Pakistan occupied Kashmir) and Islamabad and talked with Pakistani leadership and the leadership of the POK. Their main demand was that they should be involved in the peace process taking place between India and Pakistan. Pakistan denied that it could not tell India to include the Hurriyat in the peace process. Now-a-days a series of confidence building measures have taken place between India and Pakistan. One of them is Srinagar-Mujafarrabad bus service.

In fact, Pakistan is really a factor in the US-India

relationship. As long as Pakistan was the blue-eyed boy of the Americans, during the whole Cold War years, the US-Indian relations could not improve. The Post-Cold War shifts in US policy in South Asia have appeared most traumatic for Pakistan. From a front-line status which the Reagan administration accorded this country during the Afghan war, it almost came to the brink of being branded as a terrorist state by the administration of President George Bush, particularly by Islamabad's alleged involvement in the insurgency in the Indian-held Kashmir. However, while the Bush administration stopped short of calling Pakistan a terrorist state, it cut off all economic and military assistance to Pakistan under the Pressler Amendment in October 1990. The US President decided not to certify to the Congress to the effect that Pakistan was not pursuing a nuclear weapons programme. The Pressler Amendment required this Presidential certification as a condition for voting aid to Pakistan. During the whole Cold War period, Pakistan never reconciled to the idea of the US economic and military assistance, in particular for India. The Pakistanis saw this aspect of the US policy in South Asia as detrimental to the alliance relationship of 1954.

The end of the Cold War, the pullout of the Soviet troops from Afghanistan and the resultant down grading of Pakistan's standing with the United States, therefore, have constituted the lowest point in the US-Pakistan relations since their inception in 1950. With the end of the Cold War, Pakistan's "inherent strategic importance to the United States has dramatically declined". In fact, the entire edifice of the US-Pakistan relationship – which was anticommunist crumbled, turning the alliance in Washington's estimate, obsolete. Instead, a new relationship between the US and India developed after the end of Cold War.

Pakistani attitudes began to be increasingly dominated by the impression that Post-Cold War US foreign policy had an anti-Islamic component, while American policy makers suspected Pakistan's complicity in many terrorist acts in the United States and elsewhere. In May 1992, Secretary of State, James Barker wrote to Prime Minister Nawaz Sharif, "bluntly threatening to designate the country as a 'terrorist state' under a 1985 Congressional mandate if it did not cease and desist from aiding the Kashmiris. Theodore P. Wright Jr. mentioned three other incidents in early 1993 that further strained US-Pakistani relations. The first one is the assassination of two CIA agents outside the agency's Virginia headquarters on January 25 by a Pakistani, Ajmal Kansi, who fled to his country and disappeared. The second one is the bombing of World Trade Centre in New York by Muslim terrorists from Egypt and Sudan whom Pakistan allegedly helped to get entrance into the United States on false passports, and the third is the bombing of the Bombay stock exchange on March 12, which was possibly a Muslim revenge for the slaughter of Muslims in India during the post-Ayodhya communal carnage. The persons accused of this crime escaped to the Gulf by way of Karachi. These incidents conditioned American perceptions of Pakistan. Pakistan, on the other hand, complained that US policy towards their country was dictated by opportunism.

Gradually, however, the US-Pakistan relations came out of the immediate Post-Cold War downturn. Pakistan needed the US arms and economic assistance. Even though the US had good relations with India, the able leadership of Pakistan tried to make the US-Pakistan relation more fruitful. Pakistan unsuccessfully tried to get the Clinton administration release the 28 F-16 aircraft for which payment has already been made or get the money back. This 28 F-16 aircraft has been sold to Pakistan by the US in 2005 during the second tenure of George Bush. When India complained to the US about the aircraft to be used against India by

Pakistan, the Bush administration cleared that similar F-16 would also be provided to India. The Indian Defence Minister Pranab Mukharjee said that the proposal of purchasing F-16 would be considered by India.

Indo-Pakistan relations acquired an entirely new dimension with India conducting its nuclear tests on May 11 and 13, 1998 and Pakistan responding with its own nuclear tests on May 28 and 30. Actually, the issue of preventing nuclear proliferation by India and Pakistan tops the list of Washington's Post-Cold War priorities in South Asia. From the American point of view, the end of the Cold War has eliminated the need for nuclear deterrence, and proliferation of nuclear weapons will pose an increasing danger to the stability of the emerging new world order. In the case of both India and Pakistan, their perceived security needs are at the roots of their nuclear programmes. Both the countries base their programme primarily on security needs.

After the nuclear tests India offered a No-first-use Agreement with Pakistan. Pakistan rejected the No-first-use proposal of India and instead offered a Non-aggression pact which India described as irrelevant because of the existence of the Simla agreement. Pakistan's continuous refusal to consider India's proposal pertaining to no-first-use of nuclear weapons confirms suspicions that Pakistan considers nuclear weapons as not merely a means of deterrence but weapons of war which it would not hesitate to use if the need arose. Pakistan's Foreign Secretary, Sham Shad Ahmad also made a provocative statement. He stated, "We will not hesitate to use any weapon in our arsenal to defend our territorial integrity"[33].

Pakistan in the post Chagai period actively tried to link the nuclear tests with the Kashmir question by suggesting that Kashmir being an unresolved issue which has been the cause of frequent wars in the past is now pregnant with the possibilities of a nuclear conflict in the subcontinent. That's why the western media categorized this region as the dangerous zone in the world. India has declared itself as a country of no-first-use of nuclear weapons. India knows it very well that Pakistanis have no guts to use nuclear weapons against the mighty India. Pakistan did it just to attract the world's attention, particularly the attention of the United States. Pakistan always wanted a third party mediation in the Kashmir issue and openly made a bid for intervention by the United States, the United Kingdom, China and Japan after showing its nuclear capability.

The United States has a record of lengthy involvement in the Kashmir conflict both within the United Nations and outside. The Kashmir dispute has again intensified as a result of the ongoing anti-Indian insurgency in the state from late 1989. Again, Kashmir has encompassed the entire gamut of India-Pakistan relations with the added complication that both countries are now nuclear-capable. Like earlier times, Washington is concerned with the dispute because it feels it has the potential for setting off a general India-Pakistan armed hostility which may further destabilize the region. Washington has always considered such a conflictual situation in the subcontinent as detrimental to American interests. This time the problem has gained added significance for Washington because it involves all that is prominent in America's Post-Cold War South Asia policy – non-proliferation, human rights, terrorism and so forth. America stands for human rights violation, non-proliferation of nuclear weapons, anti terrorism in any part of the world.

Let us first examine Indian and Pakistanis positions regarding Kashmir. They seem rigid despite many attempts at solution of the problem by the United Nations as well as numerous bilateral negotiations between the disputants themselves. India claims Kashmir to be its integral part and at least officially does not recognize the fact that any dispute exists at all other than that a smaller portion of Kashmir which is under Pakistan's "unlawful control". In practice India wants to accept the conversion of the LOC (Line of Control) into a permanent international boundary. Pakistan still insists on a plebiscite, although in its scheme of Kashmir's self-determination there is no place for independence. At least on this one point, that is independence, both New Delhi and Islamabad are of the same view – neither would countenance an independent Kashmir.

The main focus of the US policy is to avoid confrontation between India and Pakistan. In 1990, the Bush administration perceived such a threat and that's why sent Deputy National Security Advisor Robert Gates to the subcontinent to defuse tension. He urged New Delhi and Islamabad on the adoption of confidence building measures so that war would not break out through sheer miscalculation or lack of communication.

The Clinton administration also stresses a bilateral solution as agreed upon by both sides at Simla. A more active role on the part of the United States poses problems for policy-makers. India's traditional distaste for any outside interference in the problem is well known. The Clinton administration was aware of this and that's why did not want to jeopardize the current improving trends in the US-Indian relations by showing too much concern for Kashmir. There has not been any dramatic change in the US policy regarding Kashmir, said an official of the South Asia Bureau of the State Department, reiterating the position that both disputants should seek a negotiated settlement after taking into account the views of the Kashmiri people. The official insisted that the United States has "no magic wand for an ideal solution" nor does it want to put itself as a mediator unless all the concerned parties agree[34].

Regarding the Kashmir issue, Pakistan always tries

to draw the attention of the world community that human rights violation by the security forces is going on in the valley. On 13th April, 1994, at New Delhi addressing the Army Commanders Conference, the Prime Minister Mr. P.V. Narasimha Rao, referring to the allegations of human rights violation by security forces said that India's concern for human rights was second to none. Of late, there had been better understanding of India's performance in this respect, adding "we have been successful in dispelling the motivated propaganda against our forces". He called on the interested parties to stop the futile exercise in maligning India on this score. Indeed it would amount to an insult to the concept of human rights to distort and misuse it for political exploitation and slanderous propaganda, he said.

Referring to ongoing security forces operations against militants in Jammu and Kashmir, he said the "low intensity conflict" sponsored by Pakistan in Jammu and Kashmir was a major challenge before India. Pakistan was sending terrorists including foreign mercenaries across the Line of Actual Control. He called upon the Army Commanders to gear up forces to increase vigil on the border to stop such infiltration[35].

The United States is now convinced that instead of human rights violation in Kashmir, terrorism backed by Pakistan is going on and United States is against any type of terrorism in any part of the world. The United States had said many a time that Pakistan must stop cross border terrorism and must establish the sanctity of the LOC.

It was reported in the Asian Age on 18th July 1999 that a US based human right organization "Human Rights Watch" has said that Pakistan is giving training to militants in Kashmir. It said that Pakistan's refuting the charge of not giving training to militants is not credible. The US has now felt convinced about Pakistan's complicity in aiding and abetting of Kashmir terrorists which has been the root cause of the tension. Washington has been reportedly told by Pakistan of the closure of 13 camps where Kashmir terrorists were trained and armed inside Pakistan in response to India's protest, though the authenticity of its shutdown is doubled.

On 6th February 1990, a US State Department spokesman said "We are encouraging both countries to use this framework (Simla agreement) to settle the problem". However, a significant pronouncement of the US position on Kashmir came on 6th March 1990 from John Kelly, the US Assistant Secretary of State.

Kelly categorically ruled out plebiscite on Kashmir and endorsed the resolution of the historical dispute between the tow countries by Simla accord of 1972. Referring to Pakistan's demand for self-determination in Kashmir, he contended that plebiscite could not be restricted to two choices, namely to join India or Pakistan and it was untenable for Pakistan not to allow a third option i.e. independence[36].

References

1. A. Shanmugam, "Indian Parliament and the United States", Annamalai University, 1989, pp.162-166.
2. *Ibid*, p.173.
3. *Ibid*, p.174
4. *Ibid*, pp.174-178.
5. Tanvir Sultan, "Indo-US Relations", New Delhi, Deep & Deep Publishers, 1982, pp.85-86.
6. *Ibid*, pp.84-88.
7. Emeka Ohajunwa, "Indo-US Security Relations", Chanakya Publications, Delhi, 1992, pp.32-33.
8. Speeches of Jawaharlal Nehru, Second Series, Vol.5, pp.188-90, 210-211, 218.
9. K. Subrahmanyam, "Deception on Kashmir-1965: US knew but wouldn't tell", Times of India, August 11, 1997.
10. Robert J. McMahon, "The Evolution of American Geopolitical

Strategy", in A.P. Rana, ed., Four Decades of Indo-US Relations: A Commemorative Retrospective, New Delhi, Har-Anand Publications, 1994, p.94.

11. R.K. Jain, ed. US-South Asian Relations, 1947-1982, Vol.2, New Delhi: Radiant Publishers, 1983, p.75.
12. Dennis Kux, India and the United States: Estranged Democracies, 1941-1991, Washington D.C., National Defence University Press, 1992, p.309.
13. Strategic Survey, 1990-91, London: International Institute of Strategic Studies, 1991.
14. New York Times, May 16, 1990.
15. Official Text, United States Information Services, New Delhi, February 3, 1995.
16. Pioneer, March 31, 1996.
17. Arms Control and Disarmament Agency Annual Report 1996, Excerption South Asia, USIS Test Link: 415917, File Date/ID, August 12, 1996.
18. Wireless File, USIS, May 1, 1997.
19. Hindustan Times, August 12, 1997.
20. Hindu, August 8, 1997.
21. Times of India, Hindustan Times, Hindu, August 12, 1997.
22. Times of India, August 9, 1997.
23. Hindu, August 12, 1997.
24. "US interests in India and Pakistan", USIS Release, Strategic Digest, Vol.XXII, No.7, July 1993, p.1058.
25. Maj. Gen. (Retd.) Afsir Karim, "Pakistan's Aggression in Kashmir: 1999", Aakrosh, July 1999, p.5.
26. *Ibid*, p.10.
27. Text of Joint Statement of President Clinton and Prime Minister Nawaz Sharif, at Washington on July 4, 1999, Dawn, July 5, 1999.
28. Newsline, July 1999.
29. Ayaz Amir, Dawn, July 9, 1999.
30. Altaf Gauhar's article in Nation, September 5, 1999.
31. According to IDSA database.
32. Zaigham Khan, "Allah's Armies". The Herald, September 1998, pp.28-29.

33. The News International, May 31, Pakistan.
34. Mahmudul Huque, "US Relations with India and Pakistan", Regional Studies, Vol.XV, No.2, Spring 1997, pp.67-83.
35. Editorial, The Nuclear Option, Kashmir a Indo-US Relations", Defence Today, Vol.II(2), May 1994, pp.3-5.
36. Rajan K. Sharma, "New US Policy on Kashmir", Third World Impact, August 1991, Vol.11, No.2, pp.2829.

7

The US Relations with India Under Clinton

When William Jefferson (Bill) Clinton became the President (Democrat) in 1993, it was hoped that the Indo-US relations would then grow faster as Democratic regimes were always considered more sympathetic and friendly towards India than Republican regimes. But very soon this hope was belied. In the first year of Clinton's tenure the Indo-US relations reached a new low. There was increased misunderstanding, suspicion and tension between the two largest democracies of the world.

In the first year of Clinton's tenure Clinton himself and his officials especially John Malott and Robin Raphel pinpricked India on a number of issues such as nuclear nonproliferation, human rights violation in Punjab and Kashmir, resolving complex Kashmir issue, halt on missile programme, intellectual property rights issue and move to slap Special 301 law against India.

Clinton's statement in the UN equating Kashmir problem with civil war in Angola, Bosnia, Caucasus etc. and that of his officials stating that Kashmiri people may also be made a party in resolving this issue between

India and Pakistan went against India. Then firebrand Robin Raphel's assertion that Simla Agreement has become redundant, that Kashmir is a disputed territory and that the US did not recognize the 1947 instrument of Accession by which Kashmir became a part of India annoyed the Indian Government and public. Further, Clinton's letters to secessionist leaders of Kashmir and Punjab created new apprehensions in India and embitted Indo-US relations.

When Clinton became the President there was an ill-conceived expectation that Pakistan, which had been intervening in Kashmir, would be branded a terrorist state. Instead, the United States reduced its foreign aid appropriation by 20 per cent, reneged on the delivery of promised cryogenic rocket engines and began renewing certain types of commercial sales to Pakistan that Congress thought the Pressler Amendment prohibited. Nevertheless, India, as one of the few established democracies in Asia and the second most populous country in the world, felt Bill Clinton was a candidate for positive attention from Washington. However, other parts of Clinton agenda such as stopping the spread of nuclear weapons and promoting human rights in regions affected by turbulence – worked against the improvement of relations.

The contradictory agenda of the Clinton administration was reflected by confusing messages sent from the American Embassy in New Delhi[1]. While some diplomats praised the direction of Rao's economic and foreign policies, others were critical of the government's violation of human rights in suppressing the ongoing Sikh rebellion in Punjab and especially Kashmir where half a million troops were fighting a civil war waged by Muslim militants. Incredibly, there was a diplomatic vacuum at the embassy caused by the failure to name an Ambassador for sixteen months after the departure of Thomas Pickering in March 1993. After more than a year the Clinton administration nominated career diplomat Frank Wisner, who took up his post in July 1994.

The return of Benazir Bhutto to power in late 1993 complicated the effort to improve bilateral relations between the United States and India. Well connected in Washington, she has always been perceived in the US capital as pro-American. Almost immediately upon her return to the office of Prime Minister, the Clinton administration announced its determination to do something that would bolster her fragile domestic position which was typified by the unprecedented violence that was transpiring in Karachi. Unable to promote Pakistan as a front-line state, Washington began advancing Islamabad as a moderate Islamic influence and a linchpin to the new Soviet Central Asian countries.

In November 1993 Senator Larry Pressler revealed that the Clinton administration was considering rescinding his 1985 legislation which had led to the cutoff of assistance to Pakistan in 1990. The mechanism was to be the repeal of any country-specific language in a major revision of the 1961 Foreign Assistance Act. In testimony before the Senate Foreign Relations Committee, Ms Raphel described the Pressler Amendment as an "Obstacle" to improved ties with Pakistan[2]. That act had prohibited delivery of 71 F-16 aircraft for which Pakistan had already paid $658 million dollars of a $1.4 billion arms package. Because of the Pressler Amendment, Congress could not authorize delivery of the planes and given its budgetary situation, it was unable to return the money. In the meantime, the government of Pakistan paid $50,000 a year to store and maintain each aircraft in the United States. In the guise of fairness, the Clinton administration led by the Defence Department set out to find a compromise. In a speech to the Foreign Policy Association in New York on

January 31, 1995 Secretary William Perry called the Pressler Amendment, "a blunt instrument that undermined the US influence with Pakistan". The Pentagon's lobbying efforts on Capitol Hill were vigorously resisted by Senator Presslor and John Glenn, the Chairman of the Government Operations Committee. They documented hundreds of violations of the original legislation by Pakistan, which was covertly proceeding with its nuclear programme. In the view of the non-proliferators, repeal would send the wrong message and reward Pakistan for noncompliance. At a hearing of the Senate Foreign Relations Subcommittee of West Asia and South Asia, Ms Raphel claimed that although the Pressler Amendment had served a purpose in the past, there was no more "non-proliferation mileage to be gained from it. Raphel indicated that the administration would attempt to convince Congress to enact a one-time waiver of the Pressler Amendment"[3].

The efforts to repeal the Pressler Amendment were bolstered by Hilary Clinton's trip to South Asia in March 1995 and a visit by Prime Minister Benazir Bhutto to Washington where the Pakistani leader lobbied Congressional leaders in early April. While she was in Washington, Mr. Clinton pledged "to ask Congress to show some flexibility in the Pressler Amendment so that America can have some economic and military cooperation"[4].

The repeal of the Pressler Amendment during the Clinton years was a strong blow to the US-India relations. This pro-Pakistan stand of the US was not liked by the Indians. The Indians raised their voice that the military aid which would be given to Pakistan, would be used against India as it had been done in the past.

It was Senator Hank Brown who became the administration's point person for watering down the Pressler Amendment on Capitol Hill. In a rare public attack on a visiting legislator, the Indian Government accused him of being "part of a disinformation campaign" that distorted India's position on nuclear proliferation[5]. According to Congressional sources the Colorado Republican's main motivation in resuming arms sales was to "clear the air" so that an irritant in bilateral relations with Pakistan could be removed. Beginning on March 9, 1995 he held a series of hearings where State and Defence Department officials were given a platform urging the reexamination of the Pressler Amendment. In testimony remarkable for a lack of balance, the same witnesses were repeatedly paraded before the Brown and Bereuter Committees where they branded India "as the greatest source of instability in South Asia". Anachronistic Cold War logic was resurrected to depict India as being tied to Russia, while Pakistan was described as being linked to the American security system. It was argued that the Pressler cutoff, instead of being even-handed, had produced a conventional balance of forces which favoured New Delhi. Hence, it was suggested a one-time exception to the arms embargo would not materially influence regional proliferation[6].

All of these assertions were repeated and indeed cited, on the Senate floor by its supporters when the Brown Amendment (No.2708) of HR1868 was taken up on September 20, 1995. Brown and Tom Harkin began to debate by comparing Indian and Pakistani positions on Cold War issues. Pakistan was depicted as a loyal partner of the United States on every issue, while India was portrayed as a Soviet Client always taking positions contrary to American interests.

The Brown Amendment was passed by a margin of 55-45. The dissenters included 34 Democrats and 11 Republicans. Shortly after the Brown Amendment became law, the Clinton administration was embarrassed by reports that China had secretly sold nuclear-weapons technology to Pakistan. Nevertheless,

President Clinton signed the legislation on January 27, 1996.

Critics say that the significance of the Brown Amendment is not the arms sold to Pakistan. Rather, the passage of the legislation is symbolic of the way the United States conducts policy with India. The critics also say that the manner in which the Brown Amendment was passed is also illustrative of the way in which Congress deals with the South Asia region.

The controversy caused by the Brown Amendment also demonstrates the delicate nature of the American-Indian relationship. In fact, its passage caused outrage in India, worsened relations with the United States and embarrassed Washington's friends in New Delhi. Parliamentarians from the left parties ridiculed the Rao government for pursuing what they regarded as a misguided policy of cooperation with the United States. The deterioration in American-Indian relations was signalled by a speech that Home Minister S.B. Chavan made in the Rajya Sabha on November 29, 1995. He criticized American arms sale to Pakistan and said that it was a evil design the United States had on the subcontinent. His assertion that the United States was interested in acquiring a "foot hold" in Kashmir was endorsed by the BJP opposition leader[7]. The fact that this unsubstantiated charge was widely repeated throughout India without refutation is indicative of the obstacles that advocates of better relations with the United States have to overcome.

Washington's ability to restrain India's nuclear programme was also a casualty of the watering down of the Pressler Amendment. Indeed, Washington suspected that India was preparing for a nuclear test[8]. As Foreign Minister Pranab Mukherjee decried that by selling arms to Pakistan the United States was once again forcing India to divert scarce resources to the military sector. While India had been one of the world's principal purchasers of arms in the 1980s, its military spending under Prime Minister Rao had declined by nearly 30 per cent - from 3.6 per cent of GDP to 2.6 per cent. According to Jasjit Singh, the Director of the Institute for Defence Studies and Analysis, New Delhi, "No other country in the world has cut back defence spending on this order in recent years"[9]. While Pakistan's defence expenditure is 26.72 per cent of its budget, India's had been reduced to 9.46 per cent[10]. It was expected that the additional arms sales permitted by the Brown Amendment would generate a new arms race on the subcontinent.

It was presumed that higher military spending would in turn undermine the free enterprise economy that the United States desires to see established in India. Commerce Minister P. Chindambaram claimed that the Brown Amendment "cast a shadow over bilateral commercial ties"[11]. Again the Rao government's liberalization programme slowed during the 1996 election campaign which featured demonstration against Kentuchy Fried Chicken outlets and the temporary cancellation of the Enron Power project by the government of Maharashtra. Mr. P.V. Narasimha Rao had made an official week long visit from May 14 till 19, 1994, accepting the invitation of President Bill Clinton. Like his other foreign tours, Narasimha Rao's visit to the US, has also been considered to be a successful one. The visit cleared much of the earlier misconceptions about American pressure and Indian capitulation and helped to reestablish Indo-US ties on a more mature footing. Though, there is little forward movement in political relations and giant leap forward in commercial relations as a result of P.M. Rao's visit, the two countries have overcome their reservations and established a durable framework for building a new partnership despite continuing differences over many issues. There was a shifting of focus by "low-balling non-proliferation, human rights and high-balling the economic issue".

The significant gains of the visit are that six MOUs were signed and these pertains to the following:

1. Revitalizing the Indo-US Joint Commission to enhance cooperation between the two countries. This Joint Commission was setup in 1974 and met for six times up to 1980. It last met in 1986. It was decided that this Commission would be co-chaired by the Indian Foreign Minister and the US Secretary of State. The Commission is to have four sub-Commissions on (i) Education and Culture, (ii) Science and Technology, (iii) Agriculture and (iv) Economics and Commerce. First of all fourth sub-Commission will start functioning.
2. Having regular Foreign Office consultations. These consultations will be held at the level of Minister, Secretary and division head, alternatively in India and America. India has already had such consultations with Japan, Germany, UK and France.
3. Upgrading cooperation in science and technology.
4. Revising sagging cooperation in defence in the form of holding seminars, workshops, training facilities, military exercises etc.
5. Encouraging unofficial exchange of views by setting up an Eminent Persons Group and Indo-US Business Partnership initiative.
6. Conserving of cultural heritage sites and cooperating in areas of narcotics awareness.

The Prime Minister Rao's sales talk during his weeklong visit to the US was expected to lead to an investment flow of $25-30 billion into India in the next two or three years in the infrastructure sector with an emphasis on power and energy. The US Commerce Department in a "White Paper" listed India as one of the top Big Emerging Markets (BEM).

The joint statement, which came after the summit talks between Rao and Clinton noted that the US and India have begun negotiations on a new extradition treaty and an agreement on renewable energy resources, which they hope to complete in near future.

The main points of the joint statement issued after the Rao-Clinton summit are:

1. The two leaders called for a new partnership between India and the US.
2. They agreed that democracy, respect for human rights, and economic liberalization provide the best foundation for global stability and prosperity in the Post-Cold War era. They promised to cooperate in the search for solution to global challenges posed by weapons of mass destruction.
3. The President and the Prime Minister agreed to expand the pace and scope of high level exchanges on the full range of political, economic, commercial, scientific, technological and social issues.
4. Both leaders noted with satisfaction their cooperation in support of UN peacekeeping operations, in particular in countries where forces of both countries have served. The leaders agreed to seek ways to expand their cooperation at the UN. They welcomed the progress in the West Asia peace process and hailed the recent elections in South Africa.
5. The two leaders agreed on the need for bilateral negotiations between India and Pakistan to resolve outstanding issues, including Jammu and Kashmir as envisaged in the Simla agreement.
6. Mr. Clinton and Mr. Rao offered their strong support for efforts towards the non-proliferation of weapons of mass destruction and their means of delivery and towards their progressive reduction, with the goal of elimination of such weapons, which

are among the most pressing challenges to the security of states in the Post-Cold War era. They discussed these challenges in both the global and regional contexts.

7. They pledged that their two governments would intensify their efforts to achieve a comprehensive test ban treaty and a verifiable ban on the production of fissile materials for nuclear weapons.
8. The two leaders welcomed the successful conclusion of the Uruguay round and pledged their governments would work to help the new World Trade Organization continue the process of expanding trade.

It was decided that US Commerce Secretary Ron Brown and Energy Secretary Hazel O'Leary – just two of the cabinet level officials who spoke personally with Prime Minister Rao – would make separate trips to India in 1994. Defence Secretary William Parry also discussed with the Prime Minister various ways to strengthen and deepen the US-India defence relationship including the possibility of joint military exercises in the future. By the end of 1994, Indo-US interaction was taken to a still higher plane with the forthcoming Indian visits of the US Secretaries of Commerce, Defence and Treasury. Never before in the history of India-US relations have so many US Secretaries visited India in such a short span of time. This proves the mutual desire to expand the bilateral agenda without getting stuck over points of divergence.

The US Secretary of Energy, Ms Hazel O'Leary led a 45-membered high-powered business delegation from the USA to India in the second week of July 1994. Ms O'Leary offered everything that India was yearning for. The US companies were ready to transfer the best technology and agree to mutual sharing of expertise so as to establish a sustained relationship. The only thing she insisted on was a firm counter-guarantee that the Union Government should underwrite all financial commitments which individual state electricity boards undertake. Against this, India would get the latest technology, which meant that even the coal-fired thermal plants would be environment-friendly and would not poison the air. Stressing that USA was keen to build a "sustainable partnership" with India on all aspects of sustainable development, she said that the starting point of the current cooperation initiative was the recent visit of the Prime Minister Narasimha Rao to the United States, where the government to government understanding on cooperation in the field of energy, trade and economic ties was evolved[12].

India and the USA signed a record 15 agreements on July 13, 1994 to enhance cooperation in the energy sector, 11 of them raising investment prospects of "hundreds of millions of dollars". So Prime Minister Rao's visit to the US was certainly not a flop.

Indo-US relations were undergoing the "subtle but significant" change after Prime Minister P.V. Narsimha Rao's sixday tour to the US in May. The two sides gave emphasis on the positive aspect of the relationship rather than the negative. Both sides did not gloss over their very real differences on contentious issues - Kashmir, human rights, missile and nuclear nonproliferation. Rather they admitted that "disagreements exist in every bilateral relationship and are best resolved in the context of each country's overall interests", Gomez points out[13].

On the nuclear question, both Clinton and Rao agreed that the most acceptable way in the present circumstances would be to alter the agenda from a bilateral one to a larger multilateral forum to endorse the proposed global comprehensive ban on nuclear tests and fissionable-weapons production, both points which India supports. Rao also repeated what he had stated in his excellent Congress speech: he was for first initiating a global agreement on non-first use of nuclear weapons and then ultimately aiming at elimination of nuclear weapons and a ban on missile testing and deployment. Admiringly Bobb comments: "Rao, however was at his forceful best in explaining to Clinton that India's security threat was mainly from China. Since then, all US official statements on regional nonproliferation have included China and the need for Beijing to reduce its nuclear arsenal"[14].

President Clinton said he was "disturbed" by press reports suggesting that India-America relations were marred by disagreements on nuclear nonproliferation, human rights and Kashmir, and specific issues relating to trade. "We have a very great stake, it seem to me ... in having not only friendly relationship but a constructive and operating relationship - We, the two great democracies, with a great future together", he said. "When two nations are friends, it doesn't mean that they agree on everything or that they should. But in the context of their friendly relationship, they are then able to discuss differences, problems or issues between them"[15]. President Clinton further explained, "it implies that persistent differences over nuclear issue will not be allowed to disturb the areas of agreement between the two largest democracies. These areas of agreement are economic and trade matters, secularism, democracy, political pluralism, and the rule of law".

In 1993 the US vigorously endeavoured to arm-twist defiant Asian nations like North Korea, Pakistan, Ukraine and India to roll back or cap their bomb programmes but without much success. Unwarranted pressure cannot yield result. The discussion of the nuclear nonproliferation has shown that putting pressure on small countries can be counter-productive, however much a country is in need of aid or recognition.

It seems that the US is in the habit of projecting an exaggerated, over nuclearised scenario in South Asia so as to impose or justify some kind of regional nonproliferation arrangement on the countries of this region. There was renewed US pressure on India for giving up its nuclear options, for agreeing to some regional nonproliferation arrangement or for agreeing to nine-nation multilateral forum for non-proliferation but it has declined to do so until a fair deal is assured to all countries, especially the nuclear have-nots. India sees nonproliferation not from regional but from global perspective. India will continue to keep its nuclear options open. Pakistan has also rejected the latest US proposal for unilateral verifiable capping of its nuclear programme in exchange for 38 F-16 aircrafts.

Though India has rejected Clinton administration's latest proposals on nonproliferation yet both countries agree on shifting agenda from a bilateral one to a multilateral forum to endorse the proposed comprehensive ban on nuclear tests and fissionable weapons production. Pakistan is for balance of obligation by India, on the one hand and by Pakistan on the other. It is ready for nonproliferation either through bilateral arrangement between Pakistan and India or on a regional basis, provided it is equitable and non-discriminatory.

There are various ways the US can punish India. For example, in the economic sphere it may impose cuts in loans from institutions like the World Bank, and the International Monetary Fund, Super 301 and labour law in trade. In another way, America may side with Pakistan in internationalizing the Kashmir issue and propagating human rights abuses.

But all these assumptions have not really taken place. America and Clinton have not sided with Pakistan completely, rather they have also sided with India. On the day of President's visit to India, there was terrorist killings in Jammu and Kashmir. The President said that no talk with Pakistan was possible unless Pakistan stops cross-border terrorism. When India exploded the bomb on May 1998, Clinton imposed sanctions on India. When Pakistan exploded the bomb, the same sanctions were also imposed on Pakistan. But later on economic sanctions were lifted on India and Pakistan.

Clinton's foreign policy is matured in the sense it identified India as one of the most important country. The Clinton administration did not tighten the screw by employing any of the above-mentioned punishments against India. Instead it is interested to enhance economic and trade relations between the two countries keeping aside differences on nuclear nonproliferation.

For decades India and the United States had often been described as "unfriendly friends". In more ways than one the phrase captured the essence of the five decades of Indo-US relations. The two countries shared numerous beliefs and values, including their commitment to democracy. Yet the two could not see eye to eye on many crucial issues in the Cold War phase.

The context of bilateral engagement has, however, changed in the Post-Cold War phase. There have been talks in strategic circles in the recent past, particularly in the wake of last summer's Kargil conflict, of a "paradigm shift" in Washington's South Asian policy. In the midst of these, came President Bill Clinton's weeklong visit to the region, focused mainiy on India. What is already evident is a shift in Washington's framework of engagement with India. It is clear that both India and the US are keen to rebuild the ties that have existed so far, that at different points of time, manifested in confrontation and benign neglect.

Mr. Clinton's emphasis is on forging close cooperation and on building a strong partnership in business, trade, science and frontier areas of technology.

In the Clinton administration's perception, Indian economic, scientific and technological growth in recent years and the prospects that it holds for the coming year is too important for America to wait for building new bridges with India until nagging differences on "concern" areas are resolved. That President Clinton could soften the tough posture adopted by the US towards India following the nuclear tests, at Pokhran has been evident for some time.

The "vision statement" President Clinton signed with Prime Minister Atal Behari Vajpayee on his visit to India documented the new US approach towards India. It laid down that the two sides would cooperate with one another in building a strong partnership in areas of complementarity. It recognized that there were areas of differences, real or perceived, but both would remain engaged in dialogue to narrow them down with a view to achieving agreement.

To go along the direction set out by this vision, the two leaders also committed themselves in the statement to institutionalizing bilateral dialogue through regular meetings at various levels, including at the summit level. So the vision statement is not just a definition of their vision for future bilateral ties but also a framework document.

While the document might have historic significance, the focus during Mr. Clinton's visit largely remained on two crucial issues on which agreements were neither expected nor achieved. One is the non-proliferation issue and the other the state of Indo-Pakistan relations.

President Clinton stated that the two issues remained "concern" areas for the Untied States. According to him, the full potential for a strong Indo-US partnership could be realized if the two countries got these "concern" areas out of the way.

However, keen observers of American policy have perceived a subtle shift in the Clinton administration's recent formulations on these issues. As far as the non-proliferation agenda of the United States is concerned, Mr. Clinton has stated that he would like India to forego nuclear weapons and not insist on maintaining a credible minimum nuclear determent. India should sign the Comprehensive Test Ban Treaty, join in talks on an agreement on fissile material production ban and tighten its export control regime to ensure nonproliferation of nuclear technology. While remaining committed to the non-proliferation agenda, Mr. Clinton however, put on record that America understood India's security concerns and conceded that a final decision on the issue had to be made only by New Delhi. Perhaps, the decision to hold regular Asian security dialogue emerged from this understanding.

In view of the situation, he said the best course of action for the two countries is to continue being engaged in the security and non-proliferation dialogue which the two countries started 18 months ago. Mr. Clinton appreciated Prime Minister A.B. Vajpayee's commitment not to undertake further nuclear tests and the doctrine of no-first use.

Given the fact that the Clinton administration had played a key role in getting tabled the UN Security Council resolution 1172 on Indian and Paksitani nuclear tests, requiring the two to unconditionally sign CTBT and NPT in June 1998, the President's comments here on the issue appeared rather conciliatory.

Of course, Mr. Clinton did not say anything of the sort his Deputy Secretary of State Strobe Talbott said in Washington on the eve of the visit. Mr. Talbott, the point-man for conducting the non-proliferation dialogue, said that no government in New Delhi, let alone the Vajpayee government, would give up nuclear weapons. Significantly, this was what the opposition Congress delegation led by Ms. Sonia Gandhi conveyed to Mr. Clinton when it called on him on March 22, 2000.

However, it is Mr. Clinton's remarks on the Indo-Pak front which generated the utmost interest during the visit. What the President said has become a subject of differing interpretations. But what is clear from his statements, interviews and other comments on the issue in New Delhi is that he is in favour of India and Pakistan freezing their dispute over the Kashmir issue and beginning talks with each other to at least have a working relationship.

The emphasis is on avoiding a further deterioration of relations marked by tension since their Kargil conflict last May. It is the American perception that the present situation marked by regular military exchanges can lead to a dangerous war involving nuclear weapons. Thus, the President came out with a four-point formulation on dealing with the situation. He appealed to both India and Pakistan to exercise restraint and consider ways of restarting their stalled bilateral dialogue. However, he made it known that Pakistan must stop its encouragement to cross-border terrorism and respect the Line of Control in Jammu and Kashmir. In a reference to Pakistan's Kargil misadventure, he said that the use of force could not and would not provide a solution to the problem over Kashmir. He also advised Pakistani leaders that it would not help their cause if they continued to look at their dispute with Kashmir in the same way as they did for the last five decades[16].

During his visit to India with her daughter Chelsea, the President spoke to the two Houses of Parliament. In a speech that clearly reflected the visitor's greater appreciation of India's concerns, Clinton told a packed sitting of the two Houses of Parliament: "We know the threat of terrorism all too well and we will build with you a system of justice ... We share your concern over the course Pakistan is taking but India, as a democracy has a special opportunity to prove that democracy is about dialogue". Clinton categorically told, "I have certainly not come to South Asia to mediate on Kashmir but I hope you will create an opportunity to begin a dialogue with Pakistan. One of the wisest things I have ever been told is that you do not make peace with friends"[17].

Repeatedly applauded for the warm and from-one-man-to-another tenor of his speech, Clinton also strongly pursued the nuclear non-proliferation line, but again, in suggestive fashion. "To tell you what to do is not my place", he said, "only India can determine its interests, only Indians know whether they are safer today than they were before their nuclear experiment, only Indians know what happens when the neighbour responds and that their nuclear policy can have consequences beyond their border". Clinton told that, India's nuclear explosions certainly shook the world but now your initiative on non-proliferation can move the world[18].

Speaking after Clinton's address, Vajpayee reiterated that even though India remained committed to disarmament and nonproliferation of nuclear weapons "Our decision to maintain a minimum credible nuclear deterrent is prompted by a realistic assessment of our security compulsions". In an unveiled nudge to the US to pin Pakistan down as a wrongdoer, Vajpayee said, "The problem of terrorism with its link to ideologies of extremism and funding through illegal trade in narcotics is one of the biggest challenges facing nation-states. We need to consider whether we are doing enough to strike at the root of this menace, which breeds on hatred and violence and is the very anti-thesis of democracy"[19].

Clinton, on his part, stressed the commonalities between India and the US and said, "We are, for a variety of reasons, natural allies. Our common interests lie in our love for democracy and liberty and pluralism. I hope this visit of mine will help Americans understand India better and Indians understand America better". He linked the Indo-US relationship to the elasticity of an Indian raga and said, "The basic framework for friendship is there, and like in a raga it is upon the players now to improvise and produce a harmonious symphony"[20].

The US President spoke at length on the new emerging India and emphasized the need for New Delhi to enthusiastically join the process of economic globalization. Calling globalization the "central debate of our times", Clinton said, "Many believe it is divisive and increases the gulf between the rich and the poor. This is a valid fear but I believe it is wrong. Now developing countries and especially democracies will have greater opportunities to go ahead than at any time in the past. Globalization does not favour countries with licence raj but it does favour countries with panchayatiraj".

He allayed fears of the developing nations getting hurt by globalization and said, "Sustained global economic progress should be one of the challenges that define our relationship. Disparities are unacceptable and intolerable, this we must undo because poverty is an affront to humanity".

Clinton also called for a vibrant Indo-US economic relationship and promised "all our support" to the effort to "end poverty and disease and spread better healthcare and education"[21].

Despite the pall created by the massacre in Kashmir, and notwithstanding the acknowledged differences on issues like nuclear nonproliferation and world trade, there is a stubborn optimism in Washington that President Clinton's visit to India has been an unqualified success.

This mood is best expressed by the business

community which foresees a doubling and trebling of trade and the US investment in India in the next five years.

"I think America has been saying all along, at least for the last year that India and the US could be fantastic trading partners because both are democratic societies and I think America is the biggest trading partner of India", Mr. Bose told Deccan Herald.

"So the friendship is growing. In the old days when the US was supportive of Pakistan and India was more tied to Moscow, well, those days have gone and the situation has changed and I think that could be a reason why the US wants to be with India rather than Pakistan". In every respect its been shown, from that point of view – and the Indian economy is doing much better than it has in the past – and the momentum will grow with the help from the US.

In the US House of Representatives, where India has traditionally had strong allies, the President's trip has received a standing ovation both from Staffers and Congressmen.

One Staffer, speaking off the record, said he did think Mr. Clinton should have been tougher on Pakistan by clearly condemning the Kashmir killing[22].

Mr. Bill Clinton had a historic trip to India with his daughter Chelsea. No American President had visited India after Jimmy Carter. The game plan for upgrading Indo-US commercial ties had been laid prior to the visit. The only impetus needed to push it forward was a green signal from the political leadership of both countries.

Mr. Clinton's entire trip, especially the softening of attitudes on strategic issues, laid the groundwork for the subsequent series of agreements that finally formalized the economic engagement of these two major players on the world scene.

One of the most significant announcements in the

"vision statement" issued after the Clinton-Vajpayee talks was the creation of an institutional arrangement for a Government to Government dialogue on economic issues.

The three-tier mechanism envisages regular meetings at the Ministerial level for discussion on trade and investment. The talks will be held between the Indian Finance Minister and the US Treasury Secretary at one level and at the second level between the Prime Minister's office and the US Trade Representative's office. The third tier is the Indo-US commercial dialogue for which the Commerce and Industry Minister, Mr. Murasoli Maran, and the US Commerce Secretary, Mr. William Daley, signed, during the visit, an agreement ratifying the terms of reference.

The unique aspect of the Dialogue is that it will be both at the Ministerial level and on an industry-to-industry basis. The Washington based US-India Business Council (USIBC) will act as the catalyst on the US side with the major Indian Chambers of Commerce being involved at this end. According to Mr. Michael Clark of the USIBC, the dialogue will be largely industry-led and it replaces the five-year-old largely ineffective Indo-US Commercial Alliance.

In fact, with the two Governments having entered into a formal dialogue process, the next step for strengthening business ties lies at the industry level. The business delegation accompanying Mr. Clinton appeared to be enthusiastically seeking a closer relationship and numerous agreements were concluded involving an estimated investment of $1.4 billion.

The major sectors for these tie-ups were energy, environment and information technology, the three areas where there seems to be the greatest complementarity between two countries. Energy is the area of infrastructure where India needs perhaps the biggest dose of investment from abroad. And the US power companies are eager to provide investments in case the climate is right. Similarly, there is complementarity in clean energy technologies with India seeking to upgrade manufacturing facilities and the US companies equally keen to provide the needed technology. As for IT, which remained the focus area during the entire Clinton's visit, some agreements were signed but these are probably only the tip of the iceberg. The Indo-US knowledge Trade Initiative agreement entered into by FICCI and the USIBC may signal the advent of a more formal collaboration, as the working groups will now identify specific areas of cooperation between the industries in both countries.

In any case, Silicon Valley has already had close links with India as India-born entrepreneurs play a leading role in the US IT industry. No wonder then that the business delegation comprised numerous Indian Americans especially CEOs of IT companies. In fact this was one of the criticisms against the US business delegation. Some industry representatives, however, argue that Indians are now at the helm of affairs in a wide range of industries in the US, not just in the IT sector.

Domestic industry is already quite upbeat about the long-term impact of the Clinton visit. The Assocham Secretary-General, Mr. Jayant Bhuyan, identifies three major plus points flowing out of the visit as far as economic and business ties are concerned. First, he said, India was now seen to be outward looking rather than insular. This was acknowledged by the US President in his speeches. In turn he felt the US industry would begin to recognize the presence of greater openness in the Indian economy.

Secondly, he said, the new commercial dialogue was extremely significant as it would function both at the Government and private industry level.

And finally, the visit had enabled India to sensitise the US in the area of multilateral trade as far as developing economies were concerned. It had been able to convince the US to modulate its stand on issues such as trade and environment, he pointed out.

In sum, therefore, the US President's visit has had a catalytic effect on the growth of a new economic alliance. Though India is yet to attain its potential on the world stage as an economic power, the US sees it as a major player in future. With the Indian strengths in knowledge-based industries, it is clear that closer economic and business ties can be a win-win situation for both countries in the long run.

"Even though the President is due to retire soon, his prolonged stay in India appears to tell the industry back home that it is an okay country to put your money in", added the MNC official[23].

Vision Statement Addendum

Institutional Dialogue Between the United States and India.

1. During the visit of President Clinton to Delhi in March 2000, President Clinton and Prime Minister Vajpayee agreed as part of their vision for the future relationship that a regular, wide-ranging dialogue is important for achieving the goal of establishing closer and multifaceted relations between India and the United States and for the two countries to work jointly for promotion of peace and prosperity in the 21st century. The two leaders agreed on a number of steps to intensify and institutionalize the dialogue between India and Untied States.
2. The President of the Untied States and Prime Minister of India will hold regular bilateral "Summits" in alternating capitals or elsewhere,

including on the occasions of multilateral meetings, to review bilateral relations and consult on international developments and issues. They will remain in frequent contact by telephone and through letters.

3. The two countries will also hold an Annual Foreign Policy Dialogue at the level of the Secretary of State of the United States and External Affairs Minister of India. This dialogue will be broad-based and touch upon all aspects of US-India relations, including considering the work of other groups as appropriate.
4. The two countries also consider the ongoing dialogue on security and nonproliferation between the Deputy Secretary of State of the United States and External Affairs Minister of India important for improving mutual understanding on bilateral, regional and international security matters. They agreed that this dialogue should continue and take place semi-annually or as often as considered desirable by both sides. The principals of this dialogue will establish Expert Groups on specific issues as considered desirable and appropriate.
5. Foreign office consultations between the Under Secretary of State for Political Affairs of the United States and Foreign Secretary of India will continue. The two leaders believe that close cooperation between the two countries is a factor of stability in the politically and culturally diverse and rapidly transforming Asia. A dialogue on Asian security will also be conducted as part of the Foreign Office consultations. The two sides will also stay in close touch and consult on international democracy initiatives.
6. The two leaders consider combating international terrorism as one of the most important global

challenges. They expressed satisfaction at the establishment of the Joint Working Group on counter-terrorism and its productive first meeting in February 2000. They agree that the Joint Working Group should continue to meet regularly and become an effective mechanism for the two countries to share information and intensify their cooperation in combating terrorism.

7 (a) The two leaders see an enormous potential for enhancement of economic and business relations between the two countries in the knowledge age. They decided to institutionalize bilateral economic dialogue. They will keep themselves informed and follow developments in the bilateral economic dialogue closely through a high-level coordinating group. The coordinating group will be led on the US side by the White House with the support of the State Department, and on the Indian side by the Prime Minister's Office with the support of the Ministry of External Affairs.

(b) The coordinating group will develop a common economic agenda for and undertake preparations for the Heads of Government meetings. With broad inter-agency and inter-ministerial representations at senior official levels, it would convene regularly to facilitate close coordination on the various issues raised in the ministerial dialogues and ensure that discussions therein complement and reinforce broad economic and foreign policy objectives, including the deepening of bilateral cooperation on high technology and information technology issues.

(c) The US-India Financial and Economic Forum: The US Secretary of Treasury and the Indian

Minister of Finance will host a forum on finance and investment issues, macro-economic policy and international economic developments at regular intervals. Their meetings at the ministerial level would be supplemented by sub-cabinet meetings and involve, as appropriate, the participation of the Securities and Exchange Commission, Federal Reserve, Council of Economic Advisers and other officials of the US Government and the Securities and the Exchange Board of India, the Reserve Bank of India, and other officials of the Government of India.

(d) The US-India commercial dialogue: The US Secretary of Commerce and Minister of Commerce and Industry of India will lead a dialogue to deepen ties between the Indian and American business communities. The dialogue will encompass regular government-to-government meetings to be held in conjunction with private sector meetings. Its aim will be to (a) facilitate trade and (b) maximize investment opportunities across a broad range of economic sectors, including information technology, infrastructure biotechnology and services. Participation will include, as appropriate, representatives of other cabinet agencies and ministries on both sides. Close contact will be maintained with business associations and activities will be planned with the benefit of such private sector input, including the establishment of subcommittees to pursue specific projects or sectoral issues of mutual interest.

(e) The US-India Working Group on Trade: The United States Trade Representative and the Ministry of Commerce and other concerned

Ministries/Departments of the Government of India will engage in regular discussion to enhance cooperation on trade policy. As appropriate, individual trade issues could be examined in greater depth with the participation of other agencies with corresponding responsibilities and through creation of sub-groups. The group will serve as a locus of consultation on a broad range of trade-related issues, including those pertaining to the World Trade Organization. The group will receive inputs from the private sector (including trade policy issues identified in the US-India Commercial Dialogue) as appropriate.

8. The two leaders consider cooperation between the two countries in energy and environment an important part of their vision for the future. They have agreed to setup a joint consultative group on Clean Energy and Environment. The group will hold periodic ministerial/high level meetings as desirable and appropriate and will lay emphasis on collaborative projects, developing and deploying clean energy technologies, public and private sector investment and cooperation, and climate change and other environment issues. The Co-conveners of the group will be the Department of State of the United States and the Ministry of External Affairs of India.

9. The two leaders believe that the strong scientific resources of the two countries provide excellent opportunities for scientific collaboration between them. They agree to setup a US-India Science and Technology Forum. The forum shall promote research and development, the transfer of technology, the creation of a comprehensive electronic reference source for US-India science

and technology cooperation, and the electronic exchange and dissemination of information on the US-India science and technology cooperation, and other programs consistent with the previous practices of the US-India Foundation.

10. Institutional dialogue in other areas will be considered as mutually agreed[24]. These were the institutional dialogue between the United States and India.

The Bush administration had said, "We continue to pursue a strategy that expands and strengthens market economies around the world". The Clinton administration's line on this was not much different from this. As was articulated a number of times, the priorities of the administration included: "encouraging economic reform and obtaining greater access for the US trade and investment"[25]. In that scenario, when the Indian economic reform was launched, it had at least a tenuous linkage to the American agenda with which a strong section of the Indian policy-making / intelligentsia was in complete agreement.

Another focus of the Clinton administration were nuclear non-proliferation and enforcement of human rights. The major plank of the US initiative was the Nuclear Non-proliferation Treaty (NPT). The US strategists wanted the NPT to be the kernel of all nonproliferation action. On the top of the US agenda was the task of making all those truant countries - who were yet to sign the treaty - signatories to the NPT. The other aim was to stop technology proliferation by signatories. For that, Washington devised various hard ways of rapping on their knuckles.

To achieve these objectives, the Americans produced a two-tiered plan for diplomatic arm-twisting. On one level, the American government agencies began to take a tough line with the non-signatory countries, on another level, Washington made Britain, France, Germany and Japan do the same on their respective bilateral levels.

The issue of human rights, on the other hand, was less fraught with international real politics. While initially it was born as a stick to beat the USA's political adversaries with, after the Cold War ended, it became more a tool to tackle the ethnic strifes and to extend Western liberal democratic values.

But ironically this American policy juggernaut got stalled in South Asia, a region which otherwise figured in the lowest rungs of the American priority areas. Problems cropped up with India when the Americans began exerting pressure on the country for signing the NPT. Initially, the Indian policy-makers with their erroneous judgment of the Post-Cold War and the post-Afghan War South Asia, had thought that they could negotiate with the Americans on nuclear issue. So while they were unwilling to give up the country's nuclear option, they veered around the idea of accepting some international control on the Indian programme through a process of, first, an international acceptance of the Indian right to possess nuclear weapons and then, an Indian agreement with the international control regime enshrined in the NPT.

But this grand plan fell through when the Americans decided to balance this view with Pakistan's wishes of continuing with its own nuclear weapons programme[26]. Islamabad's argument was at first based on its sense of regional insecurity stemming from the Indian conventional military superiority. But when this argument failed to cut much ice with the international community it decided to play on the American fear psychosis of getting embroiled in a South Asian war. Pakistan projected the Kashmir problem as having the potential for blowing up into a shooting war with nuclear ramifications. This cynical ploy was best manifested by the statement of Pakistan's Foreign Minister, Assef Ali, after the expected failure of the Indo-Pak Foreign Secretaries meeting in Islamabad. Ali chose this moment to articulate that the Kashmir problem could result in a nuclear exchange between the two countries.

So once this linkage of Kashmir with the nuclear issue was established, the Americans at the beginning decided to bring around the still pliant Indian policy-makers to sign the NPT by creating pressure from below through their other policy formulation, human rights. Hence, one saw the activism of Amnesty International and other organizations which castigated the Indian Government for the actions of the security forces in controlling separatism in the Kashmir valley. Till the time India decided, though belatedly, to highlight the Pak hand in training and logistically supporting these forces of terrorism which perpetrated their ghastly crimes on the unarmed populace, the human rights organizations were far too taken in with their spotlight on security forces' actions.

While this was the status of the American government till about the middle of 1993, it went through a radical shift after the Clinton administration completed its task of putting its own personnel in the key areas of the State and Defence Departments. These new personnel, unaccustomed to the travails of governance, decided to shape the destiny of this part of the world in a way that best suited the US's long-term aspirations. Wishing to gain lasting control on the potentially volatile Central Asian region, they suddenly began viewing the spectre of an independent Kashmir (or under Pakistan's effective control) as a plausible foreign policy gambit. So when the US Assistant Secretary of State, Robin Raphael, called the Instrument of Accession (through which Kashmir became an inalienable part of India) a relic of the past, she did not have Kashmir's or even the subcontinent's best interests in mind. Rather, she was articulating the American wish - list on the Kashmir issue. The only salutary effect it had was on the Indian policy-makers who finally had to shed their naivete. As if to firmly drive the point home the Americans also made it known that they planned to override the Pressler Amendment which legislated the requirement of Presidential certification of Pakistan's nuclear status for continued aid flow to the county. But in the process, the Americans by showing their hand a little too soon, again delinked the nuclear issue from the highly emotive Kashmir tangle. This again provided another opportunity to both India and the USA to begin their dialogue with a clean slate[27].

It is averred at the outset that the nuclear and missile, or WMD (Weapons of Mass Destruction) issue will continue to remain the central difference between India and the US and its management will determine the degree of realization of the joint vision statement released during the Clinton visit[28]. This centrality was more than that reiterated by Madeleine Albright, the US Secretary of State well before the visit when she cautioned: "We do regard (WMD) proliferation - any where - as our Number One Security concern. And for this reason, we must accept that significant progress in this area is necessary, before India and the United States can realize fully the vast potential of our relationship[29].

The nuclear issue came up sharply on the eve of the Clinton visit when a number of western commentators and analysts highlighted the volatile situation in the subcontinent. Kashmir was seen as the perennial flash point and concern expressed about the high probability of a nuclear exchange between India and Pakistan - unless the Clinton healing touch was applied. A random sampling of headlines and comments were "Nuclear War Between India and Pakistan is a Real Possibility" warned the Washington Post and the author opined "Experts believe existing safeguards are inadequate to prevent events from escalating rapidly to a nuclear exchange on the Asian subcontinent"[30]. This perception was further reinforced by Mr. Clinton's remark on the eve of his departure to Delhi. He described South Asia and especially the Line of Control bordering Kashmir as "the most dangerous place in the world right now"[31].

Even as the nuclear issue bobbed up and down in public articulation, the overall objectives of the Clinton visit, were spelt out by Mr. Karl Inderfurth, the Assistant Secretary of State for South Asian Affairs. The focus and thrust of the US-India relations was not predicated on a single issue. Emphasis was laid on the fact that the US was seeking "a broad, constructive engagement with India based on broadly conceived US interests[32].

The vision statement embeds the nuclear issue in a much larger framework that highlights the many potential correspondences and convergence that can bind the two states and says: "We will seek to narrow our differences and increase mutual understanding on non-proliferation and security issues. This will help us to realize the full potential of Indo-US relations and contribute significantly to regional and global security[33].

Prime Minister Mr. Vajpayee noted: "President Clinton and I had a frank discussion on the issues of disarmament and nonproliferation of weapons of mass destruction. The dialogue which is in progress between our countries on these issues has enhanced the mutual understanding of our respective concerns. I have explained to President Clinton the reasons that compel us to maintain a minimum nuclear deterrent. I have reiterated our firm commitment not to conduct further nuclear explosive tests, not to engage in a nuclear arms race and not to be the first to use nuclear weapons against any country"[34].

These positions on disarmament and the Indian

deterrent were also reflected in the address of the Indian President Mr. K.R. Narayanan who noted inter alia: "We are publicly committed to the abolition of nuclear weapons together with other nuclear powers who possess them in awesome stockpiles capable of destroying the world many times over. India does not threaten any other country and will not engage in an arms race, but India will maintain a minimum credible nuclear deterrent – no more, no less – for her own security". The Indian President added: "We continue to be anxious to work with the USA to prevent the spread of weapons of mass destruction and to promote a goal of a world free of weapons of mass destruction. On this historic, auspicious occasion of your visit to India Mr. President, let us appeal to the world to take steps, concrete and substantive, towards nuclear disarmament along with nonproliferation, so that we do not consolidate the existing inequalities and sanctify the possession of nuclear weapons in the armories of the nations"[35].

There were reasons why Indian Prime Minister declared to maintain a minimum nuclear deterrent. One is the China factor which became nuclear in 1964. Indians are very much apprehensive of a nuclear threat from China. Another is the China-Pakistan nexus. China supplied M-9 and M-11 missiles to Pakistan in the early 1990s with ranges varying from 60 to 300 miles. But this fact was ignored by the US. Otherwise the US would have imposed sanctions on china for the violation of the MTCR strictures.

This matter came up for discussion in the US Senate on March 22, 2000 (the day Mr. Clinton addressed Indian Parliamentarians) and the Director of the US CIA Mr. George Tenet in his testimony revealed that his agency – the CIA – reported to the Clinton administration the delivery of Chinese M-11 missiles to Pakistan several years ago, but the Government chose not to admit it publicly for political reasons.

India and the US have many potential strategic convergences that span the political, economic, military, technological, societal and environmental strands of the collective Post-Cold War security endeavour. India's experience as a large, diverse, secular, pluralistic state with a low technical resource base is the ultimate laboratory in which many hypotheses on modernity, globalization and free-market can be tested which was reflected in the joint Indo-US vision statement and in the Clinton speeches.

Some of the areas in which the two countries are well placed to launch a new era of cooperation are science and technology, energy, environment, infrastructure development and information technology. Apart from the two governments, cooperation is also being intensified between professional societies and business and trade representatives of the two countries[36].

President Clinton and India's Prime Minister Atal Bihari Vajpayee on March 21, 2000 resolved to "create a closer and qualitatively new relationship between the United States and India".

"We are two of the world's largest democracies. We are nations forged from many traditions and faiths, proving year after year that diversity is our strength. From vastly different origins and experiences, we have come to the same conclusions: that freedom and democracy are the strongest bases for both peace and prosperity, and that they are universal aspirations, constrained neither by culture nor levels of economic development", the two leaders said in a joint statement".

The leaders pledged to "deepen the Indian – American partnership in tangible ways, always seeking to reconcile our differences through dialogue and engagement, always seizing opportunities to advance the countless interests we have in common".

As a first step President Clinton invited Prime Minister Vajpayee to visit Washington at a mutually convenient opportunity, and the Prime Minister accepted that invitation, according to the statement.

The joint US-India statement declared: India and the United States share a commitment to reducing and ultimately eliminating nuclear weapons, but we have not always agreed on how to reach this common goal. The United States believes India should forgo nuclear weapons. India believes that it needs to maintain a credible minimum nuclear deterrent in keeping with its own assessment of its security needs. Nonetheless, India and the US are prepared to work together to prevent the proliferation of nuclear weapons and their means of delivery. To this end, we will persist with and build upon the productive bilateral dialogue already underway.

We reaffirm our respective voluntary commitments to forgo further nuclear explosive tests. We will work together and with others for an early commencement of negotiations on a treaty to end the production of fissile materials for nuclear weapons. We have both shown strong commitments to export controls and will continue to strengthen them. We will work together to prevent the spread of dangerous technologies. We will pursue our security needs in a restrained and responsible manner, and will not engage in nuclear and missile arms races. We will seek to narrow our differences and increase mutual understanding on nonproliferation and security issues. This will help us to realize the full potential of Indo-US relations and contribute significantly to regional and global security.

The true measure of our strength lies in the ability of our people to shape their destiny and to realize their aspirations for a better life. That is why the United States and India are and will be allies in the case of democracy.

We will share our experience in nurturing and strengthening democratic institutions and world over and fighting the challenge to democratic order from forces such as terrorism.

During the Presidentship of Bill Clinton the United States applauds India's success in opening its economy, its achievements in science and technology, its commitment to a new wave of economic expansion and reform and its determination to bring the benefits of economic growth to all its people. Our nations pledge to reduce impediments to bilateral trade and investment and to expand commerce between us, especially in the emerging knowledge-based industries and high-technology areas.

As leaders in the forefront of the new high-technology economy, we recognize that countries can achieve robust economic growth while protecting the environment and taking action to combat climate change. We will do our part to meet the global environmental challenges, including climate change and the impacts of air and water pollution on human health.

We also pledge a common effort to battle the infectious diseases that kill people and retard progress in so many countries. India is at the forefront of the global effort that has brought us to the threshold of the eradication of polio. With leadership, joint research and application of modern science, we can and will do the same for the leading killers of our time, including AIDS, malaria and tuberculosis.

Our partnership is not an end in itself, but a means to all these ends. And it is reinforced by the ties of scholarship, commerce and increasingly of kinship among our people. The industry enterprise and cultural contributions of Americans of Indian heritage have enriched and enlivened both our societies.

Today, we pledge to deepen the Indian-American

partnership in tangible ways, always seeking to reconcile our differences through dialogue and engagement, always seizing opportunities to advance the countless interests we have in common[37].

In 1997 50th Anniversary of India's Independence was celebrated. On this occasion President Clinton in a message said that India and the US must work more closely than ever in a way that would benefit the two of the world's greatest democracies. He said that both countries must re-double efforts to strengthen peace, stability and democracy in South Asia and around the world.

During the tenure of Bill Clinton, the United States became India's largest trading partner. Two-way trade in 1996 totalled Rs.34932 crores and is set to cross Rs.36820 crores for the first time in 1997. This is an increase of over 70% since 1991. Indian exports amounted to Rs.22713 crores as against imports of Rs.12219 crores. The level of bilateral trade is still only a very small fraction, less than 1% of USA's global trade. While the US exports to India account for nearly 12% of India's non-oil imports and the US is the destination of 18.9% of Indian exports.

The US is the single largest foreign investor in India accounting for around a quarter of all direct investment approved from 1991-1996 (December). The total FDI approved from the US during this period is Rs.28720 crores; the actual inflow till December 1995 was around Rs.1895 crores. The US investment covers a wide range of sectors including Power, Chemicals, Electricals, Electronics, Mechanical Engineering and Industrial Machinery making the US our most important source of foreign technology. Over 1500 collaborations with the US companies had been approved till 1996. Foreign institutional investors from the USA are active in portfolio investments.

While differences in certain areas such as the patent protection issue, access to textile markets, India's import regime, internal trade statutes of the US (Super 301, Special 301 etc.) and the US restrictions pertaining movement of skilled labour (HI-B visas) persist, the climate for bilateral trade is improving and businessmen from both countries are very optimistic about longer-term opportunities. Cooperation in infrastructure projects, power, telecommunications, information technology, food processing and even consumer goods is the focus of such business interests. The benefit of tapping each other's markets has become very apparent with greater flow of information following India's liberalization of trade and investment. The USA's interest in India stems from India's investment opportunities and the large market for the US products which are facing increasing competition in global markets. For India, the US remains the most promising source for both foreign direct investment and transfer of technology.

Defence relations were marked by enhanced interaction between the defenec establishments in keeping with the agreed Action Plan. Service-to-Service contacts continued, and efforts continued to identify possible areas for future joint ventures in the field of defence research and defence production.

While an amendment to existing US Law through Harkin-Warner Amendment, enabled resumption of limited economic aid to Pakistan, the US has reaffirmed its stand against delivery of the F-16 aircraft to Pakistan.

Demonstrating overwhelming support for India, the US Congress, on September 4, rejected by a 342-82 margin an amendment moved by Republican Congressman Dan Burton to cut development aid to India because of its alleged human rights abuses. The House members strongly endorsed the improvement in India's human rights record.

India and the USA signed an Extradition Treaty in Washington on June 25, 1997. The Treaty was signed by the Minister of State for External Affairs, Sri Saleem Iqbal Shervani and Strobe Talbott, the US Deputy Secretary of State.

Under a Congressional mandate, the US State Department for the first time designated 30 groups including Harkut-ul-Ansar (HUA), a Pakistan based organization, and the LTTE as foreign terrorist organizations, making it illegal to provide funds for them and denying their members or representatives visas to enter the United States.

The government of India and the US signed an agreement on 1st November 1997 to increase the maximum length of visas for ten years for tourists, temporary visitors and business visas. An Investment Agreement was also signed during the visit of US Secretary of State.

The US administration imposed export curbs on the Bhaba Atomic Research Centre, Indira Gandhi Centre for Atomic Research and Indian Rare Earths Limited for their alleged involvement in weapons of mass destruction or missiles used for delivery. The US had earlier taken similar action against Bharat Electronics Ltd. of Bangalore. Subsequently, the Federal Department removed sanctions against seven of the nine Bharat Electronic Ltd. units. Two BEL units in Hyderabad and Bangalore still continue to be under scrutiny[38].

References

1. David C. Hendrickson, "The Recovery of Internationalism", Foreign Affairs, Vol.73, Sept.-October 1994, pp.26-43.
2. Times of India, February 2, 1994.
3. Hindu, February 6, 1994.
4. New York Times, April 12, 1995, p.1, and Larry Pressler,

"Bhutto came, she saw, she conquered", *Ibid*, April 16, 1995, p.11.

5. Nuclear Proliferation News, September 8, 1995, p.20.
6. Testimony of Professor Stephen Philip Cohen before the Senate Committee on Foreign Relations. Subcommittee on New Eastern and South Asian Studies, September 14, 1995, p.5.
7. The Hindu, December 16, 1995, p.5.
8. New York Times, December 15, 1995.
9. Indian Express, January 14, 1995, p.9.
10. Indian Express, December 2, 1995, p.8.
11. Indian Express, December 8, 1995, p.1.
12. Vinay Kumar Malhotra, "Prime Minister Rao's visit to the United States and Indo-US Relatins", in V.K. Malhotra ed. *Indo-US Relations in the Nineties* (Anmol Publications Pvt. Ltd.), pp.139-144.
13. Berta Gomez, "Forging a Stronger Partnership", Span, New Delhi, June 1994, p.24.
14. Dilip Bobb, "Rao's US Visit - A Quiet Triumph", India Today, June 15, 1994, p.47.
15. Quoted in Supra n.22, pp.24 & 27.
16. Deccan Herald, 30 March 2000.
17. Telegraph (Kolkata), 23 March 2000.
18. *Ibid*.
19. *Ibid*.
20. *Ibid*.
21. *Ibid*.
22. Deccan Herald, 26 March 2000.
23. Hindu, Madras, 2 April, 2000.
24. Span, May/June 2000, p.13.
25. Testimony before the House of Foreign Affairs sub-committee on Asia and the Pacific of John Malott, Interim Director, Bureau of South Asian Affairs on 28 April 1993, USIS, New Delhi.
26. In this context, see Gen. Aslem Beg's article in The Nation on 13 December 1993, on Pakistan's Nuclear Programme. Also see A.Q. Khan on Pakistan's Bomb, Sreedhar Ed. (New

Delhi ABC, 1987) and Paksitani Bomb: A documentary Study (New Delhi, ABC).

27. Pinki Bhattacharya, "Indo-US relations", Strategic Analysis, April 1994, Vol. XVII, No.1, pp.79-88.
28. Vision Statement is the term used to describe the statement entitled, "India-US Relations: A Vision for the 21st century", signed by US President Mr. Bill Clinton and the Indian Prime Minister Mr. Atal Behari Vajpayee in New Delhi on March 21, 2000. This test is taken from Hindu (New Delhi), March 22, 2000, p.15.
29. Text of Ms Albright's address to the Asia Society, New York, WF, March 15, 2000, p.17.
30. "Nuclear War Between India and Pakistan is a Real Possibility" by Paul D. Taylor in the Washington Post; reprinted International Herald Tribune, March 16, 2000.
31. "Clinton Finds LOC most dangerous place in the World" by Ramesh Chandran in Times of India (New Delhi), March 11, 2000, p.1.
32. Official Text, Public Affairs Office of the US Embassy, New Delhi, "Inderfurth Outlines President's Goals for South Asian Visit", March 10, 2000, p.1.
33. *Ibid.*
34. WF, March 22, 2000, p.16.
35. President Clinton's visit to India, speech by the President Sri K.R. Narayanan at Banquet in Honour of the H.E. Mr. William J. Clinton, President of the United States of America. *Strategic Digest*, Vol.XXX, No.4, April 2000, pp.391.
36. India-US Political Relations, Embassy of India, Washington D.C.
37. White House text of the joint US-India Statement, March 21, 2000.
38. Ministry of External Affairs Report on USA, 1997-98, pp.78-80.

8

Other Issues and Role of Big Powers and the US-India Relations

Like the Pakistan element in Indo-American relations, China has also figured as one of the important determinants of the nature of political relations between the two countries. But unlike Pakistan, the China factor is much more complex. When the Trueman Administration adopted the policy of "Containment of Communism", it was expected that India, a democratic country, would automatically support the US. But the Indian views of Communism and the method of dealing with it were substantially different from the ones championed by the US. The emergence of Communist China in 1949, the outbreak of the Korean war in 1950, the formation of the Sino-Soviet alliance and the Indo-China crisis after the French defeat at Dien Bien Phu in 1954 did not pave the way for any Indo-US strategic understanding on the major geo-political events in Asia.

The US-India relations were affected by the Cold War and consequent Soviet equation. It is a well-known fact that unfortunately India was divided to form

Pakistan on religious grounds. This religious foundation of Pakistan and India's continued adherence to secular principles made Pakistan to see India as the only threat to its security and survival. Thus, Pakistan joined hands with the US in its global efforts to contain Communism by promoting military alliances. But after the Sino-Indian war of 1962, Pakistan became friendly with China. It is not that Americans were altogether unaware of the fact that Pakistan had joined the American-led alliance system to sub-serve her own regional Cold War with India. This was very well summed up by the then US Ambassador to Pakistan, Ronald I. Spiers when he addressed the Karachi Institute of Foreign Relations on April 20, 1982 and said:

"Most of our past problems, I think have stemmed from a different view about the purpose and open-endedness of the security ties which have existed between the US since the early 1950s. A principal focus of Pakistani concern has been India, the principal concern of the US ... is the potential threat and pressures from the Soviet Union"[1].

This was, however, overlooked by the US policy makers in the broader global context in the 1970s of containing the Soviet Union. By the time of Bangladesh war in 1971, the US-Pakistan-China axis on the one hand and India-Soviet Union axis on the other were very clear. This was also a pattern in the 1980s over the US confrontation with the Soviet Union over its invasion of Afghanistan. Mrs. Indira Gandhi, the then Prime Minister of India, neither condemned nor condoned the Soviet invasion of Afghanistan. But Reagan began his perception of India in simplistic terms – those not with the US are against the US. But by mid-1980s he changed his view of India. In an interview with Derek Davis and Nayan Chanda, Reagen said: "Mrs. Gnadhi has said that India is not pro or anti any other country, but instead is pro-India. We accept that position[2].

The end of Cold War has brought about the demise of the triangular balance of power. As a consequence, the regional pentagonal balance of power has also broken down. What has emerged in the place of bipolar world of the past is the unipolar world of the present only in terms of military predominance and the will power to commit the coercive force to achieve global foreign policy goals. But in economic and political terms actually the world can be described as multipolar.

Another important change that has occurred as a result of the end of the Cold War is the absence of a priori commitment of a security guarantee on the basis of bloc membership and also a priori threat perception arising from respective bloc membership. In this sense, with the exception of nations aligned with the US like NATO, Japan and South Korea, the world has become genuinely non-aligned in the truest sense of the term. Every nation is free to decide its policy vis-à-vis others in terms of its own national interest.

Major changes in the US-India relations came in the Bush administration in March 1990 when it clearly and categorically stated that it did not believe that old US resolutions are any longer relevant to resolve Kashmir question and a solution to the problem has to be found within the Shimla agreement of 1972[3]. This was further clarified to suggest that the US does not support any more the idea of a plebiscite in Kashmir.

It is also a significant gesture from the US that it is committed to the maintenance of territorial integrity of India. This was significant as India faced Low Intensity Conflict (LIC) promoted by Pakistan in India's north western province of Punjab and in the north Jammu and Kashmir. These states, on the grounds of linguistic and religious subnationalism are demanding secessation from the Indian union. These separatist movements are founded, equipped and supported from across the borders. The US policy makers and legislators joined together in asking Pakistan not to encourage international terrorism.

However, in the security arena the greater, though remote threat to India is from the Peoples Republic of China. Though both the countries have moved a long way from confrontationist stands of the 1970s to the uncertainties of the 1980s to develop closer bilateral relations, in the 1990s, but there remain four main Indian security concerns. First and foremost is the fact that China is a full-fledged nuclear power with all weapon systems and delivery systems. Though China recently signed the NPT as a nuclear power, it hardly had any effect on her nuclear behaviour. For instance, when Indian President was on Chinese soil in May 1992 Beijing exploded a 1000 kiloton nuclear device[4]. What does it demonstrate? China probably wants to show that her signing the NPT does not prevent her from developing further sophisticated weapon systems. Further, she would like to sit in the five-nation conference on nuclear question affecting South Asia whenever it is held, as an equal to the two other nuclear powers – US and Russia[5].

Second, there is the unresolved border dispute between India and China. Though both have decided to place the question in the back burner, Indian security concerns cannot vanish and normal bilateral relations cannot be established till the border problem is resolved. So long it is not resolved, there is so much common interest between Pakistan and China to make a common case against India and that India cannot relax her security concerns.

Third, there is the question of maintaining Tibetan autonomy and the question of violation of human rights. Though the Government of India has conceded Tibet as part of China, Indians are still not satisfied with China's treatment of Tibetans.

There is also a new dimension to China's foreign

relations in the Post-Cold War period in the context of the democratic movement worldwide. This is her close cooperation with the military dictatorship in Myanmar. China has been the main supplier of arms and equipment to the military government along with Pakistan to suppress pro-democracy movement. According to Ms. Than Than Nu, "China alone has supplied two billion dollars worth of arms in exchange for essential commodities. There is a Chinese military advisor in Myanmar where they are building a naval base for China on the southern most tip of the country"[6]. India cannot ignore its security implications for her. The remnants of communism and military dictatorship cooperating with one another is not only a sign of decay in the political thought of communism but it is also a direct security threat to India. The US as a supporter of democratic movement in Myanmar has also not taken kindly to this development.

The end of Cold War and disintegration of the Soviet Union also coincided with India liberalizing her economy by removing practically all socialistic controls and inviting foreign investment. This can be said to be more than mere coincidence because, with Gorbachev reforms in the Soviet Union, India had to look for newer markets to sell her goods and newer suppliers of defence equipment.

The US has been the largest trading partner of India. Under the new economic liberalization, India looks for greater participation by American companies in Indian economic development. This is something which the US was also looking forward because of her own domestic economic problems. It is a strange marriage between an old capitalist system with a shy and young aspiring capitalist state of India. The US economy finds it difficult to compete with industrialized economies like those of Germany and Japan. Hence, the US looks to newly industrialized economies of countries like Korea,

Taiwan, Singapore, Malaysia and India[7].

With the end of the Cold War, in a long-term perspective, the major development in the world is a new found impetus to democracy everywhere in the world. In the absence of Soviet equation coming in the way of better Indo-US relations, democracy itself becomes a natural bond between India and the US. Hence, wherever national interests of the two do not conflict and promotion of democracy worldwide could become a common global interest of the two.

We have discussed that there is improvement in the US-India relations after the disintegration of the Soviet Union. Have these changes in Indo-US relations affected in any significant way the US relations with the Peoples Republic of China? The answer seems to be affirmative. With the improvement in the US-India relations, there is an apparent cooling of relations between the US and China. The main stimulus in the 1970s for the US to be drawn closer to China was its own perception of its decline as a military power. Many American intellectuals, particularly the right-wingers thought that the US had moved from her nuclear position of superiority vis-à-vis the Soviet Union to parity in the early 1970s and likely to move to inferiority in the 1980s if the corrective steps were not taken.

The corrective steps envisaged by the US then were three: first, end of Vietnam war and secondly, signing the SALT agreement to limit the growth of nuclear weapons with the Soviet Union. Thirdly, to succeed in the above two goals and maintain a reasonable balance of power. The US saw China as a counterweight to check the growing power of the Soviet Union[8]. Professor Zigniew Brezinski described this phenomenon as two and one-half balance of power[9]. In sum, China was a factor essentially in terms of geopolitical strategy of the US vis-à-vis the Soviet Union in Cold War, as the Soviet Union was a partner of the

US in the hot war against Nazi Germany in the 1940s. In the absence of Cold War, there is nothing common between the US and China today as there was nothing common between the United States and Soviet Union during the World War II in the sense of a democratic bond.

The US has already had a status of the largest trading partner of India. In the new scenario India and the US are likely to emerge as new economic partners. With a stable working democracy in India, closer Indo-US relations are likely to liberate the US from any over dependence on China for geopolitical strategic purposes. Hence, the American pressure on China to move towards democracy is bound to be vigorous.

Another area where there is growing uneasiness in the US-China relations is the latter's human rights record. The Chinese government is widely perceived to have violated basic human rights of freedom of speech, life, and information etc. President Bush had stated that freedom of expression, religion, Press and association remain tightly constrained. In September 1992, the Chinese authorities arrested first pro-democracy leader Mr. Shen Tong who returned to China from exile.

The major problem today between the US and China is in their security perceptions. The United States as a number one power will be unable to maintain its status and influence without China's cooperation in accepting the US military preponderance of power without a challenge. Pakistan exploded the atomic bomb by China's help. Syria is also getting help from China in her nuclear programme. China has also provided medium range missiles technology to Syria and Pakistan. Not only that China is continuing its nuclear weapons programme by signing the NPT. This is a major challenge to the US because today the USA is the chief spokesman for nuclear nonproliferation. The USA is very much attracted towards India because India has abided by the rules of NPT without signing it. India is not transferring her nuclear technology to any third country. India is also committed to no first use of nuclear weapons. India has also declared and made an agreement with Pakistan not to attack each other's nuclear installations.

China's economy is growing very fast. The US knows China's ambition to emerge as a super power and even challenge the US power in the region very well. This might lead to a renewal of a Cold War with a difference of China replacing the Soviet Union. The Cold War is naturally being extended to economic relations. China had denied to the US free access to the Chinese markets. The US threatened to impose punitive tariffs on Chinese exports worth $3.9 billion. China in turn threatened to retaliate against $4 billion worth US exports.

So since the end of the Cold War, the US-India relations have improved and they are on an upward trend. One very important development since 1991 is the growing cooperation in defence areas between the two countries. This had been signalled through their cooperation during the Gulf war when India permitted the US Air Force Planes to refuel in Bombay. In July 1992 also for the first time the two navies held joint naval exercises in the Indian Ocean. There are also continuous service to service contacts through seminars and visits by high ranking officials.

On the other hand, relations between the US and China have cooled since June 1989 Tiananman Square massacre of pro-democracy students. With the end of Cold War, the triangular diplomacy that the US practised with the help of China against the Soviet Union has lost its raisond'etre.

It is not that there are no problems in the US-India relations. India and the United States have divergent viewpoints on nuclear non-proliferation and the NPT. The US wants India to sign the NPT. India has been insisting on a time bound global nuclear disarmament. There are other problems like US efforts to deny India cryogenic engines for her space programme by pressurizing Russia not to supply them by implementing the treaty obligations.

But the US and India will have to manage their bilateral relations with fine tuning by keeping in mind that in the long run democratic bond is far more durable than a relationship between a pluralistic democracy and a state governed by one party. The continued cooperation between the US and India will serve the needs of America to maintain peace in the region[10].

An interesting turnaround has taken place as far as the China factor in Indo-US relations is concerned. In the 1950s, India's policy of engaging China displeased the United States. In the 1960s, when India approached the US for assistance during the Sino-Indian war, the US military assistance came and was appreciated but it was of no use in affecting the outcome of the war. In the 1970s and the 1980s, the US strategic ties with China became a great strategic challenge for India. And subsequently in the post Cold War environment, what has come about is the widespread impression in India that the US neither appreciates nor cares about India's concerns over the rising nuclear and conventional capability of China and that while seeking to attain its regional non-proliferation goal in South Asia, confines the issue basically to India and Pakistan alone. The US attitude towards China is rather intriguing for India. To cite an appropriate example, Defence Secretary William Perry during his visit to China in October 1994, reportedly said: "... the second challenge to regional security threat that I want to focus lies in South Asia. We seem to be on the brink of a nuclear weapons race on the subcontinent, where relations between India and

Pakistan have been tense for years ... it's essential that countries with influence in South Asia should stop the potential arms race before it gathers momentum. The recent progress between the United States and China on missile technology and fissile material is a positive step in that direction. But we must do more if we want to prevent a South Asian arms race. Perry subsequently at a Press conference at the Freedom House in Washington said that non-proliferation in the region must also include China"[11].

No doubt, there is an increasing understanding in the US about the uncertainties and challenges posed by China. It is reflected in the writings of defence analysts as well as in government reports. A report prepared in the 1995 by the US Defence Department's Office of International Security Affairs made a candid remark that "China's military posture and development have a great impact on the expectations and behaviour of other states, in the region. Although China's leaders insist, their military build-up is defensive and commensurate with China's overall economic growth, others in the region can not be certain of China's intentions"[12]. Regrettably, the US understanding of the China factor has not been reflected in the US official steps to address the issue. Nor does Washington appreciate the steps taken by China's neighbours to meet the unforeseen challenges.

India is understandably not worried about a second Chinese invasion and is reasonably confident of its military capabilities to defend the country against a foreign attack. But the US attitude towards the issue is a cause of concern. As Jasjit Singh commented: "China has the most powerful military system in Asia. Although it may not match up to American military power in terms of quality and technology, we have to see its capabilities in terms of other Asian countries or its neighbours. It is modernizing rapidly both its conventional forces and its nuclear forces"[13].

Few are optimistic about Sino-American relations. Almost no one seems to envision the possibility of broad cooperation in the coming decades. As Washington and Beijing politically clash over issues such as human rights, Taiwan, Hong Kong, Tibet, arms transfer and proliferation matters, the US, at the same time, does not want to lose out to others in taking advantage of the economic opportunities offered by China. China's growing economy also poses a strategic challenge. As Robert S. Ross writes: "Japan remains the country with the world's largest trade surplus, and its economic system remains mostly impenetrable". Nonetheless, the openness of the world economy may well be facing an even greater challenge from China's emergence as an economic power. If China's economy continues to grow at current annual rates of 8 to 10 per cent, if it acquires advanced-technology capabilities, China's impact on the international economic system will dwarf that of Japan, even considering Japan's most influential period during the 1970s and 1980s. With favourable domestic economies of scale and a nearly unlimited supply of cheap labour, China could become a major export power capable of prevailing in the domestic markets of its economic competitors. If China simultaneously were to fail to offer opportunities for participation in its own domestic market, its policies could lead to destabilizing responses by all of the major economic powers. Ross and several others argue that China has to be made a member of the World Trade Organization (WTO) to make it behave on the basis of existing rules of international economy. Greg Mastel, Vice-President for policy planning and administration at the Economic Strategy Institute in Washington contends: "This view places political and security concerns above economic concerns. It has the ring of classic US Cold War foreign policy towards China for decades. Whether China becomes a member of the WTO or not, the US would not adopt a policy that would hamper its market access to China. The annual ritual over the extension of the Most Favoured Nation (MFN) status is an example of the US policy of 'economy first'. After all China "is the largest market in the world", remarked former US Secretary of Commerce Barbara H. Franklin, "for aircraft, for telephones, for construction equipment, for agricultural products and increasingly for consumer goods. The country needs virtually everything that we produce and sell". How an economically stronger China would behave politically remains a question mark. There is a possibility that China would behave like a hegemon. As James A. Baker III pointed out in an address to the Baker Institute Asia Society Conference in February 1996: "China, we should never forget, is East Asia's preeminent military power, with some three million individuals to under arms and with a significant nuclear weapons capability". Given these facts, it is vital that the United States and its allies maintain a military posture that would permit US to counter a possible Chinese bid for regional hegemony, however unlikely that might be. But the US remains militarily prepared to face a challenge from China. When China's military exercises threatened Taiwan in March-April 1996, the US did despatch its naval forces.

The Clinton administration's approach to dealing with China is "one of engagement and enlargement". It is not very different from his predecessor's who argued against isolating China. Warren Christopher, the US Secretary of State said in June 1996 that the US rejected the "counsel of those who seek to contain or isolate China. That course would harm our national interests, not protect them. Demonizing China is as dangerously misleading as romanticizing it". The Clinton administration has framed a policy of "comprehensive engagement" of China. Other countries, including India, are also in the process of working out their respective strategies to manage the rising power of China. Signing of an agreement of peace and tranquility along the border and institution of a host of confidence building measures (CBMS) are steps that indicate India's ways of engaging China.

An additional worry to New Delhi is the whole question of the US attitude to the evolving nuclear and missile collaboration between China and Pakistan. Had there been no Sino-Pakistan nuclear and missile cooperation and no biased US approach to Pakistan's nuclear weapon programme, India might have had less to complain about the US policy on non-proliferation. Two issues may be briefly discussed to understand the US attitude towards Sino-Pakistan nuclear and missile cooperation: (a) the supply of Chinese ring magnets to Pakistan and (b) the Sino-Pak M-11 deal.

Ring Magnets

Days after President Bill Clinton singed the Brown Amendment, the US media reported, citing the US intelligence sources, that China had supplied 5,000 ring magnets to Pakistan. It was on February 4, 1996, that reports appeared that China sold the ring magnets to the A.Q. Khan Research Laboratory in Kahuta in 1995. The ring magnets could enable Pakistan, according to the Nucleonic News, to double its capacity to enrich Uranium for weapon purposes. Sino-Pakistan cooperation in the field of nuclear technology had been going on for quite some time. In fact, the US sources repeatedly mentioned about the transfer of a nuclear weapon design by China to Pakistan in the early Eighties. But at that time China was outside the NPT. But after it became a party to the NPT in 1992, the legal implication of its nuclear cooperation with Pakistan no longer remained the same. The transfer of ring magnets constituted a clear violation of the NPT.

M-11 Missiles

In the midst of the controversy over the ring magnets and the debate on whether to impose sanctions, Washington made new allegations that Chinese M-11 missile parts were sold to Pakistan after US sanctions were lifted in 1994. Director John Holum of the US ACDA indicated that sanctions against China could be imposed under the Missile Technology Control of Regime (MTCR) if sales were confirmed. Close on the heels of the US decision not to impose sanctions against China over the ring magnets deal, on June 12, 1996, report in the Washington Times about Pakistan for the first time deploying a nuclear-capable Chinese supplied M-11 missile once again created sensation in the United States as well as in South Asia. The M-11 missiles, supplied by China to Pakistan, pose absolutely no security threat to the United States. Nor does Pakistan claimed nuclear capability. But Pakistan's efforts to acquire nuclear and missile capabilities have always been debated, discussed and criticized in the United States which in principle champions the cause of nonproliferation of WMD.

After weeks of confusing and sometimes conflicting signals about imposition of sanctions against China and Pakistan, the Clinton administration finally decided to go ahead with the implementation of the Brown Amendment and make shipments of weapons and military equipment to Pakistan.

The Clinton administration not only succeeded in its efforts to renew contact with Pakistan through the enactment of the Brown Amendment but also managed to implement the 1985 nuclear cooperation agreement with China. Both these efforts were made in the context of the changed circumstances of the Post-Cold War era. The Brown Amendment has enabled Washington to reestablish ties with Pakistan and redefine a role for that country in the US strategic calculus. The economic logic appears to have prompted the Clinton administration to seek implementation of the nuclear cooperation agreement with China. It would assist a beleaguered nuclear market in the US a great deal by enabling the American companies to tap the billions of dollars worth of Chinese market in the field.

Indo-US differences over proliferation issues would continue to be a feature in their bilateral relations in the 21st century. It is the US government which leads a crusade against nuclear and missile proliferation, and which has made India one of the target countries and simultaneously either condones or ignores the Sino-Pakistan nuclear and missile cooperation. Washington is following a policy of intense reengagement of China and constructive engagement of Pakistan.

However, China is going to be increasingly a major factor in Indo-American relations. And how India would deal with this factor is going to be a major challenge to Indian diplomacy. Pakistan, on the other hand, may increasingly become a marginal factor in India's foreign policy for two reasons. First, the way Pakistan has over-extended itself in Afghanistan and Kashmir and has invited in the process social instability, gun culture, drug addiction and economic chaos may lead to weakening of the Pakistan state to an extent where it would be little more than a nuisance along the border for India. Secondly, if Pakistan realizes its mistakes, mends its foreign policy ways, evolves into a resilient democracy India would welcome it.

China on the other hand, has been emerging as a super power in the making along the long stretch of Indian border. This super power would not have a global reach like the US, would be technologically backward in relation to the Western countries, would not be socially as stable as the US or West European nations or even Japan in view of its large population whose standard of living cannot be of world class in the foreseeable future despite the high economic growth rate.

Nonetheless this super power would be militarily more powerful than any of its neighbours. Its relations with its neighbours, which have an alliance relationship with the US or have much closer economic and other relations with the West, may not be very cordial. In fact, the relations between the US and China's neighbours may give rise to suspicions in Beijing. The US has good relationship with India. Economic relation between the US and India is increasing day by day. China's heavy-handed attitude towards some of its neighbours may irk Washington. China's nuclear and missile cooperation with some of the Asian countries may irk Washington much more. There are two clear examples available in this context. The renewal of the US-Japan Security Treaty has created suspicion in China of a possible anti-Chinese containment strategy of Washington. Notwithstanding the end of the Cold War, the strategy of containment has not vanished from the lexicon of international relations. The Chinese fear of a containment of their country through engagement may be psychological, but real to them. China's sale of technology and equipment related to weapons of mass destruction to Iran and Pakistan, on the other hand, causes concerns in Washington, particularly in the non-proliferation circuits. Issues related to Tibet, Taiwan, human rights, violation of intellectual property rights, unfair trade practices etc. are additional factors which contribute to political confrontation between Washington and Beijing.

China certainly has no global influence. But it has regional influence and it has been seeking to expand its influence in the region through various ways. The Clinton administration adopted the policy of comprehensive engagement of China and believed that this policy would assist in the evolution of China as a non-aggressive state that plays a constructive role in the region and elsewhere. There is thus a peculiar kind of Cold War already going on between China and the United States. This Cold War accepts China's economic reforms but targets the authoritarian state structure. This Cold War has not led to bloc or alliance politics and all the US allies are competing with one another to enter the Chinese market.

In the process, great bargaining has been taking place across the table and the compromise attitude of the US on certain issues, particularly the proliferation issues would only contribute to the growth of the Chinese economic and military power vis-à-vis its neighbours. India is adversely affected by this peculiar war and unless timely actions are taken, it would have the potential of considerably jeopardizing India's security interests[14].

Let us now examine the role of Russia. The USSR has been swept by historic changes that have created an enormous uncertainty about the future of its successor state Russia. When eleven of the republics at a summit at Mins on December 31, 1991 dissolved the former USSR and formed instead a Commonwealth of Independent States (CIS), it appeared as if a new Federation would come into being.

The CIS is, however, a group of states, not a nation. As a result, countries of Central Asia led by Kazakhstan have decided to create an alternative community. The visit of Boris Yeltsin to New Delhi removed a great deal of uncertainty. What is at stake is Russian credit in dollars worth 800 million for the purchase of military spares so vitally needed for the Indian defence industry, some 70 per cent of which is Russian in origin. India's defence Minister Sharad Pawar also visited Ukraine and sought help in procuring military spares. At the same time, strong ties have also been established with Kazakhstan. The market culture that Yeltsin has introduced into Russia has been such that India's prime adversaries, China and Pakistan, are also in the market for Russian and Ukrainian defence equipment. China was able to import weapons from Russia worth $497 million during the period 1987-91. After Yeltsin's visit to China, more deals were finalized beyond the 24 SU-27 aircraft.

Thus, India no longer enjoys a privileged relationship with Russia. Hence, the impact on India's security is likely to be quite adverse. If both its adversaries, China and Pakistan, were to procure Russian defence equipment for payment in foreign exchange or on barter terms as China is likely to, India must either look for alternative arrangements in Europe or aggressively seek credit arrangements with Russia at low interest rates (say 5 per cent). Unfortunately, European security interests do not presently impinge on South Asia. The India refusal to sign the NPT is also one major reason for disagreement with Europe. In the new world order, America itself may find it has a marginal role in Europe. Germany and France could in the future take on a more visible military role. In the Asia-Pacific region, Japan would aim for a permanent seat in the UN Security Council. India too seeks such a membership but it remains to be seen whether the European countries will agree to one seat on the Council, and allow Japan and India to have permanent membership.

European concerns presently relate to the economic union of their continent. For this reason, they are unlikely to be interested in global problems and India figures for its market. India also needs to look eastward and seek membership of the Asia Pacific Economic Community (APEC). Only if India were to become a member of such a community, can it effectively bargain with the EEC in the future?

A reunified Germany and Japan are logical candidates for a permanent membership of the Security

Council. China is a major country of the developing world that retains missiles and nuclear weapons. They are no longer relevant to European interests, but threaten both Russia and India. Also Beijing's leaders have problems dealing with a politically liberal Europe. In the past China was able to exploit the Cold War and create a visible presence in NATO's strategic planning. The collapse of Cold War and the refusal of Beijing's ageing leaders like Deng Xiaoping to give Western style freedom to his people, has only further marginalized China in the eyes of Europe's liberal leaders. India could attempt to exploit China's disadvantage and make a break in Europe.

India which has strong ties with the USSR has had both public and private sectors in the economy, and hence, has a better chance that the former USSR in integrating with the global economy even though its trade accounts for a mere 0.4 per cent of the world's total. The increasing tendency on the part of the European leaders like Mitterrand and Kohl to adopt a continental approach in the Post-Cold War era could marginalize the developing countries. India is in a sense a developed within a developing country that could still strike bilateral defence arrangements with Britain and France (which has been the case in the past) and perhaps, Germany. In the past Indo-USSR military ties enabled military relationships with the GDR, Czechoslovakia, Poland and Bulgaria.

As far as India is concerned, the location of 72 per cent of the defence production facilities in Russia and 18 per cent in Ukraine, necessitates new bilateral arrangements based on dollars as the exchange for transactions. The armed peace that raged in Europe during the years of the Cold War has now given way to Balkanizing tendencies now that the Cold War has ended.

In 1989, the USSR had announced cuts in arms production that included a 52 per cent reduction in tanks,

23 per cent in military aircraft, 60 per cent in military helicopters and 20 per cent in ammunitions as compared to the original Five Year Plan. The Russian decision to conduct all foreign trade with India in hard currency from this year has major implication for arms imports by India which has traded on a soft currency basis in the past. There was also one other important rationale for India buying arms from the USSR – obtaining political support from a super power in the context of the Cold War as it impinged on South Asia, since the other super power the US was supplying military hardware to Pakistan. In an interview at the end of 1990, Soviet Deputy Chairman of the Council of Ministers of the USSR had publicly mentioned Soviet arms export figures. According to him, India owes a debt of 8,0975 billion roubles for arms imports. It is however, not clear how reliable these figures are and how much of this debt can be desegregated from the total imports. India has now no choice but to rely on its own R&D activities in the area of defence production even as the Soviet Defence Ministry is proposing co-production of select aircraft like the SU-37, Yak-141 and Mig-31 which are presently in the design or flight testing stage. There can be little doubt that by virtue of the relations between New Delhi and Washington being strengthened, there could be further collaboration in the field of defence. One such collaboration is the Light Combat Aircraft (LCA) for which the F-404 engines were imported from the General Electric Company in the USA[15].

Certain countries like Germany have deep reservations about India's defence expenditure and perceive India as being hegemonistic towards its neighbours. Such perceptions need to be corrected through protracted dialogue. Eurocentric perceptions on South Asia have a colonial ring about them. France and Germany as ex-colonial powers can undertake interventions in the developing world. To cite an example, France invaded Zaire under the ostensible reason of establishing democracy there.

It is presumed that Moscow can transfer at lower cost its production facilities to friendly countries like India. Such an approach towards defence production in certain key areas could interest both China and India. These are the two countries that are "windows" into high technology for the USSR, apart from the ASEAN with which both Russia and India are presently seeking stronger economic ties. But ASEAN is too closely linked with Japan which has deep reservations about Russia[16].

Let us now examine the China factor in nuclear proliferation. Contrary to the common perception of an India-Pakistan nuclear contest, China was the most important influence on India exercising its nuclear option. Initially, India's nuclear capability was aimed solely at deterring aggression by China, not Pakistan. Seeing China as the reference point of India's economic, security and diplomatic policies, India's strategic analysts have long emphasized the need to cope up with China militarily.

India's obsession with China is matched by Pakistan's obsession with India. Just as India, having lost its 1962 war with China, considered nuclear weapons as a practical way to neutralize the superior conventional and nuclear strength of a much larger and powerful adversary, after the 1971 war with India, Pakistan considered nuclear weapons necessary to neutralize India's strategic advantages. China tested its first atomic bomb in 1964, 2 years after India's humiliating defeat in 1962 border war. India followed suit in 1974. The Chinese, great practitioners of balance-of-power politics, responded by providing nuclear weapons designs and technology to India's arch-rival Pakistan. Similarly, India saw its technological advantages over Pakistan in the development of ballistic missiles in the 1980s being effectively neutralized by

Chinese missile technology transfers to Pakistan in the 1990s.

The 1998 Indian nuclear tests were preceded by Indian Defence Minister George Fernandes' statements, calling China a 'bigger potential threat' than Pakistan and describing how his country was being 'encircled' by Chinese military activities and alliances with Pakistan and Myanmar. Subsequently explaining the rationale behind India's resumption of testing after 24 years hiatus, Indian Prime Minister A.B. Vajpayee noted New Delhi's 'deteriorating security environment' and put the onus on China's nuclear status and the longstanding mistrust and suspicion between the two countries.

He noted that India had 'an overt nuclear weapon state on its borders, a state which committed armed aggression against India in 1962 ... To add to the distress that country has materially helped another neighbour of ours to become a covert nuclear weapon state. At the hands of this bitter neighbour we have suffered three aggressions in the last fifty years'.

The main objective of China's Asia policy has been to prevent the rise of a rival to challenge its status as the Asia-Pacific's 'Middle Kingdom'. As an old Chinese saying goes, 'one mountain cannot accommodate two tigers'. Beijing always knows that India alone has the size, might, numbers and above all, the intention to match China. The intention of Beijing is to keep New Delhi under pressure by arming its neighbours and supporting insurgency movements in India's minority regions. That is why Beijing has pursued a policy of containment and encirclement by proxy, indeed, some 90% of China's arms sales go to countries bordering India.

Soon after the 1962 India-China war, China sought to build up Pakistan as a military counterweight to India, so as to tie India down south of the Himalayas. India has always perceived this Sino-Pakistani military nexus as threatening. Despite Chinese efforts to justify military links with Pakistan as normal state-to-state relations, India has remained unconvinced, demanding an end to China's arming of India's neighbours. What irks India most is the Chinese transfer of nuclear and missile technology to Pakistan. New Delhi's repeated protestations to Beijing have fallen on deaf ears. China provided Pakistan with a tested nuclear warhead design, M-9 and M-11 ballistic missiles and missile components, fissile materials, nuclear plants and ring magnets for enriching weapons-grade uranium. These transfers led to the imposition of US sanctions against China in 1991 and 1993.

Even the recent Sino-India rapprochement belied New Delhi's hopes that improved ties would lead to more circumspect Chinese behaviour. In fact, Beijing stepped up its nuclear and missile transfers to Pakistan as a bargaining chip in its attempts to curb the US arms transfers to Taiwan. It became obvious that China was not going to become less friendly to Pakistan, following normalization with India, primarily because the combined strategic and political advantages China receives from its relationship with Pakistan easily outweigh any advantages China might receive from a closer relationship with India. Above all, Pakistan is the only country that stands up to India and thereby prevents Indian hegemony over the region, thus fulfilling the key objective of China's South Asia policy.

In Southeast Asia, China has taken advantage of Myanmar's isolation since 1990 to satisfy its own great power ambitions, especially its desire to counter India in the Indian Ocean. China has provided US $2 billion in military aid to Myanmar and established electronic listening posts on Myanmar's Coco Islands, opposite India's Andaman and Nicobar Islands, to monitor Indian naval activity and missile testing[17]. China's strategic alliances with Pakistan and Myanmar are the linchpins of its regional strategy for the twenty-first century. Given India's long adversarial relationship with China, anything that promotes China's interests in India's immediate neighbourhood worries Indian policy makers.

India's official rhetoric notwithstanding security considerations have always been the most important factor in its stance on nuclear disarmament. It was China's nuclear test in 1964 that transformed India from a supporter of non-proliferation into its staunchest critic. In international disarmament fora, India has defended its right to build nuclear weapons on national security grounds – wedged as it is between nuclear-armed China and nuclear capable Pakistan – unless all Nuclear-Weapons States (NWS) agree to abide by a time-bound nuclear disarmament programme. From India's perspective, the indefinite and unconditional extension of the Nuclear Non-Proliferation Treaty (NPT) in 1995 (which divided the world permanently into nuclear haves and have-nots) and discussions leading up to the Comprehensive Test Ban Treaty (CTBT) shattered New Delhi's misplaced hope in nuclear disarmament in the Post-Cold War world.

Given the fact that there are genuine tensions between the world's reigning super power, the US, and the world's rising superpower, China, India had been moving closer to the US. The significant improvement in Indo-US relations following the end of the Cold War led some Indian observers to conclude that changing strategic realities – China's increasing assertiveness and its tendency to flex its muscles in the South China Sea and the Taiwan straits – would encourage Washington to look for an alternative Asian power to contain Chinese influence. In return, New Delhi wanted the US economic and military help in gaining and maintaining preeminence in the region as a counterweight to China. For its part, Beijing feared the possibility of strategic collusion between India and the US. Chinese threat analysis pointed to growing naval cooperation between the US and India, as well as Indian nuclear and naval buildup programmes. However, it soon became clear that the road to Indo-US rapprochement was littered with non-proliferation and geopolitical hurdles. The US wanted India to balance China, but not as a nuclear power, India saw its nuclear and missile capability as an integral component of its China policy and the only means to keep Beijing's ambitions in check.

Throughout the 1980s, the US strategic compulsions (i.e. the emergence of Pakistan as a 'frontline state' in the fight against the Soviet occupation of Afghanistan) had made successive US administrations turn a blind eye to Chinese missile and nuclear proliferation to Pakistan, Saudi Arabia and Iran. The 1990s saw trade and commercial considerations overtaking the US nonproliferation concerns. After 1995, the Clinton administration not only chose to acquiesce in Sino-Pakistani nuclear and missile cooperation, but also approved the first export of satellite and advanced nuclear technology to China after obtaining assurances that Beijing would limit its arms exports to Iran - but not Pakistan. Thus, while China was being rewarded for its proliferation activities, India was being punished. Unlike china, India has never exported nuclear and missile technology. The US knows it very well that even though India has not signed in the NPT and CTBT, it is against proliferation of nuclear weapons and this has been appreciated by the US. By aiding China's military modernization, the Clinton administration was heightening the concerns of India, which feared that transferred US nuclear and missile technology would eventually seep into Pakistan[18].

In an interview to the Doordarshan ex-Indian President Sri K.R. Narayanan expressed his hope that China is growing to be a power and there is no doubt in it. But China will become a responsible power and will not show hegemonistic attitude towards its neighbours. Mr. K.R. Narayanan was an ex-Indian ambassador to China during the tenure of Mrs. Indira Gandi. It is presumed that the US will be more close to India than china as India is democratic and moreover the US wants India to counter China in the region.

China is systematically campaigning for India to sign the NPT. In essence, Beijing is demanding 'decisive and clear cut' international action to force India to completely dismantle its nuclear weapons capability. As one Chinese analyst told The Hindu: "Earlier we used to speak about the three "T"s in the bilateral relationship – Territory, Tibet and the Triangular relationship among China, India and Pakistan. Now there is the fourth "T" – the non-proliferation Treaties: the CTBT and the NPT. That China is taking the lead in trying to isolate and punish India for its nuclear tests is evident from the fact that in their bilateral meetings with other countries, the Chinese have sought endorsement of their UN Security Council Resolution 1172"[19].

India's hard-line China policy was given by a commentary of one BJP ideologue:

If a bomb is good for China, why is it not good for India? ... If Beijing thinks it can keep India down by joining hands with the US, it is sadly mistaken. The US is more apprehensive of an expansionist China than of a resurgent India. If China can play games, so can India[20]. ......

This means that if China backs Pakistan's stand on Kashmir, India will play 'the Tibet card'. If China is seen as entering into anti-China alliances, New Delhi will have fewer inhibitions about joining anti-China forces, especially in the US Congress, and stirring up latent ones in the region. One Indian analyst has suggested that 'India should ... engage in aggressive diplomacy which should take into account the coming split in the American body politic on China and observe the willingness of US conservatives to reach out to India'.

China and India are competing with each other to form a strategic alliance with the reigning super power. Declaring that India and the US could become 'natural allies' in the quest for a better future in the twenty-first century. Indian Prime Minister called for a restructuring of Indo-US relations on an 'equal footing', and emphasized 'similar political cultures' and the absence of a 'conflict of interests' between the two democracies. Rarely has an Indian Prime Minister been so bold in laying out the basis for an alliance relationship with the United States, direct in demanding equal treatment from Washington, and blunt in pointing to the troubles that have dogged Indo-US ties.

Notwithstanding Sino-US rhetoric about a 'new strategic partnership in the 21st century', the US and China are likely to remain strategic competitors. China's ultimate objective is to limit the US ability to impact adversely on China's interests and influence, and eventually to displace the US power in the Asia-Pacific. The key motive behind China's assistance to countries like North Korea, Saudi Arabia, Iran and Pakistan is to balance against the US and its allies. From the regional security point of view, India could provide an effective counterweight to China's growing economic and military might in Asia. China is the party worst affected by this qualitative change in Asia's strategic balance. With India's nuclear equalizer, the power balance in the region may now be more equitable. And should a new Cold War break out between China and the US, India might come to occupy the same place in the US security calculus that China had during the US-Soviet Cold War years from 1971 to 1989.

India is seeking allies in Southeast and Central Asia to keep China on the edge. At the July 1998 ASEAN summit, Indian officials focused on the commonality of strategic and security interests, while emphasizing the absence of any territorial disputes between the ASEAN and India – a veiled reference to China's territorial disputes with ASEAN states. To assuage the Southeast Asian countries' concern, India supported the establishment of a Southeast-Asian Nuclear Weapons Free Zone (SEANWFZ) and offered to sign the SEANWFZ Treaty as a NWS. This puts China in a dilemma as it amounts to a virtual recognition of India as a NWS by its Southeast Asian neighbours.

In short, a contest between China and India over control of South, Southeast and Central Asia and the Northern India Ocean (Malacca Straits) will be the dominant feature of Asian geopolitics in the twenty-first century. Their underlying power rivalry and their self-images as natural great powers and centres of civilization and culture will continue to drive them to support different countries and causes. They are suspicious of each other's long-term agendas and intentions. India would like to remain independent, power picking and choosing its own friends. So China's grand strategy, especially Beijing's choice of allies to achieve its strategic goals, will push India into the coalition of anti-China states.

There is no doubt that China has played a very crucial role in enabling Pakistan to acquire nuclear technology and equally sophisticated missile delivery systems. There is now a fear that the nuclear technology may now go to the hands of the terrorists through Pakistan. If it happens, it would be disastrous for the world. India is a responsible country and it has not divulged nuclear technology to any second country that means it has been fully practising the NPT though it has not signed it. India's nuclear tests have upset the existing strategic equilibrium. They have also changed the Asian security environment by demonstrating India's military capability and political will in relation to China, Japan, Russia and the US. India's nuclear weapons have restored the balance of power on the Asian mainland by thwarting China's aspirations for Asia-Pacific hegemony.

The US President with her daughter Chelsea paid a state visit to India in the year 2000. As a result, China is worried by signs of a warming relationship between Washington and New Delhi. Analysts and officials say Beijing is concerned that Clinton's visit to India just two years after it tested nuclear devices in the Rajasthan desert, will amount to de facto acceptance of the country's status as a nuclear power. China is also worried about the effects of a stronger US-India relationship on regional stability.

Beijing had already made its irritation clear. In mid-February, Chinese officials told visiting US Deputy Secretary of State Strobe Talbott that Washington should uphold its commitment to the principles of nuclear nonproliferation and work to roll back India's nuclear plans.

By all accounts, China's pressure on the United States has surprised and upset India and has led to gloating in the media in Pakistan. New Delhi claims that it is the threat from China which prompted them for a nuclear device. Some in Beijing, for example, believe that in seeking a strategic partnership with India, Washington is trying to use it as a counterweight to China.

A former Indian envoy to Beijing, C.V. Rananathan agrees: "I think certainly they are worried about the US drawing India into an anti-China alliance". Jasjit Singh, Director of the Institute of Defence Studies and Analyses in New Delhi, adds: "The Chinese would have concern if the US and India were to come closer. From the point of view of the Chinese global strategy of challenging the US, it would mean a net loss"[21].

China's worries are underscored by India's technological growth as well as its link with the US – a natural one, given that the two countries are the world's biggest democracies. Indian strategist Singh charges meanwhile that one of China's motives in backing Pakistan is to keep India off-balance.

Despite their mutual distrust and misgivings, neither China nor India wants to see a further deterioration in relations. India and China held their first ever security dialogue in Beijing on March 6, 2000. Sources said the Chinese tried to get some commitment from India to halt further research and development of nuclear weapons. But China must recognize that rolling back India's nuclear power is no longer a realistic goal.

References

1. US-Pakistan Relations, New Delhi: USIA, p.5.
2. The Far Eastern Economic Review, Hong Kong, May 17, 1984, p.34.
3. The Times of India, Bombay, March 8, 1990.
4. For details on nuclear issue affecting India and Pakistan relations, see P.M. Kamath, "The Viable Alternative", The Illustrated Weekly of India, April 11-17, 1992, pp.16-7.
5. See P.M. Kamath, "Caution a Watchword", The Observer of Business and Politics, July 20, 1992.
6. In an interview with The Times of India, Bombay, April 5, 1992.
7. See P.M. Kamath, "Indo-US Relations: Future Watch", The Observer of Business and Politics", April 14, 1992.
8. For details see Seymour M Huers, "The Price of power: Kissinger in the White House", New York: Summit Books, 1983, pp.350-82.
9. "The Balance of power Delusion", Foreign Policy, No.7, Summer 1972, pp.54-5.
10. P.M. Kamath, "The US-India Relations since the End of Cold War", Strategic Analysis, Vol.XVI, No.1, April 1993, pp.93-103.

11. Chintamani Mohapatra, "Indo-US Relations in the 21st Century", pp.62-86. by Knowledge World in Association with IDSA, New Delhi, September 1998.
12. *Ibid.*, p.66.
13. *Ibid*, p.67.
14. *Ibid.*, p.82.
15. R.R. Subramanian, "India, the US and Russia in a Changing World Order", Strategic Analysis, March 1993, Vol.XV, No.12, pp.1239-1250.
16. Ibid., pp.1248-1250.
17. Mohan Malik, "Nuclear Proliferation in Asia: The China Factor", Australian Journal of International Affairs, Vol.53, No.1, 1999, p.32.
18. *Ibid.*, p.34.
19. *Ibid.*, p.38.
20. *Ibid.*, p.39.
21. Nayan Chanda in Singapore and Susan V. Lawrence in Beijing, "Nuclear Balancing Act", Far Eastern Economic Review, Vol.163, No.11, March 16, 2000, pp.26-27.

9
Concluding Observation

Even though it is the world's largest democracy, India has had a troubled relationship with the US. Washington has tended to view Indian matters through Cold War and nuclear nonproliferation lenses. This focus has restricted the growth of many aspects of the relationship, including government-to-government relations, trade and cooperation on strategic objectives and international arms control. India's policies on non-alignment, its close association with the former Soviet Union, its restrictions on foreign investment and imports, and its expectations of technology transfer and licensing rights have further narrowed the scope of relations between two nations that otherwise might have found common ground in their shared experiences of colonialism, democratic values and heterogeneous societies.

India's non-alignment policy began to take shape in the early 1950s. By the mid-1960s, New Delhi tended to side diplomatically with the Soviet Union. New Delhi became the beneficiary of Soviet arms exports and technology, much of it on a barter-or-grant basis.

For its part, the US varied the amount of aid it provided as a way to convey displeasure with India's thinly veiled support for the Soviet Union. During the 1950s and 1960s, the US provided half of the total foreign assistance India received. Half of this total came in the form of grain and agricultural commodities, but loans were also provided for industrial expansion and infrastructure, including transport, irrigation and energy. The US called for a redirection of India's development strategy, towards agriculture and away from heavy industry and a general liberalization of foreign-investment controls. When India suffered the worst drought in a century, followed by a monsoon failure in 1966, President Lyndon B. Johnson responded personally by campaigning for a massive grain-assistance programme (14 million tonnes during 1965-67). In exchange, Johnson hoped to persuade India to come closer in line with US interests. During a meeting on March 1966 with Indian Prime Minister, Indira Gandhi, Johnson laid out three US priorities.

1. Indian concessions to Pakistan on Kashmir.
2. Continued economic reform, particularly on foreign investment, which entailed accepting World Bank recommendations for rupee devaluation and import liberalization and limits on defence spending.
3. India's reassurance to the US that it 'would deal more forthrightly with the evidence of North Vietnamese aggression, and reform from publicly criticizing US policies there[1].

For the US, these requirements were deemed reasonable, given India's perceived dependence on Washington for economic assistance. Indians, however, were outraged that the Prime Minister would even consider such an exchange. The Indian government made a conscious effort to rely less on the US and began purchasing grain from other sources. Mrs. Gandhi wrote to Johnson that 'national pride made her country reluctant to accept foreign aid'. Gradually, it became clear that India's policies on direct foreign investment would not change and would continue to discourage US investors. India did not like to be coerced by the US, disagreed with many of Washington's conditions, and was suspicious of its intentions.

In the early 1950s the US first decided to sell arms to Pakistan. From India's perspective, the US was not only arming one of its enemies, but placing Pakistan in a client status that the US could use to pressure India.

It is because of the diversified views of the US and India that they could not come closer during the Cold War years. India did not believe with the US that communism needed to be contained. India adopted the socialist economic planning and rejected the free market economy during those days. The Indian government refused to allow the import technology unless a license to reproduce the technology domestically accompanied the transaction. These highly unusual expectations were made for commercial firms such as Coca Cola for its soft-drink patent and of certain US defence producers for design and production information.

India viewed the USA as an unreliable trade and food-assistance partner and an unreliable supplier of military equipment and informal ally. The sources of Indian discomfort included Washington's decision to sell arms to Pakistan in 1953 and the subsequent formation of a US-Pakistan defence alliance. There were various reasons for which the US and India could not come closer. The reasons were Washington's inconsistent and ineffective military support after China's invasion in October 1962, an arms embargo during the Indo-Pakistani war in 1965 and the perceived 'tilt' towards Pakistan during the war in East Pakistan in 1971.

The US frequently imposed unilateral restrictions on exports because of India's lack of support for US

Cold War objectives, and to prevent re-export to the Soviet Union and communist bloc. However, India was not singled out. During the Cold War, the US had difficulty in balancing its foreign policy concerns with the liberal world economic order it advocated as contributing to peace. At the same time the US was secretly preoccupied to prolong its technological advantage over the Soviet Union. India did not share COCOM's (Coordination Committee for Multilateral Export Control) objectives, until the mid 1980s. The US regarded New Delhi as having weak export controls to other states.

Till the Indian nuclear explosion of 1974 the US did not apply counter-specific export controls to India. The second major irritant in Indo-US relations has been nuclear proliferation. The US was disappointed with India's decision not to sign the 1968 Nuclear Non-Proliferation Treaty (NPT), but it was India's test of a nuclear explosive device in October 1974 that triggered several laws restricting the export of high-technology products to India (as well as to other non-NPT member States). In addition to Washington's prohibitions, other states have been pressured by the US not to assist India with or transfer nuclear technology. In 1992, the Nuclear Suppliers Group (NSG) agreed that transfers of nuclear technology, equipment or materials would require that the recipient state agrees to full-scope safeguards. As a result, since 1993 India has been unable to receive some of materials it needs to keep its nuclear facilities at full capacity. The legislation is likely to continue affecting India, especially given New Delhi's desire to expand its nuclear programme in order to meet an anticipated increase in domestic energy demands[2].

The portrayal of the US as discriminatory is exacerbated by India's rejection of the NPT's principal premise which allows declared nuclear-weapon states to continue to develop nuclear weapons, while all other members of the Treaty pledged not to develop them. From the Indian perspective, the basis for nonproliferation export controls is discriminatory; the US controls most of which go beyond international obligations, are unfair and are designed not only to limit proliferation, but also to limit the development of indigenous technology that would eventually compete with the US producers.

However, there were some exceptions made within even the sensitive category of exports. In 1982, president Ronald Regan and Prime Minister Indira Gandhi signed the 'Science and Technology Initiative', which culminated in the 1984 'Memorandum of Understanding on sensitive technologies, commodities and information'. These agreements enabled a transfer of the US technology that would be used to develop, most significantly, India's light combat aircraft (LCA)[3].

Both sides had strategic and practical reasons behind their desire to cooperate in these sensitive areas. The US was trying to justify providing economic and military assistance to Pakistan which was prohibited by the 1976 Symimington Amendment to Foreign Assistance Act, triggered by Pakistan's 1979 importation of unsafe-guarded uranium-enrichment equipment. A new waiver to this Amendment and to the 1984 Glenn Amendment (which allowed US aid to Pakistan as long as the President certified that Pakistan did not possess a nuclear explosive device) was drafted to allow the President to forgo imposing sanctions if he could certify that it was in the 'national interest' of the US. The high-technology initiative to India was a way to balance assistance to Pakistan ostensibly because the US believed that it would increase US influence over Indian military programmes. In addition, Washington wanted to pressure Moscow by trying to court the Indians.

From India's perspective, the US's effort coincided with New Delhi's desire to move closer to Washington to lessen the effect of a perceived US-Pakistan-Chinese axis developing during the Soviet Union's war in Afghanistan. India was also concerned about becoming too dependent on the USSR for military hardware.

However, the US-India cooperation at this time was neither robust nor long lasting. There were substantial disagreements over specific types of systems and technology to be exported. In one instance, India requested the Cray XMP-24 supercomputer to study the Indian monsoon. The XMP-24 also was useful in developing nuclear weapons and missiles and in deciphering cryptographic codes. Washington decided to offer India smaller supercomputer instead, the XMP-14, capable of conducting the monsoon analysts, but with no applicability to nuclear weapons, missiles or cryptography. India interpreted the offer as a lack of US credibility and an instance of US unreliability.

In 1985, exports became more difficult because of the implementation of the Missile Technology Control Regime (MTCR). India's test of the Agni intermediate range ballistic missile in 1989 caused serious concern in the US because it was believed that the US high-technology exports ostensibly for use in India's space and satellite programmes were being adopted for missiles. Despite the support of executive leadership of both countries to continue military and technological cooperation, the effort was overwhelmed by suspicion on both sides.

After the Cold War

Since 1991, both US and India have tried to improve trade and technology relations. Of course, this effort began badly in 1992, when the US pressured Russia not to transfer cryogenic rocket-engine technology to India. The US imposed meaningless sanctions on Glavkosmos, Russia's export organization for space-related goods and technology and strict sanctions on the Indian Space Research Organization (ISRO).

India had already promoted economic and trade relations by opening up its economy in 1989 and in 1991, by reducing tariffs on imports, encouraging foreign investment and liberalizing regulations on foreign-owned businesses. While the economy seemed responsive to such reforms in the early 1990s, by the second half of the decade, growth was faltering[4]. In short, India needed a boost from outside investors and technical assistance to get export to market and increase productivity.

The US became the largest trading partner of India after the Cold War. The COCOM restrictions that inhibited trade during the Cold War and the burdensome licensing procedures were scrapped by India to boost import-export. Controls are now only applied to countries that do not adhere to the MTCR or that are deemed to support international terrorism. These new criteria provide increased opportunities for technology transfer by the US.

The nuclear issue has remained as a bone of contention between the US and India since a long time. India is not a party to the NPT. India is in favour of global nuclear disarmament. First, let all the nuclear weapon states including USA eliminate nuclear weapons and then tell others do the same.

The US has already made changes to its nonproliferation policy that acknowledge the political and security-related complexities driving India and Pakistan's nuclear-weapons programmes and indicates a willingness to discuss a compromise solution to the stand-off on nonproliferation. In one recent statement of the US policy, Assistant Secretary of State for South Aslan Affairs, Karl F. Inderfurth notes that the changes occurring in the region demand a 'greater openness' in the US policy towards the region. Listing the important objectives for the region, Inderfurth includes reducing the threat of conflict, strengthening democracy, furthering Indo-US commercial relations, settling the Afghan conflict and encouraging an economic opening up of Central Asia. He notes that the nuclear weapon and ballistic missile programmes are a particularly difficult issue because they arise from very real national security concerns of both countries. These objectives are very different from those pursued even in the early 1990s that included 'rolling back' the nuclear programmes in both states. Now the US seeks to encourage India and Pakistan to exercise restraint and accept limits on their nuclear and missile programmes.

The US anti-proliferation coalition has weakened dramatically since the mid-1990s. First, strong advocates of nuclear non-proliferation objectives for South Asia such as Senators John Glen and Larry Pressler, and Representative Stephen Solarz, are either retiring or have left Congress and have not been replaced by similar voices. The lack of Congressional advocates may reflect the growing interest in the business community for investing in India and Pakistan, and greater activism by active, affluent, ethnic lobbies made up of Americans of Pakistan and Indian descent[5]. Various efforts to engage India have emerged in the last few years from the US government. (1) The Department of Commerce's official designation of India as one of the world's 'Big emerging Markets'. (2) Defence Secretary Perry's 1995 initiative to encourage military-to-military cooperation and an exploration of common strategic objectives. (3) The US Nuclear Regulatory Commission (NRC)'s current attempt to pursue a dialogue on nuclear safety. (4) The US nonproliferation objectives have undergone some change.

Relations between India and the United States appear to have entered new era with the establishment of a "commercial alliance" and the signing of the first Post-Cold War agreement on "defence cooperation" between the two countries. Visiting India in the mid third week of January 1995, the Commerce Secretary of the United States, Ronald H. Brown, signed a Memorandum of Understanding with Indian Commerce Minister, Pranab Mukharjee to create an Indo-US "commercial alliance" - a super forum for bilateral consultations aimed at forging closer business-to-business links.

The importance of Brown's Commercial Mission to India can be gauged from the fact that chief executive officers of 25 American big business houses accompanied him to conclude agreements of cooperation and collaboration in various fields. While Brown left for New Delhi with a vision to double the US exports to India - from $2.8 billion in 1994 to 4.6 billion by 2000 AD - he witnessed on the third day of his visit the signing of 11 business collaborations, six in power, four in telecommunication and one in the insurance sector, envisaging American investment of $1.4 billion in India[6].

Brown's Presidential Economic Mission as called by the Clinton administration, took place at a time when the United States had become the largest foreign investor in India and also the largest trading partner, accounting for 18 per cent of India's exports and 11 per cent of its imports[7]. But seen from the US perspective, a vast potential market in India has remained unexplored. India, in fact, accounts for only 0.6 per cent of the total exports and 0.3 per cent of the total US foreign investment. There was realization in the US of insufficient attention given to India, which according to a US Commerce Department study, figures prominently in the new concept of BEMs or Big Emerging Markets, that also includes the Chinese economic area (China, Taiwan and Hong Kong), South Korea, Indonesia, Turkey, South Africa, Poland, Argentina, Brazil and

Mexico. According to an estimate, the BEMs are to double their share of world imports in two decades to 20 per cent from today's 10 per cent. Moreover, their share in global imports is likely to exceed that of Japan and the European Community (EC) combined.

Indeed, Brown's economic mission to India in the backdrop of New Delhi's economic liberalization (after a decent burial given to the license raj) coincided with a rising percentage of annual growth in India's imports[8]. Keeping in view the political differences and the divergent strategic perceptions between Washington and New Delhi, it seems only logical that Brown's mission to India followed US Secretary of Defence William Perry's path-breaking trip to South Asia. It was symbolic enough to indicate the need for political and strategic understanding before embarking upon a massive economic initiative.

Perry visited India in the backdrop of steady growth in Indo-US cooperation in various fields and increasing appreciation of each other's security requirements and strategic compulsions. It is important to recall that the year 1993, when Clinton entered the White House, breaking twelve years of continuous Republican Administration, was not a good year for Indo-US relations. Some Indian analysts who had predicted a friendlier White House were thoroughly disappointed when a Clinton administration official quickly brandished the special and super 301 clauses, and, at the same time, the pressure on the nuclear proliferation issue was exerted by renewed noises over the nuclear Non-Proliferation Treaty (NPT) and by the efforts that went into scuttling of the Indo-Russian cryogenic rocket engine deal. The prompt recall of the US Ambassador to India for a different diplomatic assignment, undue delay in the appointment of a new Ambassador, the difficulty that the Indian Ambassador faced in getting an audience with the US President could not be convincingly justified when the political relations between India and the United States reached an all time low with Assistant Secretary of State Robin Raphel's outrageous statement over the Kashmir issue and the Shimla Agreement. Even Bill Clinton equated Kashmir issue with the ethnic movements in different areas of the globe including in Somalia and Bosnia. The heat produced by Raphel's remarks had yet to be cooled when some influential Congressman prepared a discussion draft to scrap the Pressler Amendment.

The situation, however, began to change when Robin Raphel's immediate superior, Peter Tarnoff, Under-Secretary of State made the appropriate corrective remarks on the US position on the Kashmir issue and the second high ranking State Department official, Strobe Talbot, visited India on a damage limitation mission[9], and with the Clinton administration's threats of sanctions against the M-11 missile deal between China and Pakistan. The US reports establishing the Pakistani hand in aiding and abetting the terrorist elements in the Indian state of Jammu and Kashmir also elicited some warnings to Pakistan by Washington. Significantly, Robin Raphel visited India in March 1994 and Strobe Talbot the following month, and both of them, among several expected statements, appreciated the economic reforms undertaken by the Government of India and emphasized the need to further improve Indo-US economic interactions.

In the meantime, in the area of prolonged and contentious proliferation issues, better and somewhat more sympathetic understanding over each other's security concerns began to emerge with more frequent official and non-official dialogues conducted between the two countries. The Cold War rhetoric became a thing of the past in Indian remarks - both official and non-official, in this connection, certain recommendations made in a 1993 report entitled 'India and America. After the Cold War' are noteworthy. While acknowledging the dangers of continued nuclear development in the subcontinent, the Study Group distinguishes between the US efforts to force India to give up its nuclear option, which would prove both ineffective and counterproductive to American interests and efforts to discourage and deter Indian programmes to produce and deploy nuclear weapons.

No Government in New Delhi could survive if it abandoned the nuclear option for India in a regional and global environment in which nuclear weapons continue to be the ultimate coin of power. Notwithstanding the significant steps taken by Washington and Moscow to reduce their nuclear stockpiles, the existing nuclear powers show no readiness to phase out nuclear weapons.

Instead of seeking to induce India to give up its nuclear option, the United States should shift from a focus on non-proliferation in South Asia to a policy designed to maintain nuclear restraints. Such a policy would seek to freeze the stockpiling of fissile material for weapons purposes and the development, production and deployment of nuclear weapons by both India and Pakistan.

The United State should continue to deny licenses for the sale of US technology that would contribute directly to any Indian efforts to develop missiles capable of delivering nuclear weapons. The Study Group recognizes that the Agni and Prithvi missile programmes are far advanced. They enjoy overwhelming domestic support and are not likely to be reversed by external political and economic pressures. The focus of the US efforts, therefore, should be to persuade India not to transfer its missiles technology to others[10].

Before going into other instances of improving the US understanding of India's security concerns (compared to the past US perceptions), it is perhaps appropriate to mention at this point that the Carnegie Report did suggest that "greatest potential for a rapid improvement of Indo-American relations lies in the economic sphere, and the success of India's economic reform programme will directly condition the climate both for bilateral trade and investment and for US-supported multilateral assistance"[11].

The months following the release of the Carnegie Report have witnessed not only increased economic ties between India and the United States but also certain developments, though still at a low level and largely symbolic, indicating an improvement in the security relations between the two countries. The on-going Light Combat Aircraft Project, with all its ups and downs, the naval exercises conducted by the Indian and American Navies in the Indian Ocean, the rapid rise in the number of high-level exchange visits by the military officials and increased frequency of official and non-official dialogues to thrash out contentions issues are all indicative of that improvement. The 1993 Executive Report to the US Congress, released a few months after the Carnegie Report, makes an example of the changing US perception of the security concerns of India. It points out:

"India's latent security concerns about China are a major obstacle to gaining New Delhi's support for any regional discussion in view of India's belief that the Chinese nuclear and missile programme also must be taken into consideration ... Consequently, dealing successfully with nuclear and missile proliferation in South Asia will require that the US and others take into account regional security threat perceptions, including those extending beyond these two countries themselves"[12].

The collapse of Communism in Europe and the on-going economic reform programme in the People's

Republic of China appeared to have inspired a rethinking on the economic policy and the growth strategy in India. India's adoption of a policy of economic liberalization in a changed security environment in the Post-Cold War era paved the way for smoother Indo-US relations. A series of strategic symposiums, jointly conducted by the Indian Institute for Defence Studies and Analyses and Washington's National Defence University plus Indo-US dialogue at other official and non-official levels contributed a great deal towards removal of some stereotype images and long-held mutual misunderstandings in both the capitals. By November 1993, three rounds of bilateral Indo-US dialogue by the officials on nuclear and other security issues had already taken place[13]. In January 1994, the outcome of a Conference on Technology Transfer and Weapons Proliferation, in Bangalore, hosted by India's National Institute of Advanced Studies, the Rockefeller Foundation and the Carnegie Mellon University, suggested greater US appreciation of India's commitment to non-proliferation goals[14].

When Prime Minister Narasimha Rao landed in Washington in May 1994, there was little doubt that his agenda was dominated by economic issues. Like President Bill Clinton's, Rao's foreign policy strategy aimed at improving India's economic competitiveness. In his address to a joint meeting of the US Congress on May 18, 1994, Rao said: "Perhaps the most impressive aspect of India's ambitious economic reform programme is the smoothness with which the transition from a closed, protected economy has occurred. The impact of the changes in India has had a profound effect on Indo-US economic relations ..... India's vast domestic market, huge educated, skilled and semi-skilled workforce, sound financial institutions and time-tested and democratic system offer tremendous investment opportunities for forward-thinking companies"[15]. Rao's address at the joint meeting of the US Congress emphasized the country's economic policy priorities. But he did appear to cover the nuclear issues in his discussion with Bill Clinton if we go by what is reflected in the joint statement issued on May 19. It says – President Clinton and Prime Minister Rao offered their strong support for efforts towards the nonproliferation of weapons of mass destruction and towards their progressive reduction, with the goal of elimination of such weapons, which are among the most pressing challenges to the security of states in the Post-Cold War era. They pledged that their two governments would intensify their cooperative efforts to achieve a comprehensive test ban treaty and a verifiable ban on the production of the fissile material for nuclear weapons[16].

India and the United States have similarity in their views on at least some aspects of nonproliferation goals is a novel development. India has been the votary of a comprehensive ban on nuclear tests since 1954. New Delhi, has spelled out a detailed blueprint aiming at achieving a nuclear-free world in the 1988 Rajiv Gandhi Plan on Disarmament. The Clinton-Rao joint statement has made it evident that for the first time the United States has finally come around to the Indian position on the issue by accepting in principle that the world should be rid of nuclear weapons.

On November 11, 1994 William Perry during a Press Conference at the Freedom House in Washington conceded that India could not be expected to consider the issue of proliferation only in the Pakistani context and that non-proliferation in the region must also include China. If one has to believe what Perry said, a major change in the Pentagon's approach to the proliferation issue in South Asia has occurred[17]. Two months after the Press Conference at the Freedom House, William Perry came to India on an official visit. Upon his arrival, he remarked: "The ending of the Cold War opened a new era in United States-India security relations. Old barriers to our cooperation have been replaced by new opportunities. We in the United States are excited by these opportunities and want to increase the security link between our two democratic nations. Doing so will allow us to better pursue our common security interests and provide a base of understanding for working out differences[18]. Having been aware of certain divergent strategic perceptions in India and the US and determined to enhance security relations despite those differences, Perry reiterated several times that his visit to South Asia would not aim at raking up the NPT and other contentious issues. On the very first day of his arrival in New Delhi an "Agreed Minute on Defence Relations between the United States and India" was signed. The agreement said: "The Governments of the United States of America and India recognize the importance of enhancing our defence cooperation as an important part of our overall bilateral relationship". It is an indication that such cooperation is necessary before embarking upon a bilateral "commercial alliance". The document further stated that the growth of bilateral defence relations in new areas will be evolutionary and related to convergence on global and regional issues. The enhanced defence cooperation between our two countries is designed to make a positive contribution to the security and stability of Asia. These measures will also promote the maintenance of international peace and security in the Post-Cold War world"[19].

This broad formulation of strategic cooperation is a noteworthy development in view of intense involvement of the United States in the Asia-Pacific region and growing involvement of India in the economic affairs of South-East Asia and the Far East. In addition to this, both sides have also agreed, "that such defence cooperation will cover civilian-to-civilian cooperation, service-to-service cooperation and cooperation in defence production and research[20]. Although the agreement does not include arms transfer or joint development of technologies and exemplifies little more than a good beginning in bilateral cooperation, it still heralds a new era of cooperative relationship between the two countries during the Clinton period which had been identified as "estranged democracies".

With a view to warding off any misperception and misapprehension in the neighbourhood, it has been made quite clear that Indo-US defence cooperation would not be at the cost of either Pakistan or China. Nonetheless, the China factor did come up during discussion due to the fact that Beijing's attitude and policy would constitute a significant aspect of the nuclear and missile nonproliferation/proliferation questions in Southern Asia. During a less publicized but very important breakfast meeting with William Perry and other members of his team, Jasjit Singh, Director of the Institute for Defence Studies and Analysis said:

"China has the most powerful military system in Asia. Although it may not match up to American military power in terms of quality and technology, we have to see its capabilities in terms of other Asian countries or its neighbours. It is modernizing rapidly both its conventional forces and its nuclear forces ... We have a clear goal which serves our national interests to work for (nuclear) disarmament. And we also have a problem, a dilemma to deal with the interim period between now and then (total nuclear disarmament) even if it takes many, many decades, as you (Perry) mention, to deal with existing realities, particularly when we know that China so far had shown no interest whatsoever in entering into any sort of checks or controls on its nuclear programme or posture"[21].

In reply, Perry said: "I have followed the Chinese

military closely since the early 60s .... and visited them in 1980 ... they had a very large military force but very poorly equipped, I would say , with 50s technology. From 1980 to about 1990, they only decreased the size of the military forces and the investment (in military) ... During the last two years there has been a major turn about and they have started investing (in the military) again ... My assessment at this time is, they do not pose any substantial military threat, not certainly at the global scale, not even to large neighbours like India[22].

The threat perceptions of India and the US are not identical and rightly so. The overall capabilities of the two countries are largely uneven, they are located geographically in two different continents and thus perceptions are bound to be divergent at this in this regard. But Perry's remark indirectly suggests that China poses a military threat to smaller countries in the region, if not to "large neighbours like India" and "not certainly on the global scale". Perry's concluding remark, however, perhaps would not conflict with the views of several Indian analysts as well. He said: "There is a potential that they (Chinese) could develop (their military) capability by the end of this decade and that could be a problem"[23].

How has Perry's trip to India been assessed by analysts in India? Jasjit Singh opines that during the Bill Clinton period United States "is increasingly willing to listen carefully to India's core fundamental security concerns and give them the requisite importance in its strategic thinking"[24]. In his assessment of the evolving Indo-US defence ties, he says that there, "is no cause to be euphoric about the process of defence cooperation; nor does it call for cynicism. Both sides will have to work sincerely to give partnership a chance and not demand too much of each other too soon"[25]. K. Subrahmanyam, defence analyst and former Director of the Institute for Defence Studies and Analysis, has also expressed optimism in his comments and analysis of the US Defence Secretary's visit to India. He argues that the Americans have "considerable commonality with our security concerns, though there are undoubtedly differences in translating these mutual security concerns into compatible national security policies"[26]. He suggested that in the upcoming consultations at the ministry-to-ministry level, every effort should be made to bridge the gaps between policies[27]. K. Srinivasan, India's Foreign Secretary, likewise observed that a national consensus on the Indo-US relationship is gradually emerging in India and the suspicions of the past are slowly giving away to mutual confidence on both sides[28]. This was a significant development during the time of Bill Clinton.

There is little doubt that improving ties between India and the United States in the economic sphere and the gradual emergence of a strategic consensus between the two countries not only constitutes a significant development in the Post-Cold War international relations but also exemplifies the birth of a new era of relations between the two democracies which were until recently interacting at a level that was characterized as the "dialogues between the deaf". What is perhaps necessary to give a boost to the momentum of this novel development is a balanced and cautious blend of economic ties and strategic relationship. The contentious issues in the security area, such as missile and nuclear proliferation are there to keep cropping up in the future. To facilitate smooth economic cooperation, the strategic divergences on certain key issues would have to be properly dealt with to avoid serious friction. On the other hand, improving economic ties can also contribute considerably to improvement of the security understanding between the two countries.

Actually a sea change occurred in the US-India

relation when Bill Clinton assumed office in Washington. The US became the largest trading partner with India. It is now the single largest investor in India accounting for almost $4 billion out of a total of about $12 billion worth of foreign investments cleared by the Government of India since 1991. As mentioned earlier, being the largest foreign investor in India, the US accounts for about half of all foreign equity. The US now needs Indian market. So the tremendous increase in Indo-US economic cooperation is the cornerstone of a new relationship between the two countries. What is special about Bill Clinton's relationship with India? The answer is economic cooperation and strategic relation.

There was a time when Pakistan was given utmost importance in United States. It was because of the strategic location of Pakistan and the world situation. But things changed when Clinton assumed office. Cold war had ended. The Soviet Union had been disintegrated. So Pakistan lost its importance in the new political situation. The Soviet Union and communism were no longer a threat to the USA. So Pakistan was wiped out from the USA's radar screen and instead India came up. India's opening up of the economy attracted the Americans. Recently in a T.V interview Pakistan President even complained that even though Pakistan had stood by the US in every occasion, like the Afghan crisis etc., the USA had not favoured Pakistan. It shows that everything is not well with US-Pakistan relation. There was a time when Pakistan was always highlighting the Kashmir question. But today the US says, "Stop terrorism and solve the problem through dialogue". Somehow or the other the US is convinced that the terrorist bases are there in Pakistan. When Bill Clinton visited New Delhi in March 2000, there were terrorist killings in Jammu and Kashmir. So in the Post-Cold War situation India is gainer and Pakistan is loser in terms of relationship with US. During Clinton's Presidentship the US-India relation touched new heights in economic and strategic fields.

References

1. Virginia Foran, "The case for Indo-US High-Technology Cooperation", Survival, Vol.40, Issue No.2, Summer 1998, p.73.
2. *Ibid.*, p.74.
3. *Ibid.*, p.75.
4. *Ibid.*, p.76.
5. *Ibid.*, p.81.
6. Times of India, January 17, 1995.
7. Asian Age, January 16, 1995.
8. Pioneer, January 10, 1995.
9. Statesman, April 9, 1994.
10. Selig S. Harrison and Geoffrey Kemp, India and America After the Cold War: Report of the Carregie Endowment Study Group on US-India Relations in Changing International Environment, Washington D.C., 1993.
11. *Ibid.*
12. Chintamani Mahapatra, "US approach to nuclear proliferation in Asia, in Jasjit Singh ed., "Asian Strategic Review", 1992-93, IDSA, New Delhi, 1993.
13. Span, November 1993.
14. Hindu, January 20, 1994; Times of India, January 24, 1994.
15. Address by Mr. P.V. Narasimha Rao, Prime Minister of India, to a joint meeting of the United States Congress, May 18, 1994: Strategic Digest, IDSA, New Delhi, July 1994.
16. *Ibid.*
17. Chintamani Mahapatra, ... Which is why US is seeking closer military ties with China, Asian Age, November 24, 1994.
18. Official Text, United States Information Service, New Delhi, January 12, 1995.
19. "Agreed Minute on Defence Relations between the United States and India", Official Text, USIS, New Delhi, January 12, 1994.
20. *Ibid.*

21. New Trends in Indo-American Relations, Strategic Analysis, March 1995, p.1544, IDSA, New Delhi.
22. *Ibid.*
23. *Ibid.*
24. Jasjit Singh, "Directions of Indo-US Relations", Indian Express, January 14, 1995.
25. *Ibid.*
26. K. Subrahmanyam, "Security Ties with US: Building a Commonality of Interests", Times of India, January 17, 1995.
27. *Ibid.*
28. Times of India, January 17, 1995.

Bibliography

Primary Sources

Government Documents and Publications Congressional Record 1977-2000.

US Department of State Bulletin, Kissinger, Henry *for the Record Selected Statements.*

US Congress, House Committee on Foreign Affairs.

Memoirs

Carter, Jimmy, *Keeping Faith: Memoirs of a President*, (London, 1982).

Clinton, Bill, *My Life* (Arrow Books, London, 2005).

Kissinger, Henry A., *The White House Years* (Boston, 1979).

Secondary Sources

Books

Azam J. Kousar (Ed.). *Economic Liberalization in India – Implications for Indo-US Relations*. (Delta Publishing House, Hyderabad, 1997).

Azam J. Kousar (Ed.). *Discourse in Trust US-South Asia Relations*. (South Asian Publication, New Delhi, 1999).

Banerjee, K. Pranab (Ed.). *Issues in Indo-US Trade*

and Economic Cooperation. (Kanishka Publishers, 1996).

Bertsh, K. Gary, Gahlaut, Seema and Srivastava, Anupam. "*Engaging India*" (Published by Routledge, 29 West, 35th Street, New York, NY10001).

Blechman, Barrym and Kaplan, Stephen S.Ed. *Force without war: U.S. Armed Forces as a Political Instrument*, (Washington, 1978).

Brands, H.W. *India and the United States: The Cold Peace*, (Boston, 1990).

Central Intelligence Information. *World Fact Books* (Washington D.C., 1990).

Chari, P.R. *Indo-Pak Nuclear Standoff – The Role of the United States*. (Manohar Publication, New Delhi, 1995).

Chellaney, Brahma. "*Security and Arms Control, Nuclear Proliferation – The US-Indian Conflict*". (Orient Longman, New Delhi, 1993).

Cohen Stephen, P. "South Asia and U.S. – Military Policy". In: Rudolph ed. *The Regional Imperative*.

Crunden, Robert M., Joshi, Manoj and Rao Chandrashekhar R.V.R. (Eds.) *New Perspectives on America and South Asia*. (Chanakya Publication, Delhi, 1984).

Gould, A. Haarold and Ganguly Sumit (Eds). *The Hope and the Reality: U.S.-Indian Relations from Roosevelt to Reagan*. (Oxford and IBH Publication Co. Pvt. Ltd., New Delhi, 1993).

Grover Verinder (Ed.). *International Relations and Foreign Policy of India*. (Deep and Deep Publication, F-159, Rajouri Garden, New Delhi, 110027, 1992).

Gupta S.P. and Mehra K.S. (Eds.). *Indo-US Trade and Economic Cooperation, Optimizing Relations*.

(Allied Publishers, New Delhi, 1995).

Harrison Selig S. "Dialogue of the Deaf: Mutual Perceptions and Indo-American Relations". In: *Conflicting Images: India and the United States.* Eds. S. Raghavan, Glazer and Nathan Glazer (Glenn Dale M.D., 1990).

Harrison, Selig S. and Kemp, Geaffrey Eds. India and American after the Cold War. *The Carnegre Endowment for International Peace*, (2400 4 street, N.W. Washington D.C., 1993).

Hess, Gray R. *The United States, Emergence as a South East Asian Power 1949-1950.* (New Work, 1987).

Jain, B.M. *India and the United States, 1961-1963,* (New Delhi, 1987).

Jha, Nalini K. US and India coming closer? *India Currents* (Sanjose, ed., February 1993).

Jha, Nalini K. "Sizing Bill Clinton's Policy on India", India Abroad (New York), March 26, 1993.

Juvekar D. Aditi. *Partners in Conflict – Perceptions and Realities of Indo-US Relations*. (Himalaya Publishing House, Mumbai, 1997).

Kamath, P.M. *Indo-US Relations – Dynamics of Change*. (South Asian Publishers, New Delhi, 1985).

Kheli, Shirin Tahir. *The United States and Pakistan: The Evolution of an Influence Relationship.* (New York, 1982).

Krishnan, T.V. Kunhi. *The Unfriendly Friends: India and America* (New Delhi, 1974).

Kux Dennis. *Estranged Democracies: India and the United States.* (New Delhi Sage, 1993).

Limaye, P. Satu. "*US-Indian Relations – The Pursuit of Accomodation*". (West View Press, Boulder, 1993).

Malhotra, Vinay Kumar Ed. *Indo-US Relations in Nineties*. (Anmol Publication Pvt. Ltd., New Delhi, 1995).

Mansingh, Surjit. In *India's Search for Power: Indira Gandhi and Foreign Policy, 1966-1982*. (New Delhi, 1984).

McMohan, Robert J. *The Cold War on the Periphery: The United States, India and Pakistan*. (New York Colombia University Press, 1994).

Mellor, John W. Ed. *India: A rising Middle Power*. (Boulder, 1979).

Mohite, Dlip H. *Indo-US Relations – Issues in Conflict and Cooperation.* (South Asian Publisher Pvt. Ltd., New Delhi, 1995).

Moynihan, Daniel Patric. *Counting Our Blessings: Reflections on the future of America*. (Boston, 1974).

Ohajunwa, Emeka. *India-US Security Relations*. (Chanakya Publications, Delhi, 1992).

Poulose, T.T. *The CTBT and The Rise of Nuclear Nationalism in India – Linkage Between Nuclear Arms Race, Arms Control and Disarmament*. (Lancer Books Publication, New Delhi-48, 1996).

Rahmathulla, B. *Indo-American Politics, 1970-1978*. (Delhi, 1980).

Ram Raghunath. *Super Powers and Indo-Pakistani Sub-continent, Perception and Politics*, (New Delhi, 1985).

Rana, A.P. (ed.). *Four Decades of Indo-US Relations: A commemorative Retrospective* (Har-Anand and USEFI Publications, New Delhi, 1994).

Rose, E. Leo and Gonsalves, Eric. "*Towards a New World Order: Adjusting India-US Relation*". Copyright (c) 1992 by The Regents of the University of California.

Suryanarayan, V. "*South and Southeast Asia in the 1990s – Indian and American Perspectives*". (Konark Publishers Pvt. Ltd., New Delhi, 1991)

Travis, Thom A. "*India, Pakistan and the Third World in the Post-Cold War System*". (Har-Anand Publication, New Delhi, 1997).

Tripathy, A.K. *US Foreign Policy: A Study of CIA and External Intervention in Central Asia*. (Discovery Publishing House, New Delhi, 1989).

Venkataramani, M.S. and Shrinvatava, B.K. *Quit India: The American response to the 1942 Struggle*. (New Delhi, Vikas, 1979).

Yager, Joseph (Ed.). *Non-Proliferation and US Foreign Policy*. (Washington, 1980).

Articles

Ahmed, Rashid and Shiraz, Sidhva. "Might and Menace", *Far Eastern Economic Review*, Vol.161, No.23, June 4, 1998.

Albright, K. Madeleina. "The Testing of American Foreign Policy". *Foreign Affairs*, Vol.77, No.6, Nov./ Dec. 1998, pp.50-65.

Allison, Graham. "The gravest crisis of our time". *New Statesman*, Vol.11, No.507, June 5, 1998, p.10.

Anonymous. America, India and Pakistan: Progress, Perhaps, *Economist*, Vol.331, No.2559, April 16, 1994.

Anonymous. Trading Compliments. *Economist*, Vol.339, No.7898, June 21, 1995.

Anonymons. "Why India loves the bomb". *Economist*, Vol.347, No.8068, May 16, 1998.

Anonymons. "Pakistan takes a beating". *Economist*, Vol.348, No.8082, Aug. 22-28, 1998.

Article, Alert. "Focus section weapons of Mass Destruction". May-June, 1998.

A National Security Strategy of Engagement and Enlargement, July 1998, Preface & pp.17-19.

Ayoob, Mohammed. "Nuclear India and Indian-

American Relations. *Orbis*, Vol.43, No.1, Winter 1999, pp.59-74.

Ayoob, Mohammed. "India Matters". *The Washington Quarterly*, Vol.23, No.1, Winter 2000.

Backgrounder. "A Changing India's Opportunities for the US". No.49, August 4, 1996.

Backgrounder. "A Stable Pakistan in interest of the US and India, Says Inderfuth". USIS, October 20, 1999.

Banerjee, Jyotirmayee. Implications for Asia Pacific Security. *Asian Survey*, XXXIV, No.6, June 1994.

Beinart, Peter. "The Return of the Bomb". *New Republic*, Vol.219, No.5, Aug.3, 1998, pp.22-27.

Bhambhri, C.P. "Perspective on Indo-American Relations". *Mainstream*, Vol.XXIV, No.20, Ja.18, 1986, pp.13-15.

Blair, Bruce G. Lengthening The Fuse, Global Zero Alert for Nuclear Forces. *The Bookings*, Vol.13, No.3, Summer, 1995.

Bhaskar Uday C. "Post Cold War Security". *Strategic Analysis*, Nov. 1997.

Bhattacharya, Pinaki. "Indo-US Relations". *Strategic Analysis*, Vol.XVII, No.1, April 1994, pp.79-88.

Carpenter, Galen Ted. "Rolling Asia-US Coziness with China Upsets the Neighbours". *Foreigh Affaits*, Vol.77, No.6, Nov. 1998, pp.2-6.

Chanda, Maya. India and the United States: Why Détente won't Happen. *Asian Survey*, Oct. 1986.

Chanda Nayan, Rashid Ahmen, Lutterbeck Deborah, Forney Matt, Sidhva Shiraj. "Nuclear Fallout". *Far Eastern Economic Review*, Vol.161, No.22, May 28, 1998.

Chanda Nayan, Shidva Shiraj, Rashid Ahmed, Forney Matt, Lutterbeck Deborah. "Unholy Act". *Far*

Eastern Economic Review, Vol.161, No.21, May 21, 1998.

Chanda, Nayan. "The Race is on". *Far Eastern Economic Review*, Vol.161, No.24, June 11, 1998.

Chand, Nayan. "Coming from the Cold". *Far Eastern Economic Review*, Vol.163, No.13, March 30, 2000.

Chellaney, Brahma. Nuclear Proliferation: The U.S.-Indian Conflict. Book Review, *Political Studies*, Vol.42, No.2, Jun. 1994.

Chellaney, Brahma. "Non-Proliferation – An Indian Critique of US Export Controls". *Orbis*, Summer 1994, pp.444-455.

Ching, Frank. "US, China Resume Dialogue", *Far Eastern Economic Review*, Vol.162, No.4, Jan.28, 1999.

Chittaranjan, Kalpana. "State of the CTBT". *Stategic Analysis*, Vol.XXIV, No.3, June 2000.

Cirincione, Joseph. "Asian Nuclear Reaction Chain". *Foreign Policy*, No.118, Spring 2000, pp.120-136.

Cohen, Stephen Philips. Balancing Interests: The U.S. and the Subcontinent. *The National Interest*, Fall 1987.

Cordesman, Anthony H. U.S.-Strategic Interests and the India-Pakistan Military Balance. *Paper Seminar*, June 11, 1987.

Cortright, David and Ahmed Samina. "Sanctions: Modify". *Bulletin of the Atomic Scientists*, Vol.54, No.5, Sept. 1998, pp.22-24.

Crossette's, Barbara. Essay, "India's Descent". *New York Times*, 19 May 1991.

CRS Issue Brief. "India-US Relations", updated February 6, 1997, Foreign Affairs and National Defence Division.

CRS Report for Congress. "India-Pakistan Nuclear Tests

and US Response". June 18, 1998. And updated November 24, 1998.

CRS Report for Congress. Recent Developments in Kashmir and US concerns. July 26, 1999.

CRS Issue Brief. India-US Relation. Updated Feb. 1, 2000, Foreign Affairs, Defenec and Trade Division.

CRS Issue Brief. "Nuclear Exports: The Tarapur Fuel Issue and US Interests in South Asia". Congressional Research Service, Library of Congress, date originated 6/18/80, date updated 02/12/81.

Deva, Yashwant. "Indo-US Relations and India's Security Interests". *Strategic Analysis*, Vol.XVII, No.4, Aug. 1994, pp.577-590.

Dhume, Sadanand, Mitra Pramit. "Show of Strength-China is target of New Indian Ballistic Missile". *Far Eastern Economic Review*, Vol.162, No.16, April 22, 1999.

Dhume, Sadanand. "Nuclear cloud". *FEER*, Vol.163, No.9, March 2, 2000.

Documents on Prime Minister's Visit to USA. *Strategic Digest*, Vol.XXIV, No.7, July 1994.

Dunn, Lewis A. Rethinking the Nuclear Equation: The United States and the New Nuclear Powers. *The Washington Quarterly*, Vol.17, No.1, 1993.

Fact Sheet. "Comprehensive Nuclear Test Ban Treaty", USIS, July 21, 1999.

Fact Sheet. "United States efforts to counter terrorism August 4", *USIS*, August 5, 1999.

Fact Sheet. "US Government views on Terrorism". USIS, December 8, 1999.

Facts and Files 1998. "Sarif Meets with U.S. President Clinton". pp. 929.

Fact Sheet. "New Financing to Expand India-US Trade".

March 27, 2000.

Fact Sheet. "Clinton's Remarks at Business Reception in Mumbai, India". March 27, 2000.

Frankel R, Francine. "Indo-US Relations: the future is Now". *Washington Quarterly*, Vol.19, Autumn 1996.

Freeman W. Chas Jr. "Sino-American Relations: Back to Basics". *Foreign Policy*, No.104, Fall 1996, pp.3-17.

Gaan, N. "Hopes and Realities in Indo-US Relations: From a Cold War to a Post-Cold War Perspective". *India Quarterly*, Vol.XLVIII, No.4, Oct.-Dec. 1992.

Gandhi, Indira. My Turth, (New Delhi, 1980). Franket, Francine R. Play the India Card. *Foreign Policy*, Spring, 1986.

Ganguly Sumit and Bajpai Kanti. India and the Crisis in Kashmir. *Asian Survey*, Vol.XXXIV, No.5, May 1994.

Gordon, Sandy. "South Asia after the Cold War - Winners and Losers". *Asian Survey*, Vol.XXXV, No.10, October 1995, pp.879-895.

Gosain Deepak. "Non-Proliferation Issue in Indo-US Relations". *Third World Impact*, April-May 1992.

Hagerly, Devin T. Rapporteur A Study Group, Preventing Nuclear Proliferation in South Asia. *The Asian Society*, New York, 1995.

Harrison, Selig. S. Fanning Flames in South Asia. *Foreign Policy*, 45, Winter 1981-1982.

Harrison Selig S. "South Asia and the United States: A Chance for a Fresh Start". *Current History*, Vol.91, No.563, March 1992.

Harrison Selig S. "The United States and South Asia: Trapped by the Past?". *Current History*, Vol.96, No.614, Dec. 1997, pp.401-406.

Hass, N. Richard. "Sactioning Madness". *Foreign Affairs*, Vol.76, No.6, Nov/Dec. 1997, pp.74-85.

Hass, N. Richard and Rose Gideon. "A New US Policy Towards India and Pakistan", Sponsored by the Council of Foreign Relation, USA, 1997.

Hersh, Seymour, M. A Reporter At large, Missile Wars. *The New Yorker*, Vol. 70, Sept. 26, 1994.

Hess, Gary R. Presidential Address Accommodation amid Discord: The United States, India and the Third World. *Diplomatic History*, Winter, 1992.

Historical Documents of 1998 Copy Right 'c' 1999 congressional Quarterly Inc. "UN on Nuclear Tests by India and Pakistan".

Hitchens, Christopher. Minority. *Nation*, Vol.256, No.6, March 1, 1993.

Holloway Nigel. "Limited Leverage - The US has very Little Say in the Subcontinent". *Far Eastern Economic Review*, Vol.156, April 11, 1996.

Holloway, Nigel, Karp Jonathan, Forney Matt and Rashi Ahmed. "Going Ballistic". *Far Eastern Economic Review*, Vol.159, No.26, June 27, 1996.

Holum D. John. "The CTBT and Nuclear Disarmament - The US view". *Journal of International Affairs*, Vol.51, No.1, Summer 1997.

Hoodbhoy, Pervez and Mian Zia. "Sanctions: Lift'em". *The Bulletin of Atomic Scientists*, Vol.54, No.5, Sept/Oct. 1998, pp.20-25.

Howell, Llewelly D. India: Rising Asian Economic Superpower. *USA TODAY*: The Magazine of the American Scene, Vol.121, No.2574, March 1993.

Inderfurth, F. Karl. "India-Pakistan Nuclear Tests". *US Department of State Despatch*, Vol.9, No.5, June 1998, pp.15-17.

India and the United States - Remarks by Indian Foreign Secretary at the Breakfast Session of

Conference on "India and the United States after the Cold War". *Strategic Digest*, Vol.XXIII, No.5, May 1993, pp.750-755.

India and the US: Partners for a Healthy World. *Fact Sheet*, March 28, 2000.

India and the United States - Partners in Self-Reliance. *Official Text*. USIS, April 29, 1988.

Iqbal, Badar Alam. Are Indo-US Economic Relations Really Improving? *India Quarterly*, Vol.LI, No.1, Jan./Mar. 1995.

Jayraman, K.S. U.S. Leans on Russia to Drop Rocket Agreement. *Nature*, Vol.356, No.6372, April 30, 1992.

Jayraman, K.S. Indo-US Plutonium dispute flares up. *Nature*, Vol.363, No.6430, June 17, 1993.

Jayaraman, P.S. "Pokharan II India's Security and CTBT Diplomacy". *The Indian Journal of Asian Affairs*, Vol.12, No.1, June 1999, pp.29-50.

Jha, Nalini K. "Indo-US Relations". *Third World Impact*, Vol.1, No.2, February 1990, pp.13-17.

Jha, Nalini K. "Reviving US-India Friendship in a Changing International Order". *Asian Survey*, Vol.34, Dec.1994, pp.1035-1046.

Jha, Prem Shankar. "Why India went Nuclear". *World Affairs*, No.3, July-Sept. 1998.

Kamath, P.M. "Indian Nuclear Strategy: A Perspective for 2020". *Strategic Analysis*, Vol.XXII, No.12, March 1999.

Kanwal, Gurmeet. "Pakistan's Continuing Challenge in Kashmir: Need for a Trans-LOC Pro-active Response". *Strategic Analysis*, Vol.XXIII, No.12, March 2000.

Kapur, Ashok. "Non-Proliferation-Western Biases". *The Bulletin of Atomic Scientists*, Vol.51, No.1, Jan/Feb. 1995, pp.38-43.

Kapur, K.D. "Missile Technology Control Regime: An Extension of Nuclear Non-Proliferation Regime". *Foreign Affairs Reports*, Vol.XLII, No.11&12, Nov-Dec 1993.

Karnad, Bharat. "A Sucker's Payoff"; Vinaik, Achin. "Since the Pokharn Tests". *Seminal*, No.485, Jan. 2000, pp.45-56.

Kaul, T.N. "Indo-US Relations". *Man and Development*, Vol.XXII, No.1, March 2000, pp.1-15.

Key, E. Jeffrey. "Beyond tilting Both Way's, A New Post-Cold War South Asia Policy". *Asian Affairs*, Vol.25, No.2, Summer 1998, pp.89-102.

Kitfield, James. "No Longer Untouchable". *Foreign Affairs*, Vol.32, No.12, March 18, 2000.

Kresberg Paul. The United States, South Asia and American Interest. *Journal of International Affairs*, New York, 1989.

Luce, Henry. "The American Century", Life, 17 Fe. 1941 - 61-65.

Mahapatra, Chintamani. "Indo-American Relations on the Threshold of the 21st Century". *Strategic Analysis*, Vol.XXII, 1997.

Mahapatra, Chintamani. "Indo-American Dialogue". *Strategic Analysis*, Vol.XV, No.2, May 1992, pp.113-122.

Mahapatra, Chintamani. "Cryogenic Technology Deal: American Pressure Tactics". *Strategic Analysis*, July 1992, pp.313-323.

Mahapatra, Chintamani. "The US, China and the Ghauri Missile". *Strategic Analysis*, Vol.XXII, No.3, June 1998.

Mahapatra, Chintamani. "Major Post-Cold War Trends in India's Neighbourhood". *Strategic Analysis*, Vol.XXIII, No.3, June 1999.

Manor, James and Segal, Gerald. "Taking India

Seriously". *Survival*, Vol.40, No.2, Summer 1998.

Mansingh, Surjit. "The United States and India". *World Focus*, No.197, May 1996, pp.15-18.

Mattoo, Amitabh. "India-US Relations: Sanctions and Beyond". *Agni*, Vol.3, No.3, Jan.-May, 1998.

Maynes, Charles William. America without the Cold War. *Foreign Policy*, Vol. 78, Spring, 1990.

McDonald, Hamish. "Technically Friends". *Far Eastern Economic Review*, Vol.151, Jan. 31, 1991, pp.13-14.

McDonal, Hamis and Rashid Ahmed. "Half a Deal". *Far Eastern Economic Review*, Vol.157, April 21, 1994, pp.22-23.

McMohan, Robert J. United States Cold War Strategy in South Asia Making a Military Commitment to Pakistan, 1947-1954. *Journal of American History*, 75, December 1986.

Ministry of External Affairs. *Annual Reports* 1990-91 till 1991-2000.

Morgan, Granger M., Subrahmanyam K., Sunderji, K., White M. Robert. "India and the United States". *The Washington Quarterly*, Vol.18, No.2, Spring 1995, pp.155-179.

Mukherjee, Dilip. U.S. Weaponry for India. *Asian Survey*, Vol.XXVII, No.6, June 1987.

Munshi, Miraj U-Din. "A Kashmiri Perspective I". *Asian Affairs: An American View*, Vol.22, No.1, Spring 1995, pp.20-27.

Oldenburg, Phillips. India and the Oldenburg. *Asian Affairs*, Winter, 1988-89.

Ollapally Deepa and Ramana, Raja. "US-India Tensions – Misperceptions on Nuclear Proliferation". *Foreign Affairs*, Vol.74, No.1, Jan./Feb. 1995, pp.13-18.

Palmer, Norman D. Indo-American Relations: The

Politics of Encounters. *Orbis*, 23, Summer 1979.

Panda, Snehalata. "Pokharan II: Response of US, Russia, China and Pakistan". *BIISS Journal*, Vol.20, No.1, Jan. 1999, pp.12-30.

Panda, Snehalata. "India and the United States: Perceptions and Policy". *Strategic Analysis*, Vol.XXIII, No.1, April 1999.

Parasher, S.C. "America, India and Pakistan". *India Quarterly*, Vol.LII, No.4, Oct.-Dec. 1996, pp.19-50.

Percy, charles N. South Asia's Take-off. *Foreign Policy*, Winter 1992/93.

Perkovich, George. A Nuclear Third Way in South Asia. *Foreign Policy*, Summer 1993.

Perkovich George. "Nuclear Proliferation". *Foreign Policy, Fall* 1998, No.112, pp.12-23.

Phillips, Andrew. "The Islamic Bomb". *Maclean's*, Vol.III, No.23, June 8, 1998, pp.38-40.

Pickering sees hope for increased trade/ties with India. *USIS* Press Release, August 1, 1992.

PM's Statement in Parliament on "Bilateral Talks with United States" (15 December 1998). *Strategic Digest*, Vol.XXIX, No.1, January 1999.

Pomper, A. Miles. "As the Dust Settles in India-US Rethinks Nuclear Policy". *C.Q. Weekly*, Vol.56, No.21, May 23, 1998, pp.1365-1368.

Public Diplomacy Query, Document 2 of 100, Title: Text: US-India Relations: A Vision for the 21st Century.

Public Papers of the Presidents William J. Clinton, 1997, 1998. Relevant pages.

Puri, K.K. (Lt. Col.). "NPT and Indo-US Relations". *Combat Journal*, Vol.19, No.2, August 1992, pp.41-50.

Raphel L. Robin. "South Asia after the Cold War: India and Pakistan. *US Department of State Dispatch*, Vol.6, No.39, Sept.25, 1995, pp.706-708.

Reiss Mitchell. "Safeguarding the Nuclear Peace in South Asia", *Asian Survey*, Vol.XXXIII, No.12, Dec. 1993, pp.1107-1121.

Remarks by the President to the Hyderabad Business Community. The White House, Office of the Press Secretary, Hyderabad, India, March 24, 2000.

Remarks by the President in Greeting to the People of Pakistan. The White House, Office of the Press Secretary, (Islamabad, Pakistan), March 25, 2000.

Ritcheson, Philip L. Nuclearization in South Asia. *Strategic Review*, Fall, 1993.

Rose, Leo E. United States and Soviet Policy towards South Asia. *Current History*, March 1986.

Sabur Abdus A.K.M. "India-Pakistan Security Relationship and the Kargil Crisis. *Biiss Journal*, Vol.20, No.3, 1999.

Sagar, Scott D. The Perils of Proliferation: Organisation Theory, Deterrence Theory and the Spread of Nuclear Weapons. *International Security*, Vol.18, No.4, Spring 1994.

Salitsky, Alexander. "China, India, Russia". *World Affairs*, Vol.5, No.1, Jan-March 2001.

Sangal, P.S. "Intellectual Property: Transfer of Technology to Asia and the Pacific with Special Reference to India". *Foreign Affairs Report*, Vol.XLII, No.8&9, August-Sept. 1993.

Seminal. "The US and US" a Symposium on Relations Between America and India, No.422, Oct. 1994, pp.11-54.

Seth, S.P. The Indo Pak Nuclar Duet and The US. *Asian Survey*, July 1988.

Shrivastava, B.K. India-American Economic Relations

in the 1980. Paper presented at Seminar on history of Indo-US Relations during the last four Decades, New Delhi, Jan. 1991.

Sidhu, W.P.S., Cloughley Brian, Hawes H. John and Schaffer C. Terejita. "Nuclear Risk Reduction Measures in Southern Asia". *Project Report*, No.26, November 1998. Copyright (c) 1998, Dupont Circle, NW Ninth Floor, Washington D.C. 20036.

Sieff, Martin. "Passage to India". *National Review*, Vol.50, No.11, June 22, 1998, pp.36-40.

Simpson, John and Howlett, Darryl. "The NPT Renewal Conference Stumbling towards 1995". *International Security*, Vol.19, No.1, Summer 1994, pp.41-59.

Singer E. Clifford, Saksena Jyotika, Thakar Milind. "Feasible Deals with India and Pakistan after the Nuclear Tests". *Asian Survey*, Vol.XXXVIII, No.12, Dec. 1998, pp.1161-1178.

Singh, Jasjit (Ed.). "The Road Ahead: Indo-US Strategic Dialogue". Lancer International in Association with Institute for Defence Studies and Analyses, New Delhi, 1994.

Singh, Jasjit. "India's Nuclear Policy: The Year After". *Strategic Analysis*, Vol.XXIII, No.4, July 1999.

South Asia Policy, Round Table before the Committee on Foreign Affairs and its Subcommittee on Asia and Pacific House of Representatives, One hundred third Congress Second Session. Sept. 21, 1994 U.S. Govt. Printing Office, Washington, 1994.

Special Section on Research Agendas in Indo-US Relations after the Cold War. *Indian Journal of American Studies*, Vol.21, No.1, Winter 1991.

Spector, Leonards. Neo-Nonproliferation. *Survival*, Vol.37, No.1, Spring, 1995.

Speech by the President Shri K.R. Narayanan at the

Banquet in Honour of H.E. Mr. William J. Clinton. *Strategic Digest*, Vol.XXX, No.4, April 2000.

Tomas, Raju. Propsects for Indo US Security ties. *Orbis* Summer 1988.

Thornton, Thomas P. American Interest in India Under Carter and Reagon. *SAIS* (Review Vol.5, No.1, Winter-Spring 1985).

Talbott, Strobe. "Dealing with the Bomb in South Asia". *Foreign Affairs*, Vol.78, No.2, March/April 1999, pp.110-122.

Talbott. Deputy Secretary. "US Diplomacy in South Asia - A Progress Report". *US Department of State Dispatch*, Vol.9, No.11, Dec. 1998, pp.16-20.

Thakur, Ramesh. "India After Nonalignment". *Foreign Affairs*, Vol.71, No.2, 1992, pp.165-182.

Thakur, Ramesh. "India and The United States". *Asian Survey*, Vol.XXXVI, No.6, June 1996, pp.574-591.

Thapliyal, Sangeeta. "Indo-Pak Conflict and the Role of External Powers". *Strategic Analysis*, Vol.XXII, No.7, Oct. 1998.

Thorton, Tomas P. The New Phase in US-Pakistani Relations. *Foreign Policy*, Summer 1989.

Uddin, Mughees. "Foreign Policy and Press Performance: The Case of the Kashmir Conflict, the United States and the New York Times during 1948-49 and 1989-91". *Pakistan Horizon*, Vol.45, No.4, Oct. 1992, pp.29-59.

United States Indian Relations - A Report to the Committee on Foreign Relations, United States Senate. March 1982, US Govt. Printing Office, Washington, 1982.

US State Department View on India and Pakistan. *Comparative Strategy*, Vol.18, No.1, Jan.-March 1999, pp.93-97.

US Trade Official Underscores India's Hi-tech Potential.

USIS Press Release, Jan. 25, 1988.

Venkataramani, M.S. The American Rule in Pakistan, 1947-1958. *Atlantic Highlands*, NJ 1982.

Vinod, M.J. "Nuclear India and Indo-US Relations". *Social Action*, Vol.49, No.2, April/June 1999, pp.203-212.

Wisner, "Indo-US Relations in a Bold New Era". USIS Press Release, June 20, 1995.

World Focus of May 1995, written by different writers like Zuberi Matin, Subrahmanyam, K., Raja Mohan, C., pp.3-24.

World Focus. "Indo-US Relations", February 1999.

World Focus of April 2000, pp.3-24.

World Focus. "Jammu and Kashmir", Vol.23, No.10-11-12, Oct-Nov-Dec. 2002.

Yasmeen, Samina. Pakistan's Cautious Foreign Policy. *Survival*, Vol.36, No.2, Summer 1994.

Zimmermann, Tim, Chellaney, Brahma and Moulier B. Philippe. "Nuclear Ambitions". *US News and World Report*, Vol.120, No.6, Feb.12, 1996, pp.42-46.

Zuberi, Matin. "The Proposed Indian Nuclear Doctrine". *USI Journal*, Vol.XXIX, No.537, July-Sept. 1999, pp.314-323.

Periodicals

Annals of American Academy of Political and Social Sciences (Philadelphia).

Asian Strategic Review (New Delhi).

Asian Survey (California).

Business Week (New York).

Current History (Philadelphia).

Economist (London).

Facts on File

Far Eastern Economic Review.

Foreign Affairs (New York).
Foreign Affairs Report (New Delhi).
Foreign Policy (New York).
Fortune (New York).
India Quarterly (New York).
International Affairs (London).
International Organization (Boston).
International Studies (New Delhi).
New Republic (Washington DC).
News Week.
Orbis (Philadelphia).
Pacific Affairs (USA).
Pacific Community (Tokyo).
Pacific Quarterly (London).
Political Science Quarterly (New York).
Span
Strategic Analysis (New Delhi).
Strategic Digest (New Delhi)
Survival (London).
The New Yorker (New York).
Third Concept (New Delhi).
US News and World Report (Washington DC).
Washington Quarterly (Washington).
Western Political Quarterly (Salt Lake City).
World Focus (New Delhi).
World Politics (New Jersey).
Yojana (New Delhi).